MW01009505

THE TIMBER PRESS GUIDE TO VEGETABLE GARDENING

in the
•SOUTHWEST•

THE TIMBER PRESS GUIDE TO VEGETABLE GARDENING

in the
•SOUTHWEST•

TRISHA SHIREY

Timber Press
....
Portland, Oregon

To my Mom and Dad,
who gave me the skills, the opportunity,
and the desire to garden.

Copyright © 2015 by Trisha Shirey.
All rights reserved.

Chapter opening illustrations and illustrations on pages 18, 41, 42, 43, and 93 by Julianna Johnson and Ryan Ricketts. All other illustrations © Julia Sadler.

Published in 2015 by Timber Press, Inc.

The Haseltine Building
133 S.W. Second Avenue, Suite 450
Portland, Oregon 97204-3527
timberpress.com

Printed in the United States of America
Second printing 2016
Book design by Kate Giambrone and Julianna Johnson
Cover design by Bree Goodrow

Library of Congress Cataloging-in-Publication Data

Shirey, Trisha.
    The Timber Press guide to vegetable gardening in the Southwest/ Trisha Shirey.—First edition.
        pages cm
    Guide to vegetable gardening in the Southwest
    Includes index.
    ISBN 978-1-60469-535-9
    1. Vegetable gardening—Southwestern States. 2. Vegetables—Southwestern States. I. Title. II. Title: Guide to vegetable gardening in the Southwest.
    SB321.5.A165S55 2015
    635—dc23
                                            2014020900

TABLE OF.
CONTENTS

Preface

Some of my earliest and fondest memories are from time spent helping out in our family garden when I was young. My mother would can, pickle, and freeze our harvests and we would eat from the garden throughout the year. Our pantry shelves were lined with colorful jars of pickled beets and peaches, green beans, and tomatoes. My mother cooked three meals a day for our family of eight, and every meal was made from scratch—no frozen dinners or take-out—and most of the ingredients came from the garden. My siblings and I were very involved with the preparation and cleanup with every meal. As I grew up, the idea of growing and cooking my own food was never daunting—my parents did it, their parents did it before them, and so on.

When asked why I bother with keeping a garden, I usually think of Weezer from the wonderful *Steel Magnolias* (beautifully played by Shirley MacLaine). She grew tomatoes and forced them on her friends because she didn't much like them herself. When they asked her why, she replied, "Because I'm an old southern woman and we're supposed to wear funny looking hats and ugly clothes and grow vegetables in the dirt. I don't know why! I don't make the rules." Funny hats? Check. Ugly clothes? Check. Like Weezer, it just seems like I am supposed to do this. Fortunately, I like tomatoes and certainly don't have any friends that would turn down my surplus bounty.

You don't always have to find your dinner at the grocery store; you can pick from whatever is ready for harvesting in your garden. What's more, you won't have to ask any questions about whether it's organic or nutritious and flavorful—you'll have nurtured the plant from it's beginnings as a tiny seed or transplant. You control the conditions. My garden has even turned me into a more adventurous cook—when you're eating kale three or more days of the week, you'll want to have more than a few recipes to rely on.

Unfortunately, many Americans have missed out on the experience of growing up with a food garden. Something that seems so natural to me is still mysterious and complex to so many of my friends. They're often intrigued and excited by the idea of growing their own food, but don't know where to begin. Still, from First Lady Michelle Obama's organic garden at the White House to the exploding trend of food-filled back yards and patios across the nation, more people than ever are now getting into gardening. Seed companies and garden centers are reporting that sales of herb and vegetable seeds and plants are increasing every year.

What could be fresher than produce picked right before it goes on your table? Nutrients and flavor are not lost during transportation and your food hasn't been shipped across the country, contributing to pollution and global warming. You'll learn to appreciate the variety of food that's available each season. I might not have fresh tomatoes in late winter or lettuce in midsummer, but there are so many wonderful seasonal alternatives. You can say goodbye to those transported out-of-season offerings that you find at the grocery store. You can also stop worrying about food contamination, as you'll know exactly what you used on your own garden. Growing crops organically in healthy soil can result in produce with higher levels of vitamin C, iron, phosphorus, antioxidants, and other nutrients. A study by the University of Florida and Washington State found that organic foods contain, on average, about 25 percent higher levels of 11 nutrients than their traditional counterparts. And your investment will go so much further—you can cut your food bills *and* eat healthier. The National Gardening Association found that a family that invested $70 in a garden could harvest about $600 worth of vegetables.

You'll find that there are physical rewards of gardening also. Vigorous garden work can help to increase bone density and reduce blood pressure and cholesterol. Exercising the mind and body with the planning and care of a garden can reduce stress and the risk of dementia. Studies have shown that gardeners have reduced levels of blood sugar and a lower risk of type 2 diabetes. Many gardeners find weeding, pruning, watering, and other gardening chores meditative and a great way to unwind from a hectic day. There is pleasure to be taken in watching things grow; you'll develop a connection to natural cycles and feel more self-reliant and empowered. Your children will learn that vegetables don't always have to come from a bag in the freezer and they might be more likely to eat them when they have helped to grow and harvest them. You just might instill a love of gardening that will last a lifetime!

As long as you have at least six hours of sunlight, good air circulation, and access to water, you can grow a great variety of herbs and vegetables in a garden bed or containers. Even in shady locations, parsley, chives, mint, and lettuce can thrive. And a yard isn't always necessary; determined renters and apartment dwellers can always find space to grow their favorite edibles, whether in containers or in community gardens. Sure there will be a few failures along the way, but that's how we learn. I still plant tomatoes that fail to produce a single fruit as a result of unseasonably warm spring temperatures or green beans that succumb to powdery mildew or cucumbers that won't bloom. It happens to all of us—gardening is a gamble. But at least we can compost our failures to build healthy soil for the next season!

Acknowledgments

Thank you to my dear friend Lucinda Hutson, whose garden and home have been sources of inspiration for many years. Lucinda recommended me for this project and I thank her for the opportunity to fulfill a lifetime dream of writing a gardening book. We really must get together, drink tequila, and write songs again soon!

The guidance and assistance of Michael Dempsey and Juree Sondker at Timber Press have been much appreciated. They have been very patient in helping me produce my first (and hopefully not last) book and make it something to be proud of.

When I first considered a career in horticulture I was intimidated by the heavy use of pesticides, herbicides, and fungicides—one teacher told me that I'd never make a living in the industry unless I learned to work with these chemicals. But having known only organic gardening for all of my life, I saw no reason to stop for my education. It's a decision I've never regretted. I've been fortunate to have many garden mentors throughout my lifetime of gardening: Miss Lillian Peek, John Dromgoole, Malcolm Beck, and Howard Garrett have all been valuable sources of knowledge and experience along the way. The Austin Organic Gardeners and Rodale Press have also been instrumental in my learning more about organic techniques.

Thanks to the University of Texas for giving me my first job in 1981 as a gardener at the chancellor's residence. That 5-acre estate provided me with over two years of intensive training in everything that can go wrong in a garden, but that experience was invaluable in teaching me that chemicals can often do more harm than good. Eventually, and with the help of organic practices, I got it under control and turned it into 5 acres of garden perfection. I have since moved on to new challenges, but I learned more in my time at UT's Bauer house than I would have ever learned in a classroom.

One of those new challenges was the 24-acre property at the Lake Austin Spa Resort—then a mess of dead plants, weeds, ant mounds, and bare and weedy lawns. Now, thirty years later, the grounds have been transformed—organically—winning much acclaim and attention and serving as an inspiration for the thousands of guests and employees who spend time there. Much appreciation to Deborah Evans Parker for giving me the original opportunity to learn as I grew on the property, and to Michael McAdams, Billy Rucks, and Tracy York for giving me the means to transform this oasis into something world class and wonderful and trusting me enough to do it my way. And thanks to the grounds staff through the years—you make me look good and I appreciate it! It is a place I look forward to returning to every day.

Thanks also to my associates on the Central Texas Gardener television program. Linda Lehmusvirta produces an excellent program with the help of Tom Spencer and a top-notch crew. Every show teaches me something new and I am proud to be a part of such an excellent team (watch us at www.klru.org/ctg).

Thanks to my dear, departed friend Jaci, who always believed in me and always had my back. Everyone should have at least one friend like her in their lifetime. Getting this book assignment shortly after her passing was a blessing as it helped to distract me in my grief. I know she has been cheering me on from her perch among the stars.

My sister Lisa and my friend Amy and her lovely daughters, Skylar and Ashley, have kept me grounded in this difficult year. Their kindness and encouragement are much appreciated.

GET STARTED

A LAND
OF EXTREMES

When most people think of the southwestern United States, they imagine, say, a lone cowboy riding across a dry and desolate desert with an occasional cactus dotting the landscape. And while that's somewhat accurate—a large portion of the region is a part of the North American Desert—there are also forests, mountainous areas, and grassy plains. For the purposes of this book, consider Texas, Oklahoma, New Mexico, Arizona, the eastern portion of California, and southern tips of Utah and Nevada as the Southwest. As you can imagine, the variations in the topography of this region make for some interesting weather forecasting. When the sun is shining and the temperature is 88°F in Phoenix, Arizona, only 150 miles away in Flagstaff the temperature can be a bone-chilling 26°F with a foot of snow on the ground. The mountains have an enormous effect on the climate; they block wind and change rainfall patterns and temperatures in the surrounding areas. Average rainfall amounts vary greatly as do average temperatures. Many areas will have their greatest rainfall amounts in summer while others may experience more rain in fall. Some arid regions will receive most of their precipitation as snowfall.

What most areas of the Southwest do have in common is hot summer weather and much less rain than other regions in the country. In fact, the ten driest US cities are all located in this region. Soils can range from thin, rocky caliche and sandy grasslands to nutrient-rich forest soils. Each type of soil can have its own trials, but all can produce a bountiful garden.

Gardening in this land of extremes can indeed be a challenge. But by carefully preparing your soil, effectively timing your plantings, choosing drought-tolerant, short-season varieties, and judiciously using water resources you can have a beautiful and successful edible landscape. If you can grow here, you can grow anywhere!

Growing Season Profile

The times for planting various crops are related to the temperature of the soil. Some seeds like beets, carrots, and broccoli germinate when the soil is relatively cool. Warm-season crops like tomatoes, okra, and black-eyed peas need warm soil temperatures or the seeds will simply rot in the soil. Planting times are cued to the average first and last frosts in the region. Seed packets will often recommend planting "when all danger of frost has passed," but how does a gardener know when that is? Frost dates are averaged from the data collected at regional weather stations, though that data can vary greatly from your home garden. Know the dates for your region's first and last freeze and use them as a guideline for planning your planting calendar, but adjust them according to your specific garden situation. Your garden's altitude, slope, or position near a metropolitan area (the urban heat island effect) or a large body of water could alter the dates that would be appropriate for planting. And keep in mind that each year brings its own challenges as weather patterns are altered and fluctuate. Many areas will experience relatively mild winters followed by unseasonably cold and icy or snowy winters the next year.

Invest in a min-max thermometer and barometer to help make your own forecasts; not only will it tell you the current temperature, it can record the highest and lowest temperatures of the previous day. Watching the changes in barometric pressure can warn you of instability in the atmosphere or tell you to expect pleasant weather. If the pressure drops quickly that means the air is rising and the atmosphere is unstable—storms are on the way.

Frost damage may occur at temperatures of 36°F, while a light frost or freeze occurs at 29–32°F. A moderate freeze is temperatures from 25–28°F, and a severe or hard freeze that burns all tender vegetation happens at 24°F or lower. Keep track of the first and last freeze dates each year for your area in your garden journal. That will help you to decide when to plant for optimal growth.

The number of frost-free days will determine the growing season. With the addition of row cover or cold frames and some shading in hot weather, the growing season can be extended a bit on each side of the season. Broccoli, cabbage, and kale can tolerate a mild freeze and will even taste a bit sweeter with a touch of frost,

AVERAGE FROST DATES FOR THE SOUTHWEST

CITY	LAST FROST	FIRST FROST	FROST-FREE DAYS	CITY	LAST FROST	FIRST FROST	FROST-FREE DAYS
ARIZONA				**OKLAHOMA**			
Flagstaff	6/9	9/21	104	Boise City	5/12	10/4	167
Phoenix	—	—	365	Durant	3/28	11/4	220
Tucson	3/27	11/7	324	Lawton	3/29	11/7	223
Yuma	—	—	365	Oklahoma City	4/1	11/3	215
				Tulsa	3/27	11/7	225
CALIFORNIA							
Blythe	1/25	12/9	315	**TEXAS**			
Merced	3/5	11/16	256	Amarillo	4/18	10/20	185
Modesto	2/1	12/8	307	Austin	2/17	12/6	291
Palm Springs	—	—	365	Corpus Christi	2/3	12/23	319
Tahoe City	6/18	11/19	92	Dallas	3/3	11/25	267
				El Paso	3/22	11/8	230
NEVADA				Houston	2/8	12/20	308
Carson City	5/29	9/27	120	McAllen	—	—	365
Las Vegas	2/16	11/27	281	San Angelo	3/28	11/13	230
Tonopah	5/13	10/11	151	San Antonio	2/28	11/25	270
NEW MEXICO				**UTAH**			
Albuquerque	4/6	10/28	194	Blanding	5/8	10/14	157
Carlsbad	4/15	11/2	215	Cedar City	5/21	10/1	133
Ruidoso	5/28	9/25	120	St . George	3/20	11/5	230
Taos	5/21	9/17	130				
Tucumcari	4/15	10/25	191				

Data compiled in 2005 from the National Climatic Data Center, US Department of Commerce. The dates are given for a 32°F freeze-event probability. Remember that these frost dates are an average. There is a 50 percent chance of the frost occurring earlier or later than the date listed.

but lettuce, tomatoes, and peppers will be blackened and gone with a single cold snap. Careful attention to freeze dates and planting dates will assure a longer garden season.

Water Worries

Despite the fact that some of the fastest-growing cities in the country are in the Southwest, water supplies in the region continue to dwindle. Extreme drought and heat have led to dangerous wildfires across the area and the loss of much of the native landscape. Many cities like Phoenix and Las Vegas have brought on dramatic changes in water use by pioneering the use of native plants for home and business landscapes. Water-thirsty lawns are becoming a thing of the past. The amount that you can realistically plan on growing will depend on how much water is available to you, and a large part of that will mean making the most of the rainfall in your region. Aside from choosing the appropriate crops and carefully planning planting times, tools like rainwater collection and drip irrigation are essential for efficient water management.

The timing of expected rainfall can also vary greatly. Texas and Oklahoma tend to have wetter periods in late April and May and again in the fall, while Arizona and New Mexico will receive almost half of their annual rainfall during the summer monsoons. To give you an example of how extreme the diversity of the region is, average rainfall ranges from 3.45 inches in Yuma, Arizona, to 50.31 inches in Texarkana, Texas.

A rain gauge is a wise investment. When your gauge shows you only had a quarter inch of rain, that's your cue to supplement the rainfall with a follow-up watering. Remember to empty your rain gauge before a freeze as the plastic or glass will crack and be ruined.

EL NIÑO, LA NIÑA

Weather forecasting is fairly reliable for a future period of ten days to two weeks, but longer-term patterns are beginning to be predicted. A pattern of warm ocean currents off the northwestern coast of Peru at Christmas time has been observed to flow much farther south in some years creating a weather pattern known as El Niño (little boy, or "Christ's child" as a result of its December appearance). During an El Niño year, much of the Southwest will experience record winter rains and colder temperatures. An opposite effect pattern known as La Niña (little girl) will bring warmer and drier than normal conditions in the Southwest. There is still much more to learn about these patterns and their effect on our weather but we would be wise to pay attention when these trends are predicted. Global warming is also warming the oceans and its effect on the El Niño and La Niña cycle is still uncertain. Fall is usually an excellent time for planting perennial landscape plants in many areas of the Southwest, but when a strong La Niña year is predicted it may be wise to wait. On the other hand, in many of the drought-stressed areas of the region, we cautiously welcome El Niño weather in hopes of filling lakes, reservoirs, and water tables that are becoming very dry.

Watching the Wind

Be mindful of wind direction to predict cold fronts. Before weather was forecast every ten minutes on television, farmers and ranchers always had a weather vane on their home or barn—and they were not just decorative. The direction that the wind is coming from can help you plan for the weather in store. Gardeners east of the Rockies will tend to have unsettled or changing weather when the wind is coming from the northeast, east, or south. Fair weather comes with winds from the northwest, east, or southwest. Cold fronts will generally come from the northeast. West of the Rockies you can expect dry air and pleasant days with winds from the east and cold weather and rain with winds from the west.

Since the coldest air tends to come from the northwest in my zone, plants that are located on the south or southeast side of the house will have the most protection from temperature extremes. When the wind shifts from the northwest I know I need to plan for cold, especially if there are cirrus or cirrostratus clouds.

Growing Regions of the Southwest

The states included in this region are some of the largest in the country, with extremely varied topography. The Southwest includes USDA climate zone 4 in the mountainous areas of Arizona and Nevada, where the annual extreme minimum temperatures during the period of 1976–2005 ranged from –25 to –20°F, and extends to zone 10 in the southern-most portions of Texas and Arizona, where the coldest expected temperatures are a comparatively balmy 30 to 35°F. Zone 11 covers the Death Valley region of southern California, where the lowest temperatures are 40 to 45°F, but

GET IN THE ZONE

Seed catalogs and plant tags will often include a recommended zone for planting a particular plant. The USDA produces a climate zone map dividing North America into eleven hardiness zones, with zone 1 being the coolest and 11 the warmest of the zones (available at planthardiness. ars.usda.gov). The map is based on average minimum winter temperatures over a thirty-year period with zone boundaries in 10°F increments. The map has shifted with recent changes in climate and the latest map was released in 2012, so ignore data from older maps. The states covered in this book range from zones 4 to 10.

Since it is based solely on winter temperatures, this system has its drawbacks. Extreme high temperatures in summer can have more of an effect on gardening in the Southwest than in other regions. Also, the topography of your land, microclimate in your garden, and whether you are in an urban or rural setting have all have a dramatic effect on the temperatures your garden will experience.

temperatures as high as 134°F have been recorded (not a big gardening region there!).

In the milder parts of this region (zones 8–10), the cold is not the limiting factor for gardeners, but rather the heat. Few vegetable plants thrive when daytime temperatures are over 100°F for weeks at a time in the summer, and the amount of water needed to harvest even paltry amounts of produce is not cost-effective. The plants (and the gardeners, too) give up the struggle for about six weeks in the worst part of the summer. Look for vegetable varieties that have shorter growing seasons (a 65-days-to-harvest squash instead of a 90-day type, for example) so that crops can produce before

temperatures get too high. On the bright side, these areas are blessed with mild winters that allow gardeners to grow many crops that wouldn't grow well in the spring and summer seasons (such as lettuce and other greens), so there is a wide array of vegetables for growing throughout the year.

One thing most areas in the Southwest do have is ample sunshine. In fact, a crop that would be grown in full sun in other climate zones may perform best with only morning sun here. Gardeners may find that erecting shade structures over summer gardens or placing container gardens in afternoon shade allows them to continue with their crops when the temperatures climb.

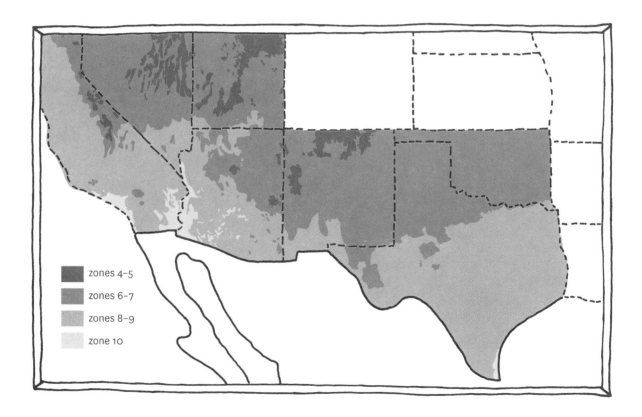

zones 4–5
zones 6–7
zones 8–9
zone 10

It is also a predominantly arid region—most crops must be provided with supplemental irrigation. One small benefit to this, however, is that weeds grow less vigorously. If plants are well mulched, weeds will be more easily controlled in areas with less rainfall.

Careful selection of plant varieties is critical to having a successful garden. Tomatoes that grow beautifully in New Jersey are not likely to perform well here. Cherry tomatoes like Sungold, Juliet, and Sweet 100, paste tomatoes like San Marzano and La Roma will produce more fruit in hot, dry conditions than large tomato types. Avoid falling for pretty pictures on a plant label or seed package and stick to the varieties recommended for your region. Potatoes, onions, corn, peppers, summer squash, carrots, broccoli, kale, collards, and okra are just a few of the crops that can really thrive in the short seasons and dry conditions in the Southwest.

When Do I Plant?

As we've already established, timing is crucial in the garden. Plant too early, warm-season crops will freeze; too late and plants may fail to set fruit or may be so stressed by the heat that they'll find themselves overwhelmed by insect damage.

The first things you'll need to determine for your region are the average dates for your last freeze in spring and first frost in fall. Fortunately, our taxes have been paying for years of climate studies by the USDA's National Climatic Data Center. They monitor weather at stations across the country and make it available for us all through hardiness zone maps on their website (planthardiness.ars.usda.gov). Just enter in your state and zip code and you'll see the frost dates from the weather station located closest to your home. Keep in mind that the numbers represent the average coldest temperature and do not reflect record cold temperatures. Even though my last freeze date is the first of March, I can recall recent freezes toward the end of March, and even one as late as 21 April—there are no guarantees.

Your local nursery, extension service agency, and master gardener organizations should also be able to share the freeze information for your area. Your garden could be colder on any given night if it is located low in a valley, near a large body of water, or far from a city. They can also share with you recommended planting dates for your area and give you a list of varieties that have done well.

Peas, spinach, mâche, and garlic are very hardy and can be planted well before the last freeze, or "as soon as the ground can be worked" in areas where the ground freezes. Other cool-season plants can tolerate a light frost and may even taste better after they have been exposed to cold weather. Cabbage, broccoli, and lettuce can be planted a few weeks before the last frost and still perform well. If covered when colder temperatures threaten, they can survive. Warm-season crops must be planted "after all danger of frost has passed." A late frost will kill cucumbers, tomatoes, squash, eggplant, and peppers.

Cold-hardy vegetables are able to withstand freezing temperatures and are planted in winter months in mild-winter areas or in very early spring and late summer in colder zones. They include broccoli, cabbage, Brussels sprouts, kale, kohlrabi, leeks, onions, garlic, horseradish, peas, rutabaga, and turnips. Half-hardy vegetables withstand light and short-term freezes. They may require cold frames or coverings to withstand more severe weather. They include beets, carrots, cauliflower, potatoes, chard, fennel, lettuce, and radishes. Tender vegetables are those that will be injured by light frosts and include tomatoes, squash, basil, corn, and beans. These plants must be planted early enough in late summer or fall so that they are harvest-ready several weeks prior to the first fall freeze. Warm-season crops need temperatures above 70°F to grow and produce crops; they include okra, cucumbers, eggplant, melons, peppers, sweet potatoes, and pumpkins. Wait until several weeks after the last freeze to begin planting these crops. They are not recommended for planting in the fall in most zones.

BY THE LIGHT OF THE SILVERY MOON

We all pay attention to the amount of sun that a plant requires, but have you given as much thought to the position of the moon when you plant? Knowing that the moon influences the ocean tides and also the motion of water in soil and plant tissues should make its influence on plant growth more credible. The tides are highest when the moon is new and full. Moisture in the earth moves higher as well, making newly planted seeds more likely to germinate and grow stronger. The migration cycles of birds may be linked to lunar cycles as well.

Lunar gardening practitioners recommend planting plants that produce aboveground crops, like kale or okra, during the first seven days of the moon's waxing phase. The time from the first quarter of the moon to the full moon is especially good for the growth of leafy plants. Plants that produce their crop underground like radishes and potatoes are planted during the first seven days of the waning moon. The fourth quarter, the last days before the new moon, are recommended for tilling, weeding, transplanting, and pruning. The days of the full moon and new or dark moon are days that are not recommended for garden activity.

There are even more specific guidelines for planting using the position of the moon in the twelve houses of the zodiac. Use a moon-sign almanac to determine which sign the moon is in for your area and plant according to its recommendations. You may find that you will water new seeds and transplants less and have better planting results.

While it is not always possible to plant or perform garden tasks at the optimal position of the moon, I have noted that crops planted at the correct moon phase are generally more successful. I record the moon's phases in my garden journal when I plant so that I can factor that in my crop evaluation notes. Look for annual calendars that include moon phases to make garden planning easier.

GARDENING
101

Gardeners have produced crops for centuries by just paying attention to the basics; every garden needs sun, soil, water, and food. Understanding the composition of your soil and providing what it lacks, figuring out where to position your garden for the best sun, and properly preparing your beds for planting will get your garden off to a successful start.

Here Comes the Sun

Most vegetables need sun, but there are some plants that will thrive in filtered or partial sun. Plants that are harvested for their leaves are usually more shade tolerant than those that produce fruit. Lettuce, most herbs, chives, Swiss chard, kale, bok choy, and fennel will all grow in partial sun. Eggplants and peppers will tolerate less sun than tomatoes, okra, or corn.

Morning sun and afternoon shade gardens can be very productive in hotter zones. Gardeners in these areas will do well to position their garden so that it is in shade from trees or the house by the hottest part of the day (from 3 to 6 PM). In colder zones, position your garden to take advantage of as much sun as possible.

I find that many gardeners overestimate the amount of sun that their yard has. We often see the back yard in the early morning before work and late at night after work and have no idea how the shade from the house or the trees moves through the yard throughout the day. Use stakes and string to mark the desired garden space and set a timer to go off each hour. Make a note of the hours that shade from surrounding structures is cast over the area. Adjust the location of the garden to have at least six to eight hours of sun, preferably in the morning. If you are preparing your garden site in winter, take into consideration the cover from deciduous trees that will provide shade in much of the growing season.

Evaluating Your Soil

Few gardeners inspect the soil around their home as carefully as they study the home interior and exterior, but I have been known to carry a trowel to check soil depth and type as part of evaluating a home purchase. But no matter what kind of soil you're working with— even thin, chalky, sandy, or rocky soils—there are ways to improve it. Building raised beds and filling them with purchased soil is always an option for fast results.

Much of the Southwest region has sticky black clay soil that clings to tools when wet, cracks when dry, and dries into cement like clods. Other gardeners have a small amount of this slick clay mixed with lime rubble—a combination known as caliche. Both soil types are less than ideal and tend to be alkaline. They are a far cry from the deep, rich soils of most of the South and the East where trees and shrubs are the dominant plant species. Prairie soils were adapted to deeply rooted grasses and were designed to expand with heavy rains and contract during dry spells. The grasses grew and constantly replenished the humus layer of the soil to hold more moisture.

Soil can vary widely from one spot to the next depending on what has grown there and how the soil was used. Your home development may have been farmland at one time. Our gardens at Lake Austin Spa Resort are fine alluvial sand, deposited there for years by the Colorado River. When you go just 200 feet from the river, the thin, rocky caliche soil most common in the region appears.

Soil Types

Sandy loam soil is the gold standard for garden soil—rich and dark but well draining. It contains a balance of organic matter, minerals, and air, and is rich with soil microbes. Sandy loam has a balance of clay, silt, and sand. It is easy to dig and does not stick to garden tools when wet. It's beautiful to work with, and an experience you can eventually have if you treat your soil properly. Adding the right nutrients can get your garden soil closer to this ideal with each season.

Sandy or rocky soils are low in organic material and do not hold moisture well. They tend to be about 80 percent sand and 20 percent silt and clay. Nutrients are easily washed from the soil because of the lack of organic material and they erode and wash away easily. The best way to improve these soils is to increase the level of organic material to improve moisture retention and add nutrients.

Clay soil has very fine particles that knit together closely, making it sticky and prone to holding water. Clay is easily compacted and can develop deep and wide cracks when it is dry. Some gardeners add sand to clay to create a better soil, but the small particle size of sand only increases the problems with clay soil—remember that sand and clay are combined to make bricks, after all. Adding organic material with compost and using cover crops and mulch will improve clay soils to make them more hospitable for edible gardens.

One simple test for evaluating your soil is done by taking a handful of moist soil and squeezing it firmly. Open your hand and see what happens to the soil: if it holds its shape but crumbles when touched, you have sandy loam; if it holds it shapes and does not crumble when touched, it is a clay soil; and if it falls apart when you open your hand, it is sandy soil. However, if you want to get a better idea as to the make-up of your soil,

there is a simple do-it-yourself test that you can perform with a glass jar.

Earthworm Test

A healthy population of earthworms, about eight to ten in a square foot of garden soil, is a good indication that the soil is healthy and well balanced. If the population of earthworms is much lower, it is likely that your soil needs more organic material. Worms will be deeper in the soil during cold and extremely hot months, so check for worms when the soil temperature is 55–65°F.

To check for worms without disrupting the soil too much, lightly scratch the soil surface and put several sheets of wet newspaper over the surface, weight the paper with rocks or board to keep it in place. Make sure there is good soil contact with the paper. The next day, dig a few inches under the paper and you should find the soil teeming with earthworms. My father had us do this the day before a fishing trip so we could harvest our own bait. When we asked why the worms came up, he told us they were "educated worms that liked to read the paper when given a chance!"

Soil pH

The pH of your garden soil is an important number to know. If the pH is over 7, your soil is considered alkaline or basic. A pH under 7 is considered acidic. Most plants prefer a pH of 6.5 to 7, just on the acidic side of neutral, though most soils do not fall into the perfect pH range.

The numbers for pH are exponential, meaning that a level of 8 is ten times more alkaline than 7, so the readings at the high or low end of the scale can be significant. Our plants will not absorb some nutrients if the pH is too high or too low. Send a soil test to a soil and plant lab to determine the pH level of your soil. You can also get a complete analysis of the nutrient levels in your soil so that you can more accurately provide the nutrients your plants require. Many labs will provide recommendations for applying chemical fertilizers, so ignore those and use organic amendments instead. Most DIY soil-testing kits are inaccurate so don't bother with those.

Sulfur can lower pH and wood ashes or lime can raise an acidic pH, but adding compost to soil with each gardening season will help to safely bring your pH to a more neutral level. Adding too much sulfur or lime at one time can make the soil toxic.

SOIL COMPOSITION TEST

Knowing the composition of your soil will help you add the soil amendments that will make your soil more ideal.

ITEMS NEEDED

quart jar with tight lid and straight sides
½ cup soil
water
1 teaspoon dish detergent to help disperse soil
    molecules

STEPS

1 Dig a sample of the soil from the area where your garden will be planted. Remove the first inch or two of soil and any mulch, stones, or sticks from the sample.

2 Add water until the jar is about ¾ full.

3 Close the lid and shake vigorously. All the soil should be well mixed, with no visible chunks of soil left. Let the contents settle without disturbing it for at least two days.

4 The contents will settle into layers. The sand is heaviest and will settle at the bottom of the jar quickly. Silt will be in a layer above the sand. Clay will be suspended in the water and organic matter will float on the surface of the water.

5 Use a ruler to measure the depth of the various elements of the soil and the total depth of the soil in the jar. Determine the percentage of each layer by dividing the depth of the layer by the total soil depth.

Perform this simple home test to determine what your soil is made up of.

Watering

Much of the Southwest has suffered from serious and persistent drought conditions for many years. There are restrictions on the days to water and the amount of water that can be used in many communities. Watering of lawns has been curtailed in many areas. Certainly, the limited use of water to grow food is a justifiable use of this precious resource, but mulching, rainwater collection, drip irrigation, and planting the right varieties can make every drop count.

Ways to Water

In order to water wisely in the Southwest, it is important to water for longer periods to ensure the water goes deeply into the soil, which encourages deep rooting of plants. Giving plants daily, brief watering encourages root growth near the surface of the soil, but when plants are allowed to dry out a bit between watering, their roots grow in search of water deep in the soil. Check the soil an inch or two from the soil surface. When that area is dry, it is time to water again.

Group plants according to their water needs. More xeric lavender, sage, and rosemary like water less often

Watering cans are great tools for various watering chores around the garden.

and don't want a heavy mulch or frequent fertilizer. Planting these next to basil or tomatoes, which like regular watering, fertilizer, and mulch, will usually lead to the death of the drought lovers. Allow the soil to dry several inches from the surface before watering xeric plants again.

Water hoses are essential for keeping plants healthy. Even with drip systems or an elaborate sprinkler system, you will still occasionally need to wash plants or use a hose end sprayer for fertilizer applications. Purchase quality hoses that will last for many years. Disconnect hoses before freezes to limit damage that can come from water freezing inside the hose. Brass hose fittings are available to make inevitable repairs.

Keep repair fittings on hand for male and female hose ends and for repairing breaks or leaks in the main body of the hose. The fittings need to be snug to prevent leaks and are sometimes difficult to install. Take a coffee cup with hot water to the garden and immerse the end of the hose to be repaired for a few minutes. The hot water will soften the hose so that you may insert the repair coupling easily. Allow the hose to cool completely before using it. You may also want to buy a larger hose and cut smaller sections of hose for certain areas. The brass repair fittings may be installed on the ends of the hose to create the perfect-size hose. Most small hose lengths available for purchase are cheaply made and don't last very long, so I buy 100- or 150-foot-long hoses and make smaller ones. I find that more than 75 feet of hose gets difficult to manage, coil up, and carry. I prefer to connect additional hoses when required. Get in the habit of coiling your hoses in one direction only as you put them away. That will limit hose kinks. Hoses that are left out uncoiled in cold weather can be difficult to coil neatly again. Hot weather in the Southwest causes hose washers to deteriorate quickly. I replace all hose washers at least once a year to keep them from dripping.

You will also probably want more than one watering can. They are handy for adding water to a thirsty plant, gently watering new seedlings, or mixing a liquid fertilizer blend and applying it to your soil. Make sure your watering can is comfortable for you to carry, especially when full. A gallon of water weighs 8 pounds, so an extremely large watering can could be very heavy. If you do a lot of watering with a can it is best to get a matching set so that you have an evenly balanced load when you carry two cans.

I look for a watering can that has a removable rosette nozzle to gently water new seedlings. Leaves and debris will clog the tiny holes in the nozzle and it is much easier to clean if it can be removed.

The use of drip irrigation and soaker hoses can make the most of the water you use on your garden. By putting

THE HOSE END SHUT OFF: A SERIOUS STEP SAVER

Do yourself a favor and put a hose end shut off at the male end of each hose connection. These brass or plastic gadgets have a lever that allows you to shut the water off temporarily without having to go back to the hose faucet at the house. You can add a spray nozzle or connect another hose or a hose end sprayer without getting wet. Don't shut the water off with a hose end shut off for long periods; they are designed for short spans of use. Hoses are not designed to withstand the constant pressure and it can cause them to leak or burst.

the water directly onto the soil, less is lost to evaporation. Additionally, your plants will stay dry, which helps curb diseases like powdery mildew.

Composting

Whether or not you've been blessed with a green thumb, the addition of beautiful black compost to your garden lets you grow anything. Compost improves heavy clay soils, making them fluffier so that the soil drains better; it increases the water-holding capacity of sandy soils and helps to move soil pH to a more neutral level, which vegetables prefer. Composting may seem like a mysterious process, but the truth is that organic materials will always decompose. We can make that process faster and more efficient or we can be patient and let nature take its own time to make compost.

Nature provides its own means of improving soil. Trees lose their leaves and those leaves fall and become leaf mold and eventually become compost that feeds the trees so they can make more leaves. Sadly, many people rake those leaves and trim tree branches and set those materials on the curb. Composting keeps garden-waste materials out of our landfills and puts them to better use improving our gardens. We save expensive landfill space and the gas for transporting the materials and turn the garden trash to treasure.

To speed up the rate of composting, shred or chop materials as finely as possible before adding them to the pile. Chopping ingredients creates more surface area for bacteria and other microorganisms to go to work. I prefer to chop up garden plants with clippers as I remove them for their next role as compost ingredients. They are more difficult to chop up when dry. Run a mower over

BUILDING YOUR COMPOST

Compost piles are mainly comprised of carbon materials (the brown stuff) and nitrogen materials (the green stuff). There are many recipes for combining those elements to make the best compost, but it's a pretty forgiving process. Some composts are better than others, but any mixture of ingredients will decompose and improve your soil. Typically, a ratio of three parts brown (carbon) to one part green (nitrogen) materials will result in a speedy composting process and an excellent finished product.

THE BROWN STUFF

- straw
- branches collected from pruning
- plants removed at the end of the season (large tomato and okra plants or cornstalks should cut into pieces)
- shredded newsprint (leave out glossy advertisements and inserts)
- pine needles
- leaves (oak leaves can be slow to decompose and are slightly acidic; shred them first to speed breakdown)
- sawdust or wood shavings from untreated wood

THE GREEN STUFF

- vegetable and fruit trimmings (keep them in a covered container in your freezer until you get a chance to add them to the pile to avoid attracting insects and creating a slimy mess in your compost container; blend them to speed up decomposition)
- spoiled food or leftovers
- spoiled dairy products in small quantities
- grass clippings
- green plant trimmings
- droppings and natural bedding from rabbits, gerbils, and hamsters
- chicken, goat, pig, cow, or sheep manure (if manure is very fresh, mix it with plenty of carbon material to control odors; horse manure may be used but is often full of weed seeds so make sure that your pile gets hot enough to kill the weed seeds)
- weeds (avoid Bermuda, nutgrass, or weeds with seed heads unless you have a very hot compost pile)
- alfalfa meal
- aquatic plants and seaweed

Coffee grounds are a great addition as well, and can have as much nitrogen as many animal manures. Their slight acidity and trace amounts of potassium, phosphorus, calcium, and copper can really perk up your compost pile and enrich your soil. Include unbleached coffee filters also as they are a source of carbon.

HOMEMADE COMPOST BINS

A structure around your compost pile is not essential but it does keep the pile more tidy and attractive. Wood pallets are usually available for free and are easily assembled into bins. Slide the pallets over metal fence posts to make them more stable. Use wire, twine, or zip ties to connect the sections. Keep the front section open on one side or provide a hinged gate to facilitate access for turning of the pile. Use pallets that have smaller gaps between the boards or line them with hardware cloth or chicken wire to contain materials more effectively.

Cinder blocks or hay bales can be stacked to contain compost ingredients. Use metal fence posts inside the corners of the cinder block walls to keep them more stable. Add a gap between blocks to eliminate excess moisture if necessary.

Wood bins or wire mesh bins can be purchased or easily constructed. Make sure that they have a panel or door that will open so that the pile can be turned easily and the finished composted can be accessed easily. Trying to empty the bin from the top may result in back strain.

Make as many compost piles and bins as your property will allow. Have one pile with finished compost, one that is completely built and cooking, and one that is in progress. I have never heard a gardener complain about having too much compost!

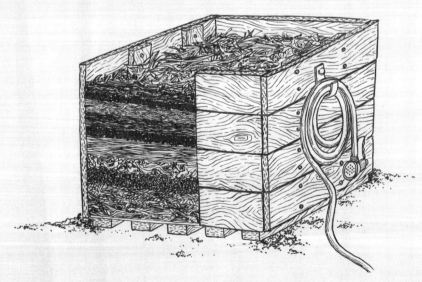

Layers of nitrogen- and carbon-rich materials will break down to become dark, crumbly compost.

leaves, especially large leaves, or put them in a metal garbage can and use your string trimmer to chop them finely. Wear eye protection and a mask when breaking down leaves with this method.

It is also helpful to keep your compost pile large and damp. The larger the size of your pile, the hotter it will get and the faster it will break down. The minimum size to get speedy decomposition is a cubic yard. Without sufficient size, materials will not heat up for rapid breakdown. Likewise, the bacteria, fungi, and other microorganisms responsible for the creation of compost thrive in damp environments. All the materials in the pile should be evenly moist, about the consistency of a damp sponge, but don't overdo it. Turning your compost frequently will also speed up the decomposition process.

COMPOST TEA: MAKE A LITTLE COMPOST GO A LONG WAY

Compost tea is a nutrient-rich liquid fertilizer that is great for new transplants and containers, among others. Make it by placing a shovel-full of finished compost or earthworm castings inside an old pillowcase or a piece of fabric. Place the "teabag" into a 5-gallon bucket with water (rainwater or water without chlorine, which would kill off beneficial microbes, is ideal). Vigorously stir the water and soak the bag for twenty-four hours. Squeeze out the excess water from the bag and add the compost back to the compost pile or to the garden. Mix enough water with the finished compost tea to dilute it to the color of iced tea. Spray on plant foliage, drench the soil around new transplants, and use on your container plants to keep them happy and healthy.

Finished compost will have a clean, earthy smell and will look like fine, dark coffee grounds. Partially finished compost will still have bits of leaves, twigs, or stems visible in it but will look more like soil than the original compost ingredients. It may be used for mulching plants and it will continue to break down and improve the soil. If your compost pile seems too smelly and damp (something that has scared off many gardeners), add air by turning the pile or add high-carbon materials like coarse mulch, shredded newspaper, or even brown cardboard pieces to absorb moisture and increase air spaces.

Organic Fertilizers: Nature's Soil Builders

Avoiding the use of chemical fertilizers in your garden is a challenge for any new gardener. Garden centers line their shelves with promises of quick fixes and miracle cures—it can be hard to resist. But it's important to realize the damage that these products do, both to your own garden and to the world at large. In the early 1980s, I learned a lesson in the leaching of chemical fertilizers when a fertilizer salesman gave me a few bags of lawn fertilizer that he said were organic with some urea nitrogen added. Our lakeside lawn, growing in very sandy soil, was generally lacking in nitrogen, so I decided to give it a try. The lawn did indeed green up quickly. What we noticed next confirmed just how rapidly chemical fertilizer moved through the soil. The water next to the shore began to develop a thick mat of bright green algae, even greener than the lawn. It took months for that to dissipate. I have not used chemical fertilizers since. High phosphorus levels in fertilizer can contribute to algae bloom and growth of water weeds in lakes and rivers, even if your garden isn't adjacent to the water.

Chemicals move into ground water and find waterways however they can.

Plants are assisted in their assimilation of nutrients by abundant soil microbes—as many as 50 billion microbes in a single tablespoon of healthy soil. Through the process of mineralization, microbes break down organic matter into humus, then humic acid, then into basic elements that are available to plants. Some microbes, like mycorrhizal fungi, actually extend the length and surface area of plant's root systems, resulting in healthier plants. Chemical fertilizers tend to bypass the plant's natural means of assimilating nutrients, and can leave salt residues in the soil that are toxic to soil microbes. Without a healthy microorganism population, the plants become dependent on the regular addition of chemical fertilizer to sustain growth. It's much like the intravenous feeding of humans, bypassing the digestive system. Patients may survive, but they don't thrive.

High levels of nitrates from chemical fertilizers are carcinogenic and are becoming a serious problem in our drinking water. Studies show that as much of 50 percent of the nitrogen from chemical fertilizers is leached out quickly and only 5–10 percent actually feeds the plants. That is one reason why nitrogen numbers are much higher in chemical fertilizers. Organic fertilizers break down slowly without leaching into streams and ground water. They improve soil tilth and structure, loosen heavy clay, and add needed humus to sandy soils.

Feed the Soil, Not the Plants

One of the most important aspects of gardening organically is realizing that we do not feed our plants, rather we feed the soil and the soil feeds our plants. Specifically, it is the soil microbes—bacteria, fungi, protozoans, amoeba, nematodes, springtails, and many other tiny denizens of the soil that break down the organic compounds in leaves, straw, manure, and other products into simple compounds that plants can actually absorb and utilize as they grow.

These tiny microbes require good working conditions—plenty of air, a constant supply of organic matter for food, and water. Mulching with layers of organic material keeps the soil cool and moist and as the mulch breaks down it provide more food for the microbes. Building raised beds and avoiding compaction of the soil ensures that the microbes get the oxygen they require. When soil gets too dry or too compacted the microbe population will die off and the soil will require compost to reintroduce the microbe population.

N-P-K: The Big Three

The first three numbers on a bag of fertilizer will indicate the proportion of nitrogen, phosphorus, and potassium present (for example, 8-2-4 or 6-2-2).

Nitrogen (N) is the primary growth nutrient. It stimulates stem and leaf growth. A deficiency will reveal stunted growth, yellowish or small leaves, and lack of vigor. Excess nitrogen will prevent flowering and fruit set.

Phosphorus (P) stimulates root growth, flowers, and fruiting. A deficiency will show reddish or purple discoloration of stems and poor root growth. Leaves may have a pale color.

Potassium or Potash (K) provides improved hardiness to heat and cold and resistance to disease. It also improves drought tolerance. A lack of K will show tough, leathery stems, small leaves, and a lack of vigor and the edges of plant leaves may appear scorched.

Other important nutrients are sulfur and lime. Sulfur is used to decrease the pH level of alkaline soils. To decrease pH by one unit, add 2 pounds granular sulfur per 100 square feet. By lowering the pH, you will also make nutrients like calcium and iron more available to the plants. Keep in mind that the effect of adding sulfur to the soil is not permanent, and the overuse of sulfur can make soil so toxic that nothing will grow. Use granular or soil sulfur as a soil amendment, rather than dusting sulfur, which is difficult to spread and can burn the skin. Sulfur dust is used for pest control and mixed with water for use as an insect spray.

If your soil is acidic you can add lime to raise the pH. If your soil needs both magnesium and lime, use dolomitic or magnesium lime to balance both nutrients. Dolomitic limestone has 46 percent calcium and 38 percent magnesium. Lime is available in a powder or granular form.

TRACE MINERALS AND DEFICIENCY SYMPTOMS

- **Magnesium (Mg).** Deficiency will show yellowing of leaves between the veins, bronzing, and shedding of leaves. Mites thrive in these conditions. Too much potassium can cause Mg deficiency. A lack of sweetness in fruit can be a result of low magnesium levels.

- **Iron (Fe).** Yellowing of outer portions of leaves while veins remain green. Symptoms are usually present on new or outer growth. Excess soil alkalinity can tie up iron and make it unavailable to plants. Treat with Greensand, Actino-Iron, or sulfur.

- **Manganese (Mn).** Deficiency is common in alkaline soils. Looks like iron deficiency followed by early death of leaves. Plants may have small dead spots or papery areas on leaves.

- **Copper (Cu).** Wither-tip, especially in cloudy weather.

- **Zinc (Zn).** Yellowing of veins, small leaves, and leaf spot. Common with excess K.

- **Calcium (Ca).** Whole plant may be yellow, and the stems tough and dry. Young leaves may cup backward and have white spots on leaves or turn brown. Calcium deficiency may cause blossom end rot in tomatoes.

   Seaweed is one of the best sources for adding trace nutrients. It contains over 55 trace minerals.

Organic Fertilizer Ingredients

When I was a young woman who wanted to learn more about organic gardening, I was fortunate enough to meet Miss Lillian Peek, who was 92 and looking for someone to help her tend the elaborate flower gardens she had developed. Iris and daylilies were meticulously labeled with variety names and she had hybridized new varieties of each. Dogwoods, roses, altheas, and many other blooming plants provided seasonal interest. She had a fertilizer shed with bags and cans of many different types of nutrient materials. I followed her hand-printed recipe cards to mix bone meal, rock phosphate, sulfur, and other nutrients in the proper proportions to feed the flowers. It was my first introduction to focusing on a particular plant's need for nutrients. She and her gardens are long gone, but I learned so much from working with her. Today, we are fortunate enough to be able to purchase balanced organic fertilizer blends and forgo the need for a fertilizer shed and the dusty mixing of materials. You can buy fertilizers designed with the specific nutrient needs of tomatoes, roses, citrus, or vegetables in mind. In fact, using single-ingredient fertilizers may make other nutrients unavailable.

Alfalfa meal (2-1-2) is a good source of trace minerals, the growth hormone triacontanol, and vitamin A. The meal and pellets are often used as animal food and are available at feed stores (don't use rabbit pellets as they have added salts). The nutrients are released within four months of application. The meal can contain viable seeds. Roses benefit from using alfalfa as a fertilizer. Use it as a soil amendment, as a compost ingredient, or in fertilizer tea. Use 2–5 pounds per 1000 square feet.

Bat guano (10-3-1) is bat feces harvested from caves where bats roost seasonally. It has one of the highest nitrogen levels of all organic fertilizers and can be mixed into the soil or used as a foliar feeding. Wearing a mask is recommended to avoid pathogens that could be present. It releases fairly quickly. Use 5 pounds per 1000 square feet.

Blood meal (12-0-0) is made from dried slaughterhouse waste and is one of the highest organic sources of nitrogen. It can burn plants if overapplied and may attract flies. It releases quickly into the soil, within one to four months. It is useful for leafy greens but can sometimes delay fruiting of plants like tomatoes, peppers, or beans. It is often used as a deer repellent. Use 5–10 pounds per 1000 square feet.

Bone meal (3-12-0) undergoes intense chemical processing which removes most of its beneficial nutrients. It is not a product that I use anymore. Adding bone meal to the soil tends to attract squirrels, rodents, dogs, and cats. It is available quickly in the soil, in one to four months. Like blood meal, this is an animal-processing waste and depending on the animals' diets, it could have high levels of metals, arsenic, and pharmaceutical waste materials. Not something we want in our organic gardens. I prefer to use soft rock phosphate instead, but

it may be difficult for some gardeners to get their hands on. Bone meal, however, is commonplace and cheap. Use 10 pounds per 1000 square feet.

Corn gluten meal (9-0-0) is an excellent source of nitrogen, but it can inhibit the germination of seeds for up to four months when added to soil. It can be added to garden beds if you are using transplants exclusively. Commonly used as a fertilizer and pre-emergent weed control for lawns, it is also added to compost as a nitrogen source. Corn gluten is used in animal feed and can be found in feed stores. It is applied at 20–40 pounds per 1000 square feet.

Cottonseed meal (6-2-2) is a rich source of nitrogen, but make sure it is from an organic source. Most cotton is sprayed with a tremendous amount of chemicals, which can remain in the seeds. Its nutrients are released fairly quickly, in one to four months. Use 10 pounds per 1000 square feet.

Earthworm castings (.5-1-1) (otherwise known as worm manure) is one of my favorite fertilizers. Not a rich fertilizer—the fertility ratio depends on the materials that the worms are given to eat—but it is full of beneficial microbes, bacteria, and enzymes and since the worms have predigested the plant material, the castings make those nutrients immediately available to plants. It has a rich black color and a nice earthy smell. Citrus trees, hibiscus, and fruit trees respond quickly to this gentle fertilizer. Brew castings in rainwater for a gentle fertilizer tea. Add to potting soil mixes and seed-starter blends and top dress any seedlings that need a nutrient boost. You can buy earthworm castings in bagged form or start your own vermiculture box for a steady supply of the perfect plant food. Think of the worms as pets—they need regular attention and food, water, warmth, and protection from predators like fire ants and from extreme heat.

Epsom salt (magnesium sulfate) helps plants to absorb nitrogen and phosphorus more efficiently. Rosarians know about the wonders of Epsom salt to keep their roses blooming and the foliage dark green. Add 2 tablespoons to a gallon of water and drench the root zone of tomatoes, peppers, and eggplants at bloom stage to increase bloom production and fruiting, or simply add a teaspoon to the planting hole. It can also be applied as a foliar spray.

Feather meal (12-0-0) is another slaughterhouse product and has high nitrogen levels but releases slowly. Use 2.5–5 pounds per 1000 square feet.

Fish meal (10-6-2) is ground and dried fish waste. Mix it into the soil well to avoid attracting flies or animals. It releases its nutrients quickly, in one to four months, and increases microbial life in the soil dramatically. Avoid applying high levels near fruiting plants as the high nitrogen level can delay blooming.

Fish emulsion (5-2-2) is a liquid fertilizer processed from fish waste. It has a very strong odor that may persist for several days, so make sure to avoid using it when you're expecting company. It releases nutrients quickly, in one to four months, and has many micronutrient benefits. Hydrolyzed fish emulsion (4-2-2) uses enzymes to digest the nutrients from fish waste instead of heat and acid. This process retains more of the protein and nutrients than regular fish emulsion and isn't quite as pungent, but it is more expensive. It may attract animals to the garden. Use 4–5 tablespoons per gallon of water.

Granite dust (0-0-5) is a source of potassium and can also help improve drainage in the soil.

Kelp or seaweed meal (1.5-.5-5) is not a rich source of N-P-K but has an amazing array of trace minerals and micronutrients. Use 1 pound per 100 square feet.

Kelp powder (1-0-4) is seaweed ground finely enough to mix with water and use for foliar sprays or soil feeding. It has growth hormones, flowering hormones, and many trace nutrients. It is typically more cost effective to buy a powdered form and mix it with water rather than purchasing a liquid concentrate.

Soft rock phosphate (0-18-0), also known as colloidal phosphate, has 18 percent phosphorus and 19 percent calcium in forms that plants can utilize easily. It breaks down slowly, so it lasts for many years and will not need to be added each season. It has many micronutrients also.

Soybean meal (7-2-1) is used as an animal feed and is an excellent organic amendment. It is quickly available to plants, in one to four months. Most soy grown in this country is genetically modified, so make sure to purchase organic meal. Use 8 pounds per 1000 square feet.

Soil activators like Medina and Agrispon have no N-P-K ratios but they act as growth stimulants for microbes in the soil. The microbes multiply more rapidly and make soil nutrients more available to plants. They aren't actually fertilizers, but they make the fertilizers you use more effective. They are particularly important to add to soil that has been neglected or that was subjected to drought, flooding, or harsh chemical treatments—things which spell death for microbe populations.

GARDEN
PLANNING

Time spent planning a garden will never be wasted effort. I have seen far too many gardeners who failed to prepare the soil well, planted more than they could care for, or grew more than they could consume of one crop. They get frustrated and sometimes give up on gardening. It is easy to be overly ambitious when we see those new transplants in the garden center and the seed racks and catalogs with dazzling pictures of perfect vegetables. But when you start with a plan, you know exactly what you have room for and where it will go when you get it home. Begin your garden journal and measure your garden space so that you know how much you have room for with each season.

If your garden beds can't quite contain all that you wish to grow there are many vegetables that will grow quite happily in containers and those containers can be recycled materials that you save from the landfill.

We will look at many ways to build garden beds and create garden spaces that maximize your food-growing potential and minimize your chances of crop failure. We can always learn from our failures in the garden, so even if you don't get a single edible morsel from a crop, it's always more material for the compost pile.

Garden Beds

Garden beds that are no more than 4 feet wide will be the easiest for most gardeners to access. That provides sufficient width for double or triple rows of plantings and it is easy to reach across the bed for sowing seeds, thinning, and harvesting. Gardeners with knee or back issues may want to keep the width to 3 feet to make reaching across easier.

Although I enjoy looking at gardens with fanciful bed layouts, I like rectangular beds and nice straight rows. They make it simpler to design, maintain, and install drip irrigation systems and to access the beds from all sides. I prefer to keep beds no more than 50 feet long in my commercial garden and I keep them 12–15 feet long in my home garden. That makes row covers and drip lines for each bed more manageable—and having to circle around longer beds creates more walking, less gardening.

The spacing between rows should be wide enough to accommodate your wheelbarrow or garden cart so that adding compost each season or bringing mulch to the beds is easily done. And you may need that cart to haul all the produce you are collecting also.

Remove weeds or grass in the planting area and loosen the soil as deeply as you can. Resist the urge to till grass into the soil, especially if you have crabgrass, Bermuda, or other aggressive grasses. Tilling just cuts the roots and stolons into more pieces and buries them deeply in the soil. You will be digging pieces of grass from deep soil depths for years. Solarize the grass for at least six weeks (see page 125) if you prefer not to dig out the grass and weeds.

Raised Beds

Most vegetables prefer a soil depth of 12–18 inches. Many Southwest gardeners have much less soil than that, so raised beds make sense. Raised beds will improve drainage and prevent plants from being washed away when a sudden deluge occurs. Raised beds also warm up more quickly in spring and allow earlier planting of cold, tender plants. The raised bed does not have a floor; whatever existing soil you have will become part of the soil in the raised bed. If you have 4 inches of decent soil and build a raised bed 10 inches tall, you will have the makings of a healthy garden bed. If desired, line the bottom of the raised bed structure with a heavy layer of newspapers, eight to ten sheets deep, tightly woven together and wet thoroughly; then top with soil. This step will suppress weed growth under the planting area and the paper becomes food for worms and beneficial soil organisms that you want to attract to the garden.

Having a bed with walkways around it will prevent soil compaction that can hinder the growth of plant roots. You never want to walk on top of the raised bed as that pushes out air spaces and turns fluffy soils hard.

(Train children and dogs to stay off garden beds with a string line tied to stakes around the garden. It will serve as a visual aid use the paths, not the beds, for walking.) Once the beds are made, with each new planting season you will lightly turn the soil and add compost and soil amendments, and you'll be ready to plant with very little effort.

Soil amendments are added only where the plants are going to grow. Gardeners who grow in furrows tend to amend the entire plot, and then make their rows, so they use more material to prepare their area—and it's just a lot more work. Frequent tilling of soil is harmful to earthworms and soil structure or tilth. An ideal soil structure has large soil particles with large air spaces between particles. Heavily tilled soil will be very porous, yet a hardpan of heavily compacted soil is created just below the depth of the rototiller tines. Water moves quickly through the top of the garden, and then sits at or below plant roots, leading to diseases.

If you choose to work the soil with a tiller, just use it long enough to turn in the organic material in each spot and move the machine as quickly as possible. My farmer friend, Carol Ann Sayle, from Boggy Creek Farms calls it "tickle tilling"—just enough mixing of the soil to break up the roots of the previous planting and mix in amendments. Lightweight mini-tillers are the best choice for working large raised beds quickly. Rear- and front-tine tillers are not necessary for permanent raised bed gardens.

The roots of the previous crop are best left in the soil. Those plants pulled nutrients from the soil and fed themselves with those roots. The roots are still full of food and will break down quickly to feed the next season's plants. Legume plant roots have nitrogen nodules which make the nitrogen very available to your next crop. Cut bean and pea plants at the surface of the soil and leave the roots. Marigold, mustard, and Elbon rye roots repel nematodes in the soil. Cut large tomato vines

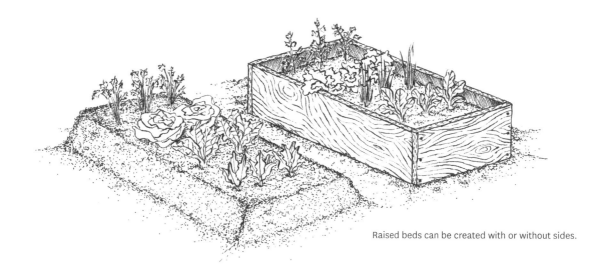

Raised beds can be created with or without sides.

or okra plants at the surface and chop the roots a bit with a shovel. The roots die quickly once the top of the plant is removed. The old roots add organic matter and prevent soil erosion.

Never work garden soil when it is wet. If the soil is sticking to your tools or the tines of your tiller, it is too wet to work. Nothing destroys soil structure and creates large, cement-like dirt clods in clay soil like working wet soil.

You don't need structures or boxes surrounding the planting beds. After the garden area has been cleaned and the soil loosened, insert stakes to mark the corners of your raised bed. Tie string from stake to stake about 6 inches high to keep the garden beds nice and straight. Dig the soil from the area between raised beds and pile it into the garden beds. Raised beds that are too high are prone to dry out too quickly in warm areas so keep beds to 10–16 inches tall if there is no structure to help hold moisture in. An exception to this is hugelkultur- and keyhole-style raised beds, usually built much higher, but because of the intense layers of organic material used in their construction, the wicking action of the soil keeps the planting bed moist.

As soon as the soil is leveled in the garden beds, add leaves or wood mulch to the pathways to keep your feet clean when the soil is wet. Well-mulched pathways will deter weeds and help hold moisture in the beds. After walking on the leaves for several months, they will be broken down into a fine leaf mold that can be dug out and used to increase the organic matter content with your next season's planting. You can even bury kitchen waste deep in the leaves to increase the organic matter and attract earthworms. I pile the leaves in the trenches until they are almost level with the top of the finished soil of the garden beds.

Raised beds built with wood can be neat and attractive but choose your wood carefully. Modern wood preservatives do not use the copper, chromium, and arsenic blend (CCA) that was banned for residential use in 2003 but are still treated with copper, which can leach into plantings. Untreated cedar and other rot-resistant wood should give you years of use in the garden but can be costly. Another option is to use untreated pine lumber and line it with galvanized metal flashing. The metal is treated with zinc and should not pose a problem with your food. The flashing comes in rolls that are 8–20 inches wide and I like to install it on the boards before they are assembled into the bed shape. Use a heavy-duty stapler to secure the flashing. Since the flashing prevents wood to soil contact, the wood will have a much longer life in the garden. Galvanized angle braces will protect the corners when the sides of the bed are joined together.

Wood alternatives have become more readily available and affordable, also. Typically created from recycled plastic and sawdust, they look like wood and can be cut like wood, but will last for years, don't splinter, and stay cool in the heat. This material is not always available in widths deep enough for a raised bed, but they can be lined with heavy plastic or flashing to keep soil in place. These materials are also ideal for making rot-resistant compost bins (Trex is one of the most popular brands).

Many gardeners choose galvanized metal or plastic stock tanks to create large raised gardens easily. They need to have holes drilled to provide drainage. They are ideal for gardeners who have difficulty stooping or bending. Railroad ties and tires contain toxic chemicals which can transfer into the soil and plants so are best to avoid as materials for edible gardens.

Use brick or stone for raised beds to match the materials used on your home. If you are building a home and decide where you want your gardens before construction begins, have the masons that are installing the stone or brick on the house make the raised beds for you. The material and masonry style of the garden beds will match your home and you can often get the work for less since the workers are already on the site. Cinder blocks or stackable paving stones can make raised beds quickly. Paint the cinder blocks to make them more aesthetically pleasing. Recycled concrete from sidewalks or patios can be used to create raised beds.

If you were not blessed with carpentry genes and the thought of stones and mortar terrifies you, don't worry. There are easy-to-assemble kits available at many gardening stores and online outlets. Some kits will provide the corner brackets and you provide the boards to assemble your own garden beds in a short time. Fill with soil and you are ready to plant.

Sunken Beds

For many gardeners in the arid Southwest, a sunken garden bed will protect plants from drying winds and help soil retain moisture. Sunken beds collect rainwater and their high walls give plants wind protection. They work well for sandy soils but are not the best solution for clay soils or wet climates. Simply planting garden seeds in a shallow trench will keep them moist enough to germinate in warm, dry areas. It is often recommended that squash, cucumbers, and melons be planted in small hills to allow better drainage; however, in arid regions, instead dig shallow basins several inches deep to prevent the soil from drying out, crusting over, and inhibiting germination.

Lasagna Gardening

If you want to build raised beds without digging or purchasing new soil, or even spending any money at all, lasagna gardening is worth a try. After hearing gardeners rave about this labor-intensive but quickly successful style of bed building, I decided to try it myself. I built it in the winter months and planted it in spring. That summer was one of the hottest and driest in Austin's history and I gave up on my other garden beds and my little patch of lawn, but the lasagna bed kept going even after I stopped watering. The soil is still rich and productive years later, so this method is one that I am very keen on.

One of the best aspects of lasagna gardening is that the lawn or weeds that are growing in the garden area need not be removed. When I built my bed, there was a pretty healthy patch of Bermuda that was completely composted by the first layers of newspaper and cardboard.

The process of building the bed goes fairly quickly but assembling sufficient materials for the bed may require more effort. You will collect the same types of items that you would utilize in building a compost bed, but with a few additions.

For the carbon components, stockpile newspapers (without the shiny ad inserts), brown cardboard (white boxes may contain bleaches and chemicals best left out of the garden; make sure to remove all tape), lots of mulch, bags of leaves, straw, untreated hay, or sawdust. The nitrogen materials may include kitchen waste, coffee grounds, animal manure (if you can get it), grass clippings, lake plants, or seaweed.

Water the area and mow the grass if necessary. Lay the newspapers down, at least ten pages thick, overlapping the sections so that they form a tightly knitted covering. Wet the newspapers as you get a 4-foot square section down so that they will not blow away. The next layer will be cardboard. Use several layers, especially if you are covering a weedy area. Extend these two layers around the perimeter of the actual planting bed to make a weed-free path around the planting area. Cover the pathways with a thick layer of mulch.

Now add about an inch of your green materials. Cover with 4 inches of brown material, and another of green, wetting the bed after each addition of the brown materials. Add a sprinkling of garden soil or finished compost to each layer to speed up the soil-making process. The bed will settle a bit, so build it at least 6 inches taller than you would like the ultimate height to be. You can always add soil and compost to the top to increase the depth as needed.

Keep the bed moist to assist with decomposition. Add some finished garden soil and compost to the top of the bed if you want to plant right away. Shallow-rooted plants like beans or lettuce will perform best until the bed layers have cooked together. I covered my lasagna bed with leaves and left it for a few months, watering it when needed. The bed can be built all at once or gradually as materials are collected.

This method is a great way to recycle materials that might end up in landfills and the resulting soil is so rich that much less water is needed. Build the beds higher if stooping and bending to care for the garden is a challenge for you. The beds can be formed into any shape you choose. I plan to edge my lasagna bed with a stone border to keep nutgrass and Bermuda from creeping in around the edges.

1–2 feet tall or more

mulch
garden soil and compost
carbon
nitrogen
carbon
nitrogen
cardboard
newspaper

existing sod

Recycle common materials to create rich garden soil by building a lasagna garden bed.

Hugelkultur: German Engineering for the Garden

Hugelkultur is a German term for "hilled garden," and is basically a lasagna bed built on rotting logs, branches, and twigs. The base of the bed is filled with tightly stacked wood—preferably old and dry, but some green wood can be mixed in. The wood absorbs water as it rots and becomes a water reservoir for the plantings in the garden bed above. The wood is also a rich source of organic material as it breaks down. It generates heat and keeps the bed warmer in cool seasons.

As the wood base disintegrates it takes up a good deal of nitrogen, so the bed is best used for plants that have low nitrogen needs for the first few years or you will need to add nitrogen-rich fertilizer like coffee grounds, fish meal, or kelp to compensate. Potatoes would be an ideal crop, as would any legume crop since they would obtain their own nitrogen. Tomatoes, okra, and corn are big crops that need steady supplies of nitrogen, so they're not good choices for a new hugelkultur bed.

These beds can be built as high as you wish and can be dug into the ground. They will settle over the years. This is an ideal option for anyone who has dead trees or old wood that needs to be cleaned up. Anyone with very shallow soil might benefit also. Some gardeners report that their hugelkultur beds did not require any supplemental water or fertilizer, but I found it necessary to provide both—at least through the first summer season.

Rot-resistant wood like cedar or redwood are not ideal for this system and black walnut wood could be toxic to your plants.

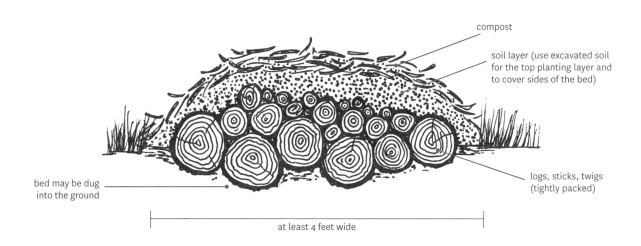

compost

soil layer (use excavated soil for the top planting layer and to cover sides of the bed)

bed may be dug into the ground

logs, sticks, twigs (tightly packed)

at least 4 feet wide

Construction of a hugelkultur bed.

Keyhole Garden

Keyhole gardens are constructed in a fashion similar to lasagna and hugelkulter beds but with a compost bin in the center to provide moisture and nutrients. They can be built rather high to accommodate gardeners with special needs. Gardeners in drought-stressed regions are finding them very successful as the sheer volume of organic matter keeps them moist. The sides and tops of the bed may be planted to increase yields.

The beds are typically built in a horseshoe shape about 6 feet in diameter. A circular wire compost bin is installed in the center with an access path left open to the bin so that new kitchen wastes and garden trimmings can be added regularly. The soil slopes downward from the center bin so that when the center compost is watered, the nutrient-rich water trickles into the surrounding bed, feeding and watering the garden.

The beds generally have stones, logs, or bricks on the outside edge to support the base. Layers of newspaper and cardboard will suppress weed growth and attract earthworms to the soil. Once the bed is built, the compost bin can be emptied periodically to enrich the top of the bed before planting.

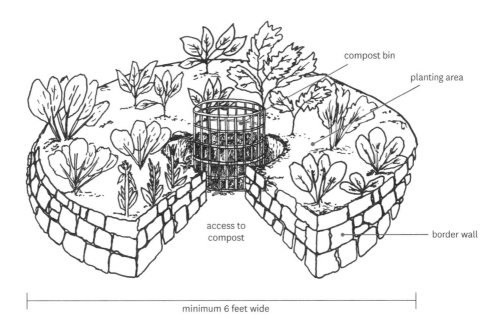

Keyhole garden plan

Small-Space Gardens

Don't think that you need to have separate flower gardens, herb gardens, vegetable gardens, and rose beds. When you use organic methods for growing in all your gardens there is no worry about planting your bell peppers right next to your rose bush. Many edibles are just as beautiful as plants grown for ornamental gardens.

When you plant new perennials at their optimum spacing, it can take some time for them to fill in, so use that space between landscape shrubs or roses to add a few more eggplants or broccoli plants. Use chives, parsley, thyme, and shallots for ornamental borders instead of useless liriope or monkey grass. Fragrant rosemary, basil, and sage can help to keep pests from neighboring

COMMUNITY GARDENS

Community gardens are an excellent alternative if digging a garden isn't a viable option at your home, or if your space doesn't get enough sunlight. Some community gardeners use their plots to grow rambunctious sweet potatoes or space-hogging corn or potatoes when their home garden doesn't have enough space. There is a wealth of knowledge and years of gardening expertise at most community gardens so you can learn a lot by just visiting. Gardeners usually share tools in a tool co-op and share communal garden chores also. Plant sales, potlucks, and harvest parties make community gardens a fun and exciting place to grow.

ornamental plants and they can attract butterflies and beneficial insects.

You'll want to use caution when preparing the soil around perennial plants like roses and shrubs. Their roots might be damaged by overzealous tilling or burned by too much soil amendment. Leave the area just beyond the width of the perennial plant's foliage undisturbed. Another method of adding perennials to garden beds is to dedicate the ends of your rows to perennial plants. Add a rose bush, rosemary, or a grouping of perennial herbs at the end of the row so that their roots remain undisturbed at planting time.

Gardeners with limited space will probably want to avoid growing widely spreading crops like pumpkins, sweet potatoes, and melons. Look for bush-type squash and cucumbers to make the most of small gardens. Use a trellis or other garden structure and train sprawling crops to grow up instead of out.

Succession Planting

Some plants produce their crop quickly and will have a limited period of harvest. Radishes will often be ready in two to three weeks and can be woody and bitter tasting if left in the garden too long. Planting an entire packet of radishes would produce more radishes than most households can manage to eat at one time. Instead, plant a few short rows of carrots, lettuce, radishes, beans, or turnips every two to three weeks so that you have a continual, but manageable, harvest. Once the plants are harvested, follow with another planting.

Crop Rotation

Crop rotation is the practice of alternating the location of crops to assist with insect and disease management and to help maintain the balance of nutrients in the garden soil. Plants will take certain nutrients out of the soil where they grow. If you plant corn in the same spot each year, that area will become depleted of the nutrients that corn requires and the corn will not perform as well. Diseases that affect tomatoes will have the opportunity to multiply and grow when their host plant is returned to the same spot each garden season.

Since some soilborne diseases can persist in the soil for as long as seven years, it may be difficult to avoid planting crops in the same spot for that long in a small garden. Rotation to avoid diseases is probably more important for large-scale farms than for home gardeners. If you keep garden records and attempt to rotate the location of squash family members (squash, melons, and cucumbers), nightshade family members (tomatoes, potatoes, eggplants, peppers), and legumes (beans and peas), you should have fewer issues with pests and diseases affecting your harvests.

Planting nitrogen-producing legume crops followed by heavy nitrogen users like tomatoes, corn, and okra will ensure more successful harvests. Grow soil-building legume or cover crops as often as possible to add organic matter and add compost with every planting when your garden is small to ensure that your plants will have all the nutrients they need.

Sowing Your Seeds

Once your garden beds are built and prepared with compost and amendments, you are ready to plant seeds. There are many techniques for planting seeds but always look at the seed packet for information about the proper depth for planting, the spacing between seeds, or how much thinning is required.

You may see that planting in hills, rows, or blocks are recommended on the seed packets. Furrows or row planting is recommended for large plants like okra and sunflowers. You make a small trench at the recommended depth and place the seeds in the trench at the proper spacing. Gently cover the seeds and lightly tamp the soil to remove air spaces around the seeds. Leave sufficient room between rows as recommended on the seed packet. Crops like beets and radishes may need to have soil pulled toward their growing roots so leave enough room between rows to make that possible.

Block planting (or broadcast sowing) is often used for lettuce and carrots to create "living mulch" and limit the chance of weed seeds sprouting. Seeds for beets, carrots, onions, and spinach will fail if planted too deeply and this method helps to keep them at the proper depth. The planting bed is smoothed and the seeds are broadcasted over the area. I like to build a small raised berm around the edges of the planting area to keep the broadcast seeds from washing away. Gentle watering with a water breaker nozzle is required to keep the seeds in place.

The hill method is recommended for cucumbers, squash, melons, and pumpkins. Making small raised hills ensures that these seeds will have excellent drainage and the soil will warm up a little more in the raised area. You can add the extra dose of compost and nutrients that make these hungry crops flourish as you create the raised soil area.

Use a soil sifter to strain out clumps, rocks, and sticks and cover your seeds with the soft, sifted soil or compost. What seems like a small rock to you will be a giant boulder for a tiny seedling that is trying to burst from the ground.

No matter which method you choose for sowing seeds, remember that watering gently and keeping the soil moist is crucial for germination. If the garden is very dry, wet the soil the day prior to planting. Use a water breaker nozzle on your hose to provide a gentle watering or use a rose nozzle on a watering can to give a gentle sprinkling over the seed bed. Drip irrigation systems will not provide the consistent moisture over the seed bed that is required for seed germination and watering overhead with a sprinkler can compact the soil and create a crust on the surface that requires more effort than most delicate seedlings can muster.

Even one day of drying out can spell disaster for your newly planted seeds. Shade the seed bed with lightweight row cover, damp burlap, or sheets to keep them from drying quickly when the weather is warm. In very dry regions, plant seeds in shallow trenches, water them

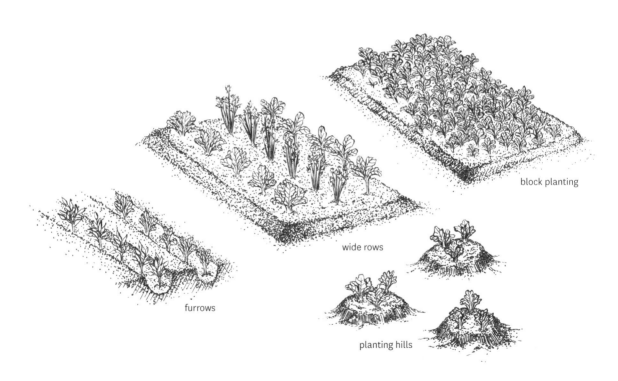

block planting

wide rows

furrows

planting hills

Planting methods will vary depending on the seeds planted and your garden beds.

well, and place a board over the row or seed bed until the seeds germinate. Once seedlings are about 2 inches tall, or they have their second set of true leaves (the first leaves are called seedling leaves), thin the crop as directed on the seed packet. I like to include the spacing for thinning on my plant labels for easy reference. Use a pair of scissors to snip the plants at the soil line so that the roots of adjacent seedlings will not be disturbed. When thinning plants in a hill, choose the most vigorous of the seedlings to keep and thin those that are smaller.

Pest and Disease Management: Control Without Chemicals

Coping with insects is an ongoing challenge in the garden, but there are many options to try before resorting to chemical sprays. Washing plants with a strong blast of water, especially the underside of the leaves where insects tend to congregate, can get insects under control. Aphids knocked off by the water will generally not have the strength to climb back up on the plant. If you catch an infestation early and repeat the daily washing ritual for a few days, you might take care of spider mites as well.

Vacuuming your plants might look a little odd to your neighbors, but it can be a very effective means of controlling bugs. Use a small hand-held vacuum to suck up harmful insects; try inserting a length of drip irrigation tubing into the vacuum intake to extend the reach. Be sure to empty the vacuum contents into soapy water to ensure the bugs are dead and to avoid a smelly mess. A wet-dry shop vacuum fitted with a crevice tool can make removal of stink bugs, caterpillars, and other pests a quick project. Here you can just add soapy water to the canister so that bugs drown when they hit the suds. I find that the crevice tool makes it easier to skip over beneficial insects and target the pests.

There are many tricks you can use to trap insects. Shallow containers like a tuna can, filled with about an inch of beer, will attract snails, slugs, pillbugs, earwigs, and other pests. The pests crawl in them to drink and will then drown. Sink the cans into the ground to provide an easy entrance and dispose of them or rinse them out after a few days as they will get very smelly. Aphids are attracted to the color yellow, so you can coat bright yellow cardstock with a sticky substance like Tanglefoot and suspend the cards in a greenhouse or over transplants to reduce the numbers of these pests. Red balls can be coated with the same material and hung in apple trees to catch apple maggot flies.

Plants can also become insect traps. I found that cardoon plants are a great host to ladybugs because they often have an aphid infestation in late winter. They also shelter the lygus or leaf-footed bug in early spring. These pests mate, lay their eggs, and the nymphs cluster around the plant. I keep a spray bottle with soapy water near the cardoon to spray the nymphs and adults when I see them. This has kept the numbers of this prolific pest down so that my tomatoes and peppers have fewer problems.

Snails and slugs dislike copper so using copper pipe or copper tape around a garden bed can keep them out. In our grandmother's gardens, pennies were often glued around the rim of pots that were favorites of stealthy slugs and snails. The penny collar kept them at bay back then, but today's pennies have so little copper this trick no longer works.

Wrapping the stem of a transplant loosely with aluminum foil creates a barrier to the cutworm. Roll a square of heavy duty foil diagonally so that there is a thick middle area and two thinner ends. Twist the ends around each other, forming a loose ring around the plant stem. Tomato, pepper, and eggplant stems still have room to grow and expand while cutworms are, well, foiled. Remove the foil rings at the end of the season and save them for the next planting.

Lightweight row covers can keep flea beetles from pelleting arugula leaves with tiny holes, squash vine borers from squash, and aphids from many plants.

Handpicking insects, of course, is the world's oldest form of pest control. Remember that an insect's metabolic rate increases as the temperature increases. That

HOMEMADE PEST REMEDIES

- **Soap spray.** Use a mild soap and avoid dish detergents, which will burn plants. Soap can burn on hot, sunny days, so spray late at night and wash plants the next morning (or spray early and rinse plants after a few hours). The soap spray may affect some beneficial insects as well, so spray directly on the pests you're trying to target. Castile soap or Dr. Bronner's soaps are mild enough to use on plants.

- **Pepper and garlic spray.** Remove most of the exterior papery layers from a bulb of garlic (there is no need to peel the individual cloves) and add the cloves to a blender along with several hot peppers (use jalapeño, serrano, or habanero peppers; or ½ teaspoon cayenne powder). Add 2 cups of water and blend well. (Avoid inhaling the fumes from this mix unless you are in need of a serious sinus cleanse!) Add more water to fill the container and allow the mix to stand for several hours. Strain the blender contents through a fine strainer or cheesecloth. Add ½ teaspoon of soap to allow the mix to stick to the leaves. Refrigerate any unused spray and wear gloves to protect your hands while spraying.

- **Coffee grounds.** Not only a good source of nitrogen fertilizer, coffee grounds can also act as a deterrent to insect pests. Dry the grounds so that they are more easily distributed in the garden. A light sprinkling around the base of plants discourages pillbugs, snails, slugs, and cutworms.

- **Milk spray.** Use one part milk to nine parts water and mix well. Used as a spray, it is effective at controlling powdery mildew on members of the squash family.

- **Dried red pepper flakes.** These are an effective deterrent for a number of pests. If rabbits, squirrels, or other rodents are digging in the garden or in container gardens, sprinkle the soil with dried hot pepper flakes. This is also effective at keeping my dogs out of my recently fertilized containers. I buy large containers at discount stores but also use any extra packets that come with pizza deliveries. Reapply after watering or rain.

means the hotter it is, the faster they move. Grasshoppers can be handpicked in the early morning but not so easily at noon. Mist the garden on hot afternoons to cool down insects and make hand picking easier. Wear gloves if you are squeamish about the task.

Keep a pitcher filled with soapy water in the garden to make dispatching insects fast and easy (a container with a handle makes it easier to maneuver). Most insect will fly straight up or drop down, so position the container under the bug with your hand over the insect. With practice, you can get the insect to drop down into the soapy water or knock them into it with your hand.

If you have to spray your plants, hose end sprayers are not ideal; they're fine for fertilizers but they are not accurate enough to deliver the proper amount of pest-control product. You'll end up using more product than necessary, and thus putting more product than necessary into your garden soil. A pump-type sprayer or a hand-held spray bottle will enable you to mix products accurately and apply only what is needed.

The pump sprayer's seals may be adversely affected by many organic products. Treat the seals on the sprayer with petroleum jelly before using and rinse the sprayer well afterward. After you've emptied the sprayer, fill it with water and spray to clean the wand thoroughly. Store your sprayer pump separate from the base. Twisting the pump into the sprayer causes the seals to wear out prematurely as they expand and contract with temperature extremes. A properly maintained sprayer will last for years. If a sprayer is not pressurizing, it's generally the result of a faulty seal. Look for a sprayer brand that offers a set of replacement seals. I bought my current sprayer in 1986 and I am still using it today.

Root-Knot Nematodes

Root-knot nematodes are parasitic worms that infest plant roots and rob them of water and nutrients. Although they are microscopic and not visible to our naked eyes, the knob-shaped damage they cause to roots is very apparent. They are more common in sandy soils and can be introduced when soil is added to the garden—from soil on tools and garden implements or from infected plants. Note that these are not the same as beneficial nematodes, which are often added to soil to help reduce pest problems.

The nematodes form colonies that block the normal root plumbing and rob the plants of the nutrients and water they are pulling from the soil. The colonies form stunted and distorted roots. These are not like nitrogen nodules, which are found on the roots of beans and other legumes. Nitrogen nodules can be easily pulled off the plant roots; root knots from nematodes are not removable. Plants wilt quickly and may look chlorotic or yellowed due to their malnourished state. A soil test can determine how severe the problem is and identify the specific type of nematode that may be present in the soil.

Certain crops are more affected by nematodes than others. Tomatoes, pumpkins, and okra may be impossible to grow in severe nematode infestations. Peppers, cucumbers, beets, watermelons, eggplants, and even roses are affected to a lesser degree. They rarely kill woody plants like trees and shrubs, but can weaken them and make them more susceptible to other problems. Nematodes rarely affect cool-season crops in mild-winter areas since they are not active in soil below 64°F. However, late plantings of carrots and radishes may be affected.

Unfortunately, root-knot nematodes may never be fully eradicated, but there are measures you can use to control them so that crops can be successful.

- Increase organic matter in the soil to encourage the life of beneficial soil microorganisms.

- Drip irrigate to avoid plant stress and mulch plants well.

- Plant nematode-resistant varieties. Tomatoes will include the letter *N* to indicate resistance. Use Nemaguard rootstock for fruit trees and Freedom rootstock for grapes. Grafted tomatoes and peppers may have nematode-resistant root stock.

- Plant spring and summer crops as early as possible to get a jumpstart on growth before nematodes are a problem in warming soil.

- Use chitin-containing products like Clandosan to treat your soil in advance of planting. The nematodes have a chitin shell and microbes that are stimulated by the introduction of chitin will help to reduce nematode numbers. (The chitin comes from crab and shrimp shells and can attract flies, so you may want to use lightweight row cover over treated areas.)

- Add cornmeal to the soil to boost soil life.

- Treat soil with Actinovate, a biological fungicide. It is expensive, but you only need 6 ounces per acre.

- Treat with sesame oil products like Dragonfire, Ontrol, or Nemagard.

- Monterey sells an organic nematode-control product that has a *Quillaja saponaria* extract (Chilean soapbark tree).

- Plant cereal or elbon rye in the cool season. Cut it back before it seeds and turn into the soil several weeks before planting time.

- Allow the soil to lay fallow for a season, keeping it moist and turning it often to expose it to the sun.

- Solarize for four to six weeks in summer to kill many of the nematodes in the top layers of soil.

- Use French and African marigolds, mustards, brassicas, and castor beans as repellant crops. They produce chemicals toxic to nematodes. Follow nematode-sensitive crops with these plants.

- Add citrus peels and pulp to the soil and treat the soil with citrus oil before planting a crop susceptible to nematodes.

PLANTS NOT AFFECTED BY NEMATODES

PLANT	VARIETY
corn	all varieties
English peas	Wando
tomatoes	Beefeater VFN, Beefsteak VFN, Carnival, Celebrity, Early Girl, Roma II, Lemon Boy, Small Fry, Sweet Chelsea, Tycoon, Viva Italia
sweet potatoes	Jewel, Nugget, Red Jewel

GET PLANTING

.JANUARY.

PLANNING
FOR THE YEAR

Just like a new year, the new garden season is full of possibilities. While some southwestern gardeners will be strictly armchair or window-sill gardeners in January, others will be making daily harvests in the garden. Either way, the busy spring season will be upon us soon, so this is the time to prepare for it. Careful planning of your next garden venture—making sure you have the seeds, tools, and equipment at the ready—can make the difference between success and failure. Take time now while the garden chore list is a bit shorter to get organized for the year by making a master plan, getting your equip-ment organized, and starting a garden journal. Establish a foundation for success for the gar-dening year.

TO DO THIS MONTH

PLAN

- Organize a garden tool kit.
- Measure your garden areas and create a master plan.
- Create a garden plan for the new season.
- Inventory and order seeds needed for the coming year. Compost old seeds.
- Study your landscape to determine locations for new plantings or structures.
- Observe planting areas that hold water and improve the drainage or convert them to a rain-garden feature.

PREPARE AND MAINTAIN

- Clean and sharpen garden tools, oil wheelbarrows and carts.
- Check supplies of fertilizers and purchase items as needed.
- Clean and organize seed-starting supplies.
- Create or purchase seed-starter mix.
- Water plants well before freezing temperatures occur. Make sure plants are mulched to protect them from cold.
- Watch the forecast and protect garden plants with row cover if temperatures will be below 28°F. Remove or open covers if daytime temperatures will be warm.
- Use lightweight row cover to protect crops from insects.
- Renew mulch in areas where it is thinning.

ZONES 5–6

- Replant perennials heaved out by freeze and thaw cycles
- Knock heavy snow off of garden plants and structures to prevent damage.

ZONES 7–10

- Clean up winter weeds.
- Weed and fertilize asparagus and strawberry beds. Cut back dried asparagus fronds.
- Top dress garden beds with compost to prepare them for planting.
- Transplant trees, shrubs, or roses.
- Apply foliar fertilizers to keep vegetables in production and promote harvesting.

ZONES 9–10

- Prune, feed, and mulch roses.
- Prune fruit trees and spray for insects and diseases if necessary.
- Water as needed—the winter season can be dry and dry soil can increase frost damage.
- Trim citrus blossoms and enjoy them indoors. Allow bees access to citrus tree blooms for pollination.

SOW AND PLANT INDOORS

ZONES 4-6
- Plant a crop of microgreens for winter salads.

ZONES 5-6
- Start seeds of onions, leeks, cabbage, and cauliflower.

ZONES 7-8
- Start cabbage, lettuce, broccoli, and cauliflower seeds.

ZONES 9-10
- Sow seeds for peppers, tomatoes, and eggplant.
- Start melons, cucumbers, and squash seeds.

SOW AND PLANT OUTDOORS

ZONES 7-10
- Set out transplants of broccoli, cabbage, spinach, and lettuce.
- Sow seeds of arugula, bok choy, fennel, carrots, radishes, spinach, beets, turnips, and peas directly.
- Plant dill, parsley, cilantro, and chervil from seeds or transplants.
- Plant asparagus crowns and strawberry transplants.
- Shop for bare root fruit trees, asparagus crowns, blackberries, artichokes, and rhubarb.

ZONES 9-10
- Purchase seed potatoes and cut if large; dust with sulfur and pre-sprout in preparation for planting.

HARVESTING NOW

ZONES 4-6
Dig parsnips and Jerusalem artichokes left in the ground over winter.

ZONES 7-10

arugula	cabbage	fennel	leeks	spinach
broccoli	cauliflower	green onions	mustard	Swiss chard
Brussels sprouts	collards	kale	radishes	

Some of the highest-yielding and most nutritious garden plants are grown in mild-winter areas in the Southwest. Kale, Swiss chard, spinach, and other garden greens will provide weekly harvests of vitamin-rich leaves, and their flavor is even better after a mild frost. Lettuce and cilantro grow lush and flavorful in January, but become bitter and are likely to bloom when temperatures start to rise in spring. Winter is my favorite time to garden—there are fewer bugs, less heat, more regular rainfall, and the variety of crops that we can grow is astounding. Still, providing protection for tender plants is essential to keeping garden vegetables alive and thriving. Row covers, hoop houses, and cold frames or greenhouses allow most of us to maintain our gardens during unpredictable winter weather.

Take Measure

One of the most common mistakes that I see new gardeners make is planting too many plants and crowding them too closely together. It is easy to be overwhelmed with new varieties of peppers and tomatoes when standing in the garden center come springtime. But if you've already established a garden plan that only has space for six of each then it is easier to stick to the plan! Crowding plants leads to more insect and disease issues and less produce. A clear garden plan will allow proper spacing and help you to maximize the yield of your garden. Take the time to make a scale drawing of your garden and use it to plan out the season. I use graph paper with

¼-inch-scale lines and make a master copy for my files. Each garden season I fill in a copy of that master with everything that was planted because it is easy to forget where the squash was planted the spring before.

If your garden space is limited, careful selection of vegetables is important. Cabbage is a slow grower and is harvested only once while lettuce, spinach, and greens may be harvested continually throughout the growing season. Brussels sprouts and cauliflower are also slow growers and harvested for a short time. There are many plants like lettuce that will grow happily in 4- to 6-inch-deep containers so that you can save garden beds for the space hogs—broccoli and kale, for instance, prefer at least 10–12 inches of soil depth.

Your garden plan is invaluable for making sure that certain plants are rotated and it will help you to plan succession plantings. Diseases and insects that might remain in the soil can affect squash and tomatoes between plantings, but moving those plants to a new spot each season will help avoid these problems. On the other hand, peas and beans add nitrogen to the soil so you can follow those plantings with plants that will benefit from the higher nitrogen availability—large-growing, heavy feeders like corn, okra, and tomatoes. Potatoes planted in February won't be harvested until late May or June, so I make a notation that those will be followed with okra, melons, or other crops suited for summer seed germination. Rambling squash and pumpkin need to have plenty of space to roam and a scale drawing ensures that you leave sufficient room for these ramblers.

BASIC MATH FOR GARDENERS

Do you find yourself wishing you had paid more attention in math class when it is time to order a load of mulch or soil? Here are some basic equations to ensure you order the correct amount of materials for your garden.

SQUARE-FOOTAGE CALCULATIONS

To determine the proper amount of fertilizer to add to your bed or how many pavers an area requires, you will need to know the square footage.

Square or rectangle beds. Multiply the length by the width to calculate the surface area of the bed ($l \times w = a$).

Triangle beds. The longest side of the bed will be the base. Find the center of the base and measure from that center point to the point of the triangle opposite. That will be the height measurement. Multiply the base and the height and divide in half to calculate the area ($(b \times h) \div 2 = a$).

Circular beds. Locate the center point of the circle and measure to the edge to find the radius. Multiply the radius by itself and multiply that by π (3.14) to calculate the area ($r^2 \times 3.14 = a$).

For irregularly shaped beds, try to break up the space into squares, rectangles, or circles and determine the area of each of those and add them together.

To calculate how much soil you will need to fill a raised bed or how much compost you need to top off those beds, measure the length of the bed (feet) and multiply that by the width of the bed (feet). Then multiply that number by the desired depth in inches. Divide that total by 324. That will give you the number of cubic yards of material you will need.

Most small and medium pickup beds will hold a cubic yard of compost when loaded level with the top of the bed. Larger truck's beds may hold 1½ yards, but pay attention to the hauling capability of the vehicle. A cubic yard of compost may weigh between 800–1200 pounds depending on the materials used in it and the moisture content. Soil blends with high levels of sand or rock dust will weigh much more. The weight limit for most trucks will be in the owner's manual or will be posted inside the driver's door panel.

Bagged and bulk materials are typically sold by cubic volume. You will need to determine the volume required when ordering soils, rock, or compost. If the material in a bag is sold in cubic feet and you need to convert that to cubic yards, divide by 27, the number of feet in a cubic yard.

HOW MANY PLANTS WILL FIT IN THIS SPACE?

You have a bed that you want to fill with lettuce or broccoli. How do you determine how many to buy? Find out the proper spacing distance (from the center of one plant to the next one) for that plant and calculate the area of the space you wish to plant. Then multiply the plants per square feet by the area in square feet. A bed that has 30 square feet that you want to plant with lettuce plants that are 8 inches apart will need 68 lettuce plants to fill it.

RECOMMENDED SPACING	NUMBER OF PLANTS PER SQUARE FOOT
6 inches	4
8 inches	2.27
12 inches	1
18 inches	.512

Record Keeping

Your garden journal is a valuable guide for keeping track of your successes and failures. Keep notes on which tomatoes performed well for you and which succumbed to disease. Note the date you planted those snow peas and had excellent germination and an excellent harvest. When you see that a crop was affected by insects or underperformed, it may mean that it was planted too late and you should plant earlier next year.

Record significant rainfall and other weather events, including freezes, and make notes of planting dates for each item planted. Keep track of when the first item of a crop was harvested and how long the harvest lasted. I like to keep a record of when I have enough of a crop to freeze, can, or dry some of the yield. Some do this with a calendar while others will use a three-ring binder and keep adding to it throughout the years. You can also do this easily on your computer, along with regular photographs of the garden as the season progresses. Strive to make notes at least monthly. No matter how you decide to pull it together, a well-kept garden journal will pay you back handsomely.

SKILL SET

THE GARDENING TOOL KIT

I have a job that keeps me working long hours and often my time in the garden is limited to a few minutes each day. Rounding up tools or searching for items in the shed or tool box cuts into what little time I have to garden. My gardening tool kit has eliminated much of that wasted time. I use a washable canvas bag that has a several large center sections big enough for my pruners, hand trowel, and hand-weeding tools and lots of other pockets that hold a variety of handy implements. A 5-gallon plastic bucket would also make an excellent tool tote (you can purchase inserts to divide the bucket and hold tools) or you might use a plastic or wooden tool caddy or metal toolbox.

Here are some of the indispensable items in my tool bag:

Gardening gloves: I include disposable gloves for messy jobs, plastic-covered gloves for working in damp soil, and leather gloves for tough jobs with pruning or rocks

Large ziplock plastic bag: to protect seed packets

Plastic bags: for harvesting

Small paper bags: for seed collecting

Plant labels: I recycle these from purchased plants (write on the blank reverse side) or use metal or plastic mini blinds cut into sections; I note the date that I plant, the brand and type of seeds, the number of days to harvest, and the recommended final spacing

Marker or pen: make sure it is durable for outdoors

Folding saw

Pliers: handy for pulling out oak, pecan, and other deep-rooted tree seedlings

String or sisal twine: for tying up plants; to keep the twine clean and untangled, find a plastic jar large enough for the bundle of twine and make a hole in the lid to pull the twine through

Pieces of pantyhose or knee-high stockings: for tying up rambunctious tomatoes or supporting melons and squash on a trellis

Natural insect repellant

Scissors

Rubber bands: for tying bundles of herbs or flowers for drying

Extra washers for hoses and emitters for the drip irrigation lines: I use metal tins that mints come in to store these

Bandana or rag: for quick cleanups

Small sharpening stone: for quick tool touchups

Foam kneeling pad: to protect my aging knees

Folding knife

Small notebook and pen: to make reminders about what to plant next or what seeds I need to purchase

My garden journal: encased in a plastic bag for protection

Water breaker nozzle: for gentle watering of new seed beds

You may also want to include sunglasses or a hat, hair ties if your hair is long, and some sunscreen. I know that sounds like a lot, but the bag is lightweight and easy to carry.

Another smaller tool tote is used for my irrigation supplies and hose-repair items. It has all of the tools needed to mend a leaking water hose or to add a new drip irrigation line. Each spring I replace all of the washers on my water hoses, hose attachments, and drip lines. Summer heat and winter cold make washers brittle, which leads to leaks.

·FEBRUARY·

GEAR UP

As the season sets into motion, February is a great time to make sure all your tools are in order and get seeds started for your garden. Tools are as important for gardeners as they are for carpenters, chefs, or surgeons—having the right tool for the job at hand makes for cleaner and more efficient work. I occasionally pick up a shovel, hoe, or rake at a garage sale since it is nice to have an extra tool available if I have a garden helper (they're also the tools that I'll loan out if someone is in need). Years of use have shown me that you get what you pay for with garden tools, so I am rather particular about my gardening equipment. Well-made garden shears allow me to prune for hours without developing tendonitis and a nice sharp trowel goes through rocky soil with ease so I

CONTINUED ON PAGE 66

TO DO THIS MONTH

PLAN

- Look for winter sales on tools and pots.
- Replace grow light tubes if they are over two years old.

PREPARE AND MAINTAIN

- Water plants well before freezing temperatures occur. Make sure plants are mulched to protect them from cold.
- Watch the forecast and protect garden plants with row cover if temperatures will be below 28°F.
- Remove or open covers if daytime temperatures will be warm.
- Renew mulch around plants where it has thinned.

ZONES 5–6

- Start broccoli, cabbage, cauliflower, lettuce, and onion seeds.

ZONES 7–10

- Purchase seed potatoes and pre-sprout for planting

- Purchase onion sets and soak them in seaweed for a half hour before planting them.
- Add compost and fertilizer to planting beds.
- Prune, feed, and mulch roses.
- Prune fruit trees and spray for insects and diseases if necessary.
- Clean purple martin houses before scouts arrive.

ZONES 9–10

- Hill up soil around potatoes as new growth emerges.
- Cut back and turn in cover crops to prepare beds for planting.
- Use cover crop trimmings to make compost.

SOW AND PLANT INDOORS

ZONE 4

- Start onions, leeks, and celery seeds under lights.
- Start containers of lettuce in sunny windows for indoor winter salads.

ZONES 5–6

- Start broccoli, cabbage, cauliflower, kohlrabi, lettuce, celery, leeks, and Brussels sprouts seeds.

ZONES 7–8

- Start tomatoes, peppers, and eggplant seeds.

SOW AND PLANT OUTDOORS

ZONES 5–6

- Plant spinach, radishes, peas, fennel, leeks, onions, and shallots.

ZONES 7–8

- Plant lettuce, cabbage, and onions.
- Plant radishes, lettuce, beets, turnips and spinach seeds. Repeat every two weeks for regular harvests.
- Plant transplants of broccoli, cabbage, cauliflower, bok choy, collards, and mustard greens.

- Plant peas and protect them from birds with row covers.
- Plant potatoes in trenches.

ZONE 10

- Begin planting beans, corn, cucumbers, melons, squash, peppers, and tomatoes but be prepared to protect them from frosts and freezes.

HARVESTING NOW

ZONES 7–10

arugula	chervil	leeks	parsnips
beets	chives	lettuce	sorrel
carrots	fennel	mâche	spinach
chard	kale	onions	turnips

plant transplants more quickly. If you purchase high-quality tools and care for them properly, they can last a lifetime and possibly even be handed down to the next generation of gardeners.

Starting your own seeds, on the other hand, is a great way to save money and ensure that you'll get the varieties that you *want*, rather than just what your local nursery stocks. Keep in mind, however, that tiny seedlings are delicate and require daily attention. One day of neglect can spell disaster, so if your work schedule is already keeping you busy and you have neither the time nor the space or energy to devote to growing your own transplants, don't despair. Purchased transplants cost a little more but can still result in significant cost savings compared to the price of produce in your grocery store. After you have a few garden seasons under your belt, you may want to venture into saving your own seeds and growing transplants yourself.

Tools

Even though a few good knives and a cutting board will handle most of your cooking needs, most of us have drawers and cabinets in the kitchen full of things that we never use. It's no different in the garden—garden stores are full of gadgets and tools that would likely languish in the tool shed after a couple of uses. It's best to focus on purchasing just a few high-quality tools that will last for years and tackle most of your garden chores.

A well-made pair of garden shears is a must for me, just like that quality chef's knife in the kitchen. When I tried my first pair of Felco No. 9 left-handed shears over thirty years ago, I was in heaven. I still have them, in fact, though I have since replaced the blades along with a few other parts. Lopping shears are also essential for larger branches and for pruning and cutting spent plants into smaller pieces for faster composting (my Felco loppers have also seen years of use).

I also heavily rely on a strong hand trowel for planting and digging up small weeds along with a long weeding tool known as a dandelion fork. Look for tools

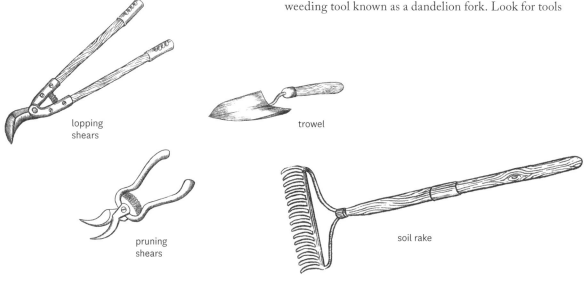

lopping
shears

trowel

pruning
shears

soil rake

with brightly colored red or orange handles so that you can find them more quickly when you need them (they're also not as likely to disappear in the compost pile!). I use a trowel with a ruler etched into the blade to help with spacing plants and planting bulbs. I prefer cast aluminum blades because they won't rust, are difficult to bend or break, and last for years. If you struggle with arthritis or wrist issues, there are many ergonomically designed hand tools available that you can look for.

You'll also want to have a sturdy spading fork for turning planting beds and compost and digging holes for plants. Some of the newer all-aluminum forks are lightweight and it is almost impossible to bend the tines. They are also rust free and should survive a lifetime of use in the garden. More petite gardeners will appreciate a short border fork with a round handle (border forks have shorter tines and handles and are suitable for shorter gardeners and children). Standard spading fork handles are 28 inches long, though taller gardeners may want to look for 32-inch handles to save their backs.

A round, pointed shovel with a long handle is useful for digging and moving soil and gravel. You can use a file to sharpen the edges when it starts to dull. A turned edge at the top of the tool that provides a spot for your foot to rest during use is helpful. A transplant shovel or a lady's shovel is a smaller version that makes digging up and dividing perennials or potatoes quick work. Later you may want to add a spading shovel that has a long, slim head to assist in digging up plants for transplanting and digging narrow trenches.

Hoes are used for shaping beds, cultivating, and weeding. There are many styles of hoes to choose from depending on your needs. The handle should be long enough to allow you to stand up without bending over,

which will cause back strain if done for long periods. The scuffle hoe one of the best time- and back-saving tools you'll find. The blade cuts on both sides and is used in a back-and-forth fashion on the top of beds or in pathways to remove tiny, newly sprouted weeds. It is less effective for large or deeply rooted weeds, but it will clear a large area of small weeds rapidly. Get some mulch down quickly in garden beds to prevent the weeds from reappearing.

Soil rakes allow you to quickly level planting beds or rake mulch away from plantings for end-of-season cleanup. Leaf rakes with metal or bamboo tines are essential for gathering leaves and grass clippings. A pitchfork is handy for moving mulch and turning compost quickly. It also comes in handy for moving large piles of garden debris.

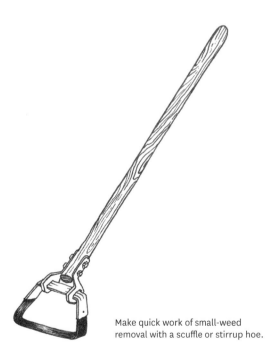

Make quick work of small-weed removal with a scuffle or stirrup hoe.

Maintenance

Since garden tools can be quite an investment, regular maintenance is important to ensure that they last. Lightly sand wooden handles and treat with linseed oil at least once a year. Use a wire brush to scrape off any rust from your tools and treat them with oil. Avoid leaving tools outdoors in the elements—wood handles become dry and brittle and are more easily broken.

A flat metal file called a mill bastard file and a sharpening stone are essential for keeping tool edges sharp so that the tools do their work more efficiently. If you've never sharpened your tools before, you'll be amazed at how much easier it is to work in the garden. A bench vise to hold the tool steady during sharpening is a plus or you can simply use clamps to secure the tool to your worktable. Apply sharpening oil to the file and begin with the coarse side of the file. Move the file in one direction, starting at the bottom of the blade and moving toward the handle. Match the angle of the file to the angle of the tool blade. Switch to the finer side of the file for a few strokes. Check the edge after a few strokes and pass over the blade with the oiled sharpening stone to remove any metal burrs. However, if you are planning on shoveling gravel or coarse material, wait to sharpen until you're finished. Always wear gloves while cleaning and sharpening tools.

I also make sure to mark all of my tool handles with paint. A couple of colored stripes—my signature is purple—on the tool handle will make ensure that you can quickly find them in your neighbor's garage after loaning them out. I even spray paint my garden hoses. If your property is large and you have tools in different locations, you can even color code tools for certain areas so that you will always have the right tools where you need them.

Seeds: Taking Stock

Now would be a great time to take an inventory of and organize your seed supply before the gardening season hits full speed. Check the dates on seed packets and labels and compost those that are well past their useful life. You can perform a simple germination test by placing seeds on a moist paper towel inside a plastic bag or container to see if they'll sprout. That said, I prefer to simply plant them more densely than recommended and see what happens. Since I'd replant them anyway, it's not a great loss if they don't come up.

One of the more common problems that I see with new gardeners is that they can never find the seeds they want when it is time to plant them. So each season they buy more and end up with lots of excess seeds. Some will end up at the garden store with no recollection of what they have or need. I keep all of my seeds in a large decorative box. Each type of seed is in a large manila envelope labeled by category: beans, carrots, cucumbers,

EXPECTED STORAGE LIFE OF SEEDS

ONE TO TWO YEARS	THREE TO FOUR YEARS	FIVE TO SIX YEARS
corn	carrots	turnips
leeks	chard	celery
onions	mustard	cucumbers
parsley	pumpkin	lettuce
peas, beans	squash	melons
spinach	tomatoes	watermelon
parsnip	beets	eggplant

and so on (you could also categorize them by season). The envelopes fit neatly inside the seed box.

In late winter I go through the box and make a note of each type of seed I have and which I need. Armed with this list and my garden plan, I get just the seeds I need for the next planting season. Keep a planting guide for your area and a list of recommended varieties with the seed box. I also keep ziplock bags in the box for seeds to be planted; this will protect them from an errant spray with the hose or a sudden rain shower. I include a few large paper clips to close bags that are still holding seeds. You can even organize seeds for each month's planting in a separate bag so you will be prepared for the entire season.

Seeds should be stored in a cool, dry location. A hot, humid garage or shed is not an ideal location. If you use an air conditioner in the hottest months, your seeds should fare well indoors as long as they are kept in a well-ventilated area. Glass or plastic jars with tightly fitting lids may be used for seed storage in the refrigerator if your home's temperature is not moderate.

Is It Warm Enough to Plant?

Each type of seed germinates in a specific range of soil temperatures. When soil is too cool or too warm, seeds will fail to germinate or germination rate may be greatly reduced. Planting-recommendation charts give the dates when the desired soil temperature is generally reached, but what if you have a warmer spring or a cooler late summer (one can dream!)? A soil thermometer can help you determine exactly when to plant for your area. When temperatures are not ideal, you can plant more seeds. It's better to thin more when needed than not have enough plants to work with. When planting cool-season crops in summer, it helps to mulch the soil or shade the planting bed for a few weeks to reduce the temperature. A 40 percent shade cloth might reduce the temperature of the soil by 5–6°F, enough to allow seeds to germinate. In spring, pull back mulch to allow the soil to warm to the optimal temperature.

OPTIMAL TEMPERATURES FOR SEED GERMINATION

PLANT	TEMPERATURE
beans	75–85°F
beets	75°F
broccoli	65–75°F
carrots	75°F
corn	75–85°F
cucumbers	75–85°F
lettuce	65–70°F
okra	80–85°F
peppers	78–85°F
squash, summer	75–85°F
squash, winter	75–80°F
tomatoes	75–80°F

SKILL SET

STARTING SEEDS INDOORS

There are many benefits to starting your seeds indoors. It allows for more control over soil temperature and gives you a head start on the growing season, and there are a vast number of seeds to choose from for planting instead of the few varieties available as transplants. Transplants also pose the problem of not always knowing where they came from; there's a possibility that they were grown with chemicals that you would prefer not to use in your garden. By starting them yourself you control the process. You will also reduce the possibility of introducing soilborne diseases from infected transplants into your garden. And saving seeds from the healthiest plants in your garden each year will allow you to develop plant strains that are ideally suited for your soil and climate.

Growing your own transplants will require some special equipment purchases, but by reusing these materials each year you will quickly start saving money from buying seed packets instead of transplants. A single seed packet will often provide sufficient crops for several years of gardening. Most gardeners would not require twenty-five eggplants of the same variety each year. You can also partner up with other gardeners to share seeds and plants.

To get started growing indoors you will need:

Seeds suitable for transplanting. Some seeds like radishes, beets, sunflowers, and carrots prefer to be started directly in the garden. Their roots dislike being disturbed in the transfer process to the garden. Refer to the instructions on the packet if you have questions.

Sterilized seed-starter medium. Regular potting soil is generally not sterile and would hold too much moisture for seed starting. Garden soil is full of naturally occurring fungi and bacteria that could be lethal to your tiny seeds. Seed-starter mix is light and uniform in texture and has the ability to hold moisture well without being too soggy.

Clean containers that allow the soil to properly drain. I use plastic nursery flats that I line with several sheets of newspaper to hold in the soil. Wash and reuse 4-inch pots and flats for transplants. Plastic containers from the produce section, soda bottles, aluminum pans, or milk cartons may be recycled for excellent seed habitat. Punch plenty of holes in them for good drainage. Be sure to wash all containers first and get rid of any residual soil or food that might harbor disease. Dip them in a 10 percent bleach solution to be certain they are sterile.

caption needed

A good light source. Even the sunniest window would be inadequate for most seeds, so florescent lights are ideal. A 4-foot shop light fixture that holds four bulbs works well. Use two cool spectrum bulbs and two warm light bulbs for the broadest array of light. Attach a chain to the fixture that will allow it to be moved closer to the seedlings initially and then moved up as they grow taller. Foil-covered cardboard or mirrors placed around the seedlings will help reflect and intensify the light.

A warm location that has good airflow. Damping off and other diseases can be a problem where the air is not circulating. Water plants with a gentle mist from a hand sprayer to keep the soil from being waterlogged. Substitute chamomile tea, which contains natural fungicides, for the water to prevent damping off. Brew four chamomile tea bags in a quart of water and bring to room temperature before spraying on the seedlings. Use a fan set on low speed to circulate air to keep plants healthy.

Warming mats. These will help increase the soil temperature and enhance seed germination. Placing flats over florescent bulb fixtures or on top of the refrigerator for a few days where it is warm will aid in germination if you don't have warming mats.

Plan your seed-starting dates as carefully as you do your outdoor planting dates. You will not want to have your transplants ready too early or too late for the correct time for planting outdoors.

·MARCH·

TOMATO TIME

This month's focus is on the real star of the home garden, the tomato. Undoubtedly the most popular crop for home gardeners, there are hundreds of varieties, from tiny patio tomatoes perfect for small pots to mammoth vines that can grow up to 15 feet long. Still, they can be a bit temperamental. Knowing the right type of tomato to suit your garden space or container will help to guarantee success. Preparing the soil properly, feeding your plants well, and watching for pests and diseases are also vital to producing that bumper crop. We all like to boast about having the earliest crop or the largest fruit, as well as the number of jars we've managed to can each season. With the right amount of care and attention, your tomatoes will be something to brag about this summer.

TO DO THIS MONTH

PLAN

- Make notes in your garden journal about plant growth and harvests. Record significant weather events and plant problems.
- Make sure there are plants to provide food for insects and wildlife: blooms on rosemary, basil, parsley, cilantro, and dill provide food for bees, butterflies, lacewings, and ladybugs, while dill and fennel feed swallowtail larvae; milkweed is vital for monarchs.

PREPARE AND MAINTAIN

- Loosen soil and add compost and soil amendments
- Control weeds and check plants for insects and diseases.
- Renew mulch where needed.

ZONES 5–6
- Prune grapes, fruit trees.

ZONES 9–10
- Prune and feed citrus trees.

SOW AND PLANT INDOORS

ZONE 4
- Sow broccoli, Brussels sprouts, cabbage, cauliflower, eggplant, head lettuce, okra, onions, peppers, tomatoes.

ZONES 5–6
- Start peppers, tomatoes, and eggplants indoors.

ZONES 7–10
- Move tomatoes, peppers, and eggplants to 6-inch or 1-gallon containers.

SOW AND PLANT OUTDOORS

ZONES 5–6
- Move broccoli, cabbage, and cauliflower transplants outdoors to a cold frame or protected bed.
- Plant peas and potatoes.

ZONES 7–10
- Plant chard in an area with afternoon shade to provide harvests late into summer.
- Make plantings of beets, carrots, kohlrabi, radishes, lettuce, turnips, and spinach.

- Plant transplants of peppers, tomatoes, and eggplants and provide protection when temperatures are below 45°F.
- Begin planting corn, squash, cucumbers, and beans.

ZONES 9–10
- Begin planting okra, sweet potatoes, and melons.

HARVESTING NOW

ZONES 7–10

arugula	broccoli	chard	kale	mâche
beets	cauliflower	fennel	lettuce	peas
		fennel		

Depending on your zone, you'll be either starting your tomato seeds indoors, caring for your transplants, and waiting until temperatures are warm enough for them to venture outside or have them in the ground already and awaiting the first blooms. The popularity of tomatoes is no mystery—there is no substitute for a juicy, sun-warmed, homegrown tomato. It's a crop that has inspired poetry, songs, festivals, and recipe books. However, this is one fussy fruit (perhaps this is part of why it inspires such passion in gardeners). If it is too wet or too dry, too early or too late, if there is too much or too little wind or too much or too little fertilizer, they will fail to set fruit. Still, if you familiarize yourself with the plant and adhere to some fairly simply instructions, you can have beautiful tomatoes every summer.

Determinate vs. Indeterminate

The two common classifications of tomatoes are *determinate* and *indeterminate*. Determinate tomatoes are so called because they will grow to a determined size. Often called bush tomatoes, they will grow to 36 inches.

TOMATO TERMS

Since you and your gardening friends will be talking about your tomatoes throughout the growing season, it would be good to get familiar with the following terms. You'll sound like a tomato pro around the office water cooler when you complain about how your heirloom beefsteaks are cracking!

Beefsteak: a large tomato with thick, solid flesh and small seed cavities

Blossom end rot: brown areas at the bottom of tomatoes due to poor calcium uptake caused by inconsistent watering

Catfacing: misshapen fruits caused by incomplete pollination, cool weather during fruit set, or from the use of herbicides

Cherry: small fruiting tomatoes that typically have wild indeterminate vines; they set fruit in warmer conditions than those for large fruited types; and they produce a large number of blooms so have the potential for lots of fruit at one time

Cracking: deep breaks in the skin caused by irregular watering

Heirloom: tomatoes that have been grown by generations of gardeners who save the open-pollinated seeds; they generally have less disease resistance and thinner skin, but have wonderful flavor, texture, and come in a variety of colors from green and yellow, orange and purple. Since they do not store or transport well, they are not typically grown by large commercial growers

Paste: a type of fruit with thick, meaty flesh and smaller seed cavities; ideal for drying, preserving, and making sauces

Slicing or salad tomatoes: medium-sized tomatoes like the popular Celebrity; they generally produce well and have a shorter period until they are harvest size compared to larger beefsteak-type tomatoes

Sunscald: a white or yellowish patch that may appear on the side of the plant most exposed to the sun; poor foliage cover for the fruit is usually to blame

Semi-determinate types get a little larger, usually up to 3–5 feet tall. The typical tomato cage will suffice for these types and they may even be planted in containers of at least 5 gallons in size, although 7- to 10-gallon containers would be better. Dwarf determinate varieties like Patio will be about 2 feet tall and will grow in hanging baskets and smaller pots. They typically do not produce many fruit and tend to be short lived. Determinate tomatoes will typically produce fruit in abundance at one time so they are ideal for canning and freezing. Once their main crop is finished the plants are done for the season.

Indeterminate, of course, means the size is not predetermined. These are the tomatoes that will climb over fences and sprawl across the rest of the garden unless you keep them under control. Most cherry tomatoes are indeterminate. Many gardeners make the mistake of thinking that a small-fruited tomato like a cherry will grow well in a small pot but that is not the case. Give these tomatoes a seriously strong cage and prepare to prune them to keep them in bounds. They will typically grow up to the top of a 6-foot cage and then back down to the ground. Their roots match the vines in size, so they are not suited for containers unless you've got really large containers. These tomatoes produce less fruit at one time but over a longer period they will produce many—they can go from spring planting to the first hard freeze. Most heirloom tomatoes are indeterminate types.

DETERMINATE OR SEMI-DETERMINATE	INDETERMINATE
Better Boy	Carmello
Better Beefsteak	Champion
Better Bush	Cherokee Purple
Bush Champion	Early Girl
Bush Celebrity	Juane Flamme
Bush Early Girl	Large Red Cherry
Bush Goliath	Oxheart
Corona PS	Improved Porter
Early Wonder	Stupice
Homestead	Sweet 100
Tycoon	Sungold

Tomato Diseases

Tomatoes may experience a number of diseases. Many of these diseases will remain in the soil from year to year so rotating the location of your tomatoes to avoid reinfection of the next crop is a good idea. The leaves closest to the soil are the first infected when the soil around the plant is contaminated. A layer of mulch under the plants will stop some of the disease transfer, but pruning leaves can eliminate most of those problems. Start trimming leaves that touch the soil at planting time and prune all lower leaves up to 12 inches high by the time the tomato plants are about 3 feet tall. Water new transplants with care to avoid getting soil onto the leaves and transferring diseases. Use a water breaker nozzle and drip irrigation to water gently. Planting disease-resistant varieties will give you even more insurance for a bountiful crop.

Early blight. Dark brown spots with dark circular rings will develop on older leaves. Spotted leaves will die early. Stems have brown, elongated sunken lesions. Usually occurs in warm, wet weather conditions. The fruit may develop leathery, sunken spots near the stem. The disease can be transmitted by seeds, by transplants, or by fungus overwintering in the soil from the previous year.

Late blight. Leaves show large brown lesions that look similar to sun scald. Stem lesions may have a white, moldy appearance. Fruit have irregular greenish brown patches that appear greasy and rough. Greenish black lesions may be found on stems. Occurs in cool wet weather.

Fusarium wilt. Leaves turn yellow, wilt, and then turn brown and are still attached to the stem. It will progress upward from the soil. Sometimes only half of a leaf or branch will die. Stems will show brown discoloration. The disease enters the plant from the roots and can be spread easily from plant to plant. It can remain persistent in the soil for years. Plant resistant varieties to avoid it.

Leaf roll. High temperatures will not only cause tomato plants to abort their blooms, it can also cause physiological leaf rolling where the leaves curl up. While not a disease, it is a sign of stress. Provide shade to prevent further stress. Drought stress and prolonged wet soil conditions can also cause leaf roll.

Southern blight. A gradual wilting of the entire plant occurs and it dies without changing color. The fungus damages the stem at the soil line and brown lesions with a white fungal mat may appear. Remove and discard damaged plants quickly. The fungus can be spread by infected tools or seed and can survive from year to year in the soil.

Verticillum wilt. Older leaves begin wilting on their edges and turning yellow, then brown. Wilting is not alleviated by watering. Cut stems will show tan discoloration. Early treatment can save the plant.

Alphabet Soup

If you have been plagued by diseased tomatoes in the past you will want to look for varieties that have capital letters after their name. These are hybrid tomatoes that have had disease resistance bred into them. The letters are the disease-resistance code and each capital letter stands for a specific disease or pest that the plant will not be troubled by. The more letters the better!

WHAT THOSE LETTERS MEAN

A	Alternaria alternate fungus
EB	Early blight
F	Fusarium fungus
N	Parasitic root worms
St	Stemphylium or gray leaf spot fungus
T	Tobacco mosaic virus
TSWV	Tomato spotted wilt virus
V	Verticillium fungus

Heirlooms

Many tomato growers swear that heirloom tomatoes are the most flavorful. They are certainly a colorful group—yellow, orange, purple, green, and combinations of all of those in addition to the usual red tomatoes. They also come in exotic shapes and enormous sizes. But they do have their downside. The skin of heirloom tomatoes tends to be thinner and more delicate, making them difficult to ship for commercial markets. They have less disease resistance and can be susceptible to cracking, catfacing, and many other maladies. Most are rampant, indeterminate vines and the larger tomatoes are less likely to set fruit in the warmer parts of the Southwest. With so many strikes against them it is amazing that we continue to plant heirloom tomatoes at all. But once you taste one it all starts to make sense. I typically harvest only eight to ten fruits in total from my Cherokee Purple tomatoes, but the taste of those tomatoes makes the poor showing totally worth it. They are often consumed right in the garden with the juice dribbling down my chin.

If you have a small garden or want to can or freeze a lot of tomatoes, then heirlooms are probably not for you. If you've had issues with tomato diseases in the past you may want to stick with hybrids. In my garden, though, I always save a couple of spots for some of my favorite heirlooms like Cherokee Purple, Orange Jubilee, Green Zebra, Black Krim, and the oddly shaped Constoluto Genovese. Mortgage Lifter, Brandywine, and German Johnson are also popular and delicious.

Vine Ripe?

Leaving tomatoes on the plant until they are fully colored is often an invitation to birds. They seem to know just when that tomato is perfectly ripe and they swing by to take a large chunk for themselves. Stink bugs are more likely to attack tomatoes as they get closer to harvest. To thwart these and other pests, collect your tomatoes as they start to show color. They ripen indoors just as well and there is no difference in the flavor. Just don't refrigerate them! The temperatures in the refrigerator destroy enzymes that give tomatoes their garden-fresh flavor, which is why tomatoes from the grocery store that are picked green, refrigerated, and then gassed to ripen are lacking in flavor.

Studies have shown that storing tomatoes with the stem side down actually makes them last longer. My kitchen island is adorned with beautiful platters of ripening tomatoes in summer, along with vases of fresh basil, and I prefer that to any flower arrangement! I keep cherry tomatoes in a shallow bowl on the counter and sort through them daily to find the ripest ones.

SKILL SET

GROW YOUR TOMATOES FROM CUTTINGS AND ROOT LAYERING

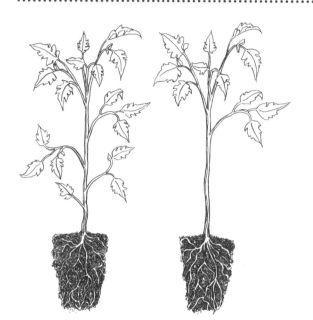

If your tomato plants are still looking healthy in early summer you can propagate them for more plants for your fall garden. Wash the vines well to remove any insects, carefully remove the lower leaves, and bury a portion of the tomato vine about a foot from the tip with a mixture of soil and compost. Keep the soil moist and the buried portion will form new roots. In a few weeks you can cut the rooted tip and there's your next tomato plant. Pot it up in a small container with potting soil for a few weeks.

Another means of propagating your healthy spring plants is taking cuttings from the plants. Cut several healthy tips from your plants and place in water in bright indirect light. Cut any lower leaves and any blooms off and change the water frequently. When the cuttings form roots, pot them up in small containers for a few weeks and then they will be ready for the garden.

Tomatoes have the ability to produce roots along their stems. To encourage more roots for a stronger plant, trim the first set of leaves at the soil level and plant them just above where those leaves grew.

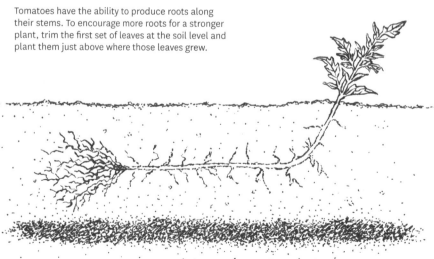

If your tomato transplants have gotten tall and leggy, remove several sets of leaves and plant the stem in a trench parallel with the surface of the soil, leaving several sets of leaves above the soil surface. The plant will produce roots all along the stem resulting in a sturdier, more vigorous plant.

•APRIL•

SPRING IS IN
FULL SWING

Spring has arrived and garden chores keep us occupied. Many of us are still harvesting produce from the winter garden as we continue to plant for spring. Careful planning now will pay off later. Providing needed support for sprawling plants, choosing the healthiest transplants, and thinning seedlings are essential for garden success and are this month's focus. Remember that many of us can still expect to have wintry blasts this month and in some areas daytime temperatures could soar to near 100°F. Be prepared for whatever nature sends your way and you'll be on the road to a productive spring garden season.

TO DO THIS MONTH

PLAN

- Insects are on the increase, so inspect daily and control quickly. Check first to see if beneficial insects are on the job and let them do their work.
- Set out traps for snails, slugs, and pillbugs if they are a problem.
- Update your garden journal with the successes and failures for the month.

PREPARE AND MAINTAIN

- Turn compost piles and make additional compost.
- Add compost and soil amendments to planting beds.
- Add mulch to cool-season crops to keep the soil cooler.
- Cut down and turn in winter cover crops several weeks before planting time.
- Foliar feed vegetables to keep them healthy and producing.
- Begin thinning fruit on fruit trees to every 6 inches to prevent damage to the trees from too much fruit.

ZONE 4

- Purchase seed potatoes and pre-sprout before planting.
- Uncover strawberries and weed and mulch if needed.

ZONES 7–8

- Thin earlier plantings of carrots, lettuce, beets, and chard.
- Remove row covers from peas and provide a trellis for support.

SOW AND PLANT INDOORS

ZONE 4

- Cabbage, squash, melons, okra, corn, tomatoes, and broccoli.

TO DO THIS MONTH CONTINUED

SOW AND PLANT OUTDOORS

ZONE 4

- Asparagus, beets, carrots, cauliflower, collards, endive, horseradish, kale, leaf lettuce, onion from seeds, sets and transplants, parsley, peas, potatoes, radishes, rhubarb, spinach, turnips.
- Plant raspberries.

ZONES 5–6

- Transplant tomatoes outside with protection.
- Sow lettuce, spinach, radishes, beets, carrots, turnips, outside and repeat plantings every two weeks for continual harvests.
- Plant peas outdoors and provide a trellis for support. Protect seeds from birds with row cover.

ZONES 7–10

- Plant black-eyed peas, okra, squash, melons, cucumbers, and pumpkins.
- Plant beans and corn every two weeks for continual harvest.
- Plant basil to replace cilantro as it goes to seed.
- Plant nasturtiums, amaranth, Malabar spinach, and purslane seeds.

HARVESTING NOW

ZONE 4

- Dig and eat carrots and parsnips that overwintered from the fall crop.

beets	kale	spinach
collards	lettuce	

ZONES 5–6

arugula	kohlrabi	radishes
carrots	lettuce	spinach

ZONES 7–10

asparagus	broccoli	cucumbers	peppers	tomatoes
beans	cabbage	kale	squash	

There is so much to do at this time of year that it seems as if there's never enough time to complete all the tasks needed in the garden. Garden centers are full of eager planters, anxious to find what they need to complete their spring garden. Find out when your garden center gets their deliveries of herbs and vegetables and try to visit on those days. If you wait until the weekend the best of the plants may be gone. Some of our local garden shops stay open later one day each week in spring to allow working gardeners a chance to stock up without the traffic jams and frenzy of spring weekend business.

Choose Your Transplants Wisely

When it comes to choosing transplants, bigger is not better. Choose a short, stocky plant with deep green color. Gently remove the plant from its container to inspect the roots. They should be healthy and white, not beige or brown or wound tightly around the base, which would indicate that the plant has been sitting in the container too long. Avoid container plants that have set fruit already or with roots that extend outside the pot; they have outgrown the container and are likely to be stressed and more prone to insects and diseases. A 4-inch or smaller container is not large enough to provide sufficient nutrients for a tomato or pepper plant with fruit. If such transplants are your only choices, however, gently remove the fruits to allow the plant to focus on roots and leaves again in your garden. Once they are well established, they can focus on fruit production once again.

Support Your Plants

If you're looking to harvest loads of peppers, eggplants, or tomatoes, you'll need to plan on giving them lots of support. Supporting plants keeps them off the ground where they may come in contact with diseases. Cucumbers and beans will grow straighter and be easier to find with support structures. Allowing plants to go vertical lets you plant other crops at the base to make the best use of space and enables gardeners to add companion plants to keep crops healthier. I use galvanized wire cages that don't rust and that fold up for easy storage. They are sturdy enough to support branches laden with lots of heavy eggplants, peppers, and tomatoes without bending. After years of searching, I found my cages from the Texas Tomato Cage Company in Edinburg, Texas, and have used them for many years.

Many gardeners rely on concrete reinforcing wire for vegetable cages. You may need to add wooden stakes or concrete reinforcing bars to hold them upright when plants get top heavy or if you garden in a very windy area. In my experience, the wire tends to rust and can take up a lot of storage space when not in use.

Galvanized fence panels and steel T-posts may also be used to support garden plants. The posts and wire panels can be moved in order to rotate crops. The fence panels come in lengths of 4 ft. × 16–20 ft. I cut them into 6-foot sections and use the T-posts to support them. I found that if the sections are taller than 6 feet I need a ladder to harvest green beans. The fence panels can also support peas, tomatoes, and melons. They are easy to store when not in use, but I find them useful for year-round gardening and for building compost structures. You will need a post setter tool to drive the posts into the ground securely. Be sure there are no water or electrical lines under the locations where the posts will be driven. I cover the top of the T-posts with a thick sock to keep them from being scratched and dented by the post driver.

Larger fruiting plants like spaghetti and butternut squash or cantaloupe can grow on a trellis with a little extra support for the heavy produce. The panty portion of a pair of pantyhose can cradle the produce and the legs can be tied to the trellis structure. Mesh produce bags can also provide support.

Bamboo stakes will hold up for a season or two and can be used to build structures for supporting peas and beans or for tying up corn that gets blown over. Stick three strong bamboo stakes in the ground and tie the tops together with a zip tie to make a bamboo tepee structure. I like to use sisal twine to wind around the bamboo stakes to give bean, pea, and cucumber tendrils an easy surface to attach to. The twine will biodegrade after a season in the garden. Be careful not to go too tall with your support structures because the plants will follow and you don't want to have to pull out a ladder for harvesting.

More formal and attractive trellis structures that provide support beautifully are available in garden centers. Be wary of tomato cages sold in garden centers—most are pretty flimsy. They can be useful for peppers or eggplants but often collapse under the weight of even a sturdy determinate tomato plant. If you have already purchased some, try doubling them up for more support.

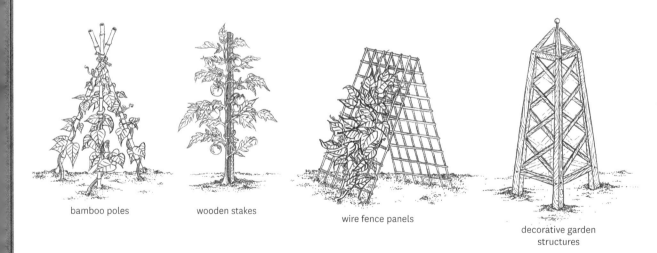

bamboo poles   wooden stakes

wire fence panels

decorative garden
structures

Thin is In

Seed packets will tell you to plant seeds more closely than is recommended for final spacing since the seeds may not all germinate and some that do might be eaten by insects or birds. As the old saying goes, "Plant one for the cut worm, one for the crow, one for the blackbird, and one to grow."

Since we're all in this to plant seeds and nurture the plants as they grow, getting rid of (or thinning) the extra seedlings can be a painful process. Make a note of the plants' final spacing recommendations on your garden plant tag to save time, and use scissors to clip the unneeded plants to the ground. Failing to thin seedlings will leave them overcrowded and they will begin to strangle each other as they grow and struggle for sufficient food, water, and space.

If you would like to save your thinned plants, you can move them to a new location. Use a kitchen fork to gently pry the seedlings from the dirt and hold them by the leaves, not the tender stems. Once you've replanted them, gently water them well and keep them shaded for a few days. Some plants, like carrots and beets, do not transplant well. Transplant seedlings by the time you see their second set of true leaves (not including the seed leaves, or cotyledons), or they may not survive the move.

WEED TEAS

We spend a lot of our garden time weeding, so why not make our weeds work for us? Fast-growing weeds are a rich source of nitrogen, phosphorus, and potassium, as well as hormones and trace minerals. When we drink a cup of tea, the vitamins, minerals, and essential oils are extracted from the plants and our body takes up the nutrients. It is much the same with plants. Weed teas are especially good for giving transplants a boost when they are actively growing.

For transplants, make a blender tea with fresh chard, alfalfa, or comfrey leaves:

1 Place two cups of coarsely chopped plant material in a blender.

2 Cover with hot water and blend thoroughly; allow to cool.

3 Strain with cheesecloth, coffee filter, or pantyhose; add the strained herbs to the compost pile or use as mulch.

4 Use the tea as a soil drench for indoor or outdoor plants. Tomatoes and peppers can really benefit from this treatment.

To make a weed tea that you can apply more broadly to your garden, use any weeds you have and mix as many as possible for the best array of nutrients. Some to consider: comfrey, chard, horsetail or equisetum, lamb's quarter, nettles, burdock, willow branches, chickweed, sorrel, plantain, pigweed, dandelions, dried and chopped egg shells, used coffee grounds and filters (especially for acid-loving plants), bedstraw or cleavers, chamomile, and lawn clippings. Weeds will have their highest nutrient content just before flowering.

1 Coarsely chop the weeds and place in an old pillowcase or a mesh bag (I use produce bags from onions or citrus) or just dump them in a bucket. (The mesh bag strains out the larger particles and makes it easier to use the finished tea.)

2 Place bag (if using) in a 5-gallon bucket and cover with rainwater or chlorine-free water (chlorine will kill the microbes that break down the plants).

3 Let stand for several days, up to two weeks. Like many other organic fertilizers, these weed brews can be a bit smelly, so store them away from the house and keep them in shade during the summer months.

4 To keep out mosquitos, cover the container with screening or row cover and tie it into place. An elastic bungee cord will secure the mosquito cover.

5 Stir every few days.

When you're ready to start using the tea, add one part tea to four or five parts water and apply it around your plants, but not on the foliage. Avoid using the tea on edible plants at harvest time as it could contain bacteria that might be harmful to ingest.

BEATING
THE BUGS

The weather has warmed and the battle of the bugs has begun. Early detection and response to insects is crucial if your plants are going to make it out alive. There's an old saying that the best way to control insects is to let them see your shadow, and while that's not entirely true (our shadows don't have super powers!), it is true that the more time you spend inspecting your plants, the better. You'll have much greater success if you can catch insects at early stages or find the eggs of problem insects before they hatch. This may include nighttime visits with your flashlight or headlamp to collect worms, snails, and slugs.

TO DO THIS MONTH

PLAN

- Make notes about the successes you had with spring planting. Is there something that should have been planted sooner or later? What insects are you seeing this month?
- Keep up with the weeding chores and reapply mulch where needed.
- Check irrigation systems to ensure they are working correctly.

PREPARE AND MAINTAIN

- Feed fruit trees with compost and mulch them.
- Continue thinning fruit on fruit trees to every 6 inches while fruit is small.
- Make the top of exposed compost piles concave so that they absorb rainfall rather than shed it.

ZONE 4

- Remove winter protection from cool-season crops (but keep it handy for late cool snaps).
- Harden off annuals before transplanting them outside.

SOW AND PLANT INDOORS

ZONE 4

- Start seeds of melon, squash, and cucumbers under light.

TO DO THIS MONTH CONTINUED

SOW AND PLANT OUTDOORS

ZONE 4

- Plant transplants of beans, celery, chard, corn, cucumbers, kale, leaf lettuce, melons, parsnips, peas, potatoes, pumpkin, radish, rutabaga, summer squash, and tomatoes.

ZONES 5–6

- When soil reaches 60°F, begin planting tomatoes, peppers, and eggplant transplants outdoors.
- Direct sow seeds of melons, cucumbers, squash, corn, okra, lettuce, and sweet potato slips.

ZONES 7–10

- Begin to remove heat-stressed cool-season crops and replace them with heat-loving black-eyed peas, Malabar spinach, yard-long beans, eggplant, okra, sweet potatoes, peppers, purslane, and basil.
- Plant heat-tolerant tomatoes like Heat Wave, and cherry-type tomatoes like Sweet 100 and Juliet.

HARVESTING NOW

ZONES 4–6

arugula	greens	green onions	lettuce	radishes
asparagus	garlic	kohlrabi	peas	spinach

ZONES 7–10

tomatoes	squash	cucumbers	sweet peas
peppers	eggplant	green beans	snow peas

Keeping Insects Under Control

Good soil will have a balance of both good and bad insects—it's just part of the package. But by understanding a bit more about why insects target certain plants, we can more effectively address the problem. Insects are generally drawn to plants that are stressed or unhealthy—a kind of natural selection to eliminate the weakest of the species. When we notice insects targeting a plant, instead of asking, "How can I kill these bugs?" we should ask ourselves, "What am I doing wrong with this plant?" Plants may be too wet, too dry, in need of fertilizer, or may be a poor variety choice or planted at the wrong time. When harlequin bugs are swarming on my radishes, greens, and broccoli in the spring, I know what they're trying to tell me: it's too hot for these cool-season plants and they need to go into the compost bin. Aphids can indicate a need for more nitrogen, while spider mites are attracted to plants that are stressed by lack of moisture. Manage what your plants are lacking, and you may succeed in curtailing the bug attacks.

The regular application of seaweed to plants will also prevent many insect infestations. The broad array of nutrients and trace elements in seaweed provides a well-balanced diet for healthy plants. Applying seaweed to the leaves of plants also leaves a salt residue on the leaf surface that most insects find distasteful. Plants that have been ravaged by bugs need extra nutrition to grow leaves to replace those that have been eaten or damaged and seaweed can provide the needed boost.

Friend or Foe?

Only about 2 percent of all insects are actually harmful to people or our crops, but resorting to chemicals for pest control will likely kill them all. Many of those bugs are beneficial and actually help to control damaging insects. By killing off those good bugs, we inherit their jobs and end up creating more work for ourselves.

Every gardener should own an insect book that clearly shows all of the stages of life for both beneficial and harmful insects. There are also sites on the internet that will aid in proper identification of insects but I like the portability factor of a book. Knowing insects in all their forms and stages is essential to maintaining beneficial insect populations and controlling pests. When you recognize the yellow, jellybean-shaped eggs of the ladybug on the underside of plant leaves you will want to leave them in the garden. Most people know the adult form of the ladybug, but many do not know that its larval form is a black and orange alligator-shaped creature that moves quickly and is a voracious eater of aphids and other insects.

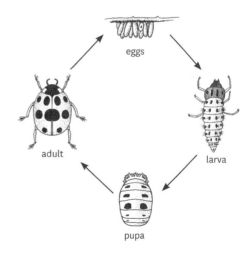

eggs

larva

pupa

adult

Life cycle of the ladybug

The egg case of the praying mantis is a fuzzy, gray-brown capsule that looks similar to a stinging caterpillar known as the puss caterpillar or stinging asp. A gardener might think they are saving themselves from a painful sting in the future, but they actually may be killing off about 50 mantises. The praying mantis is not a picky eater; it will happily eat a honeybee, a small lizard, or a stink bug but they are interesting to watch in the garden. They will also attack and eat many harmful insects, so I like to see them around.

Poison Ivy and Other Burning Questions

Poison ivy grows throughout the Southwest and the leaves can take many forms—smooth, deeply lobed, or with toothed edges—and it can vary in color from bright red or purplish to dull or glossy green. Remember the old adage, "leaflets three, let it be." If there are three leaflets growing on each leaf stalk and the stems are reddish, it is likely to be poison ivy. Poison ivy has flourished in our recent droughts and looks hale and hearty along roadsides where trees are stressed and dying.

Poison ivy varies in form from a single sprout to a low shrub and can even become a thick vine that climbs trees. The vines are sometimes confused with wild grape vines and with other native vines like Virginia creeper and cow-itch vine that look somewhat similar, but do not have the same dangerous oil. California and Nevada have a shrubbier poison oak that has oak-shaped leaves. Poison oak has the same grouping of three leaves and the waxy berries that birds love.

Since birds spread the waxy green or white berries, there is always a chance to encounter new sprouts of poison ivy or oak in your gardens. Even the smallest plant can provide a nasty rash, so use caution when dealing even with infant plants. I wear an old garden glove or a disposable glove and wrap a plastic bag over my gloved hand. Grab the new seedling and pull the bag over the plant, seal it, and dispose of it.

Some people are fortunate enough to not have any reaction to the plant but there is still the danger that you can develop an allergy to it. I was around it for years without problems but have since become very sensitive to it. All parts of the plant contain an oil called urushiol that causes the allergic reaction. Some people may get a few itchy bumps, others get a blistering rash, and some people may have a serious reaction that could require hospitalization.

Even dead vines and dried plants up to 18 months old can have nearly the same toxicity as fresh plants. Indirect contact from plants is common for gardeners. Mowing or using a weedeater or shovel in areas with the plant can cause the oil to be transferred to your skin when you handle the tools. The oil can remain on tools or clothing to infect you up to a year later. My dogs have run through the plants and transferred the oil to my skin on several occasions.

Act quickly to remove the oil if you have a reddened, itchy area on your skin that could be poison oak or ivy, as the oil enters the skin rapidly. Wash with soap and cool water only, since warm water opens the pores and could cause more of the urushiol to be absorbed. There are commercial products like TecNu Cleanser or IvyCleanse that can help to clean the oil off the skin.

An antihistamine may be helpful if you are having a bad reaction.

After washing the skin, mix a little white, green, or bentonite clay (such as those used for facial masks) with enough cool water to make a thin paste and apply it to the affected area. Let it dry, rinse with cool water, and reapply until the clay pulls the oil from the skin. After cleansing and several clay treatments, I seldom get a blistering rash if I catch it quickly enough.

There are barrier oils that can prevent the plant oil's contact with your skin, but in my experience several layers of clothing is safer if you're going to battle with a hefty number of these plants. Be sure to wash your clothes separately several times in the hottest water possible after wearing or simply wear something you won't mind discarding when you're done. I wear double or triple layers of disposable gloves when weeding the plant—remember to pull your gloves off with the insides out to avoid contacting the oil.

And don't ever burn poison ivy! The oil can be inhaled as smoke and the same blistering rash can affect the respiratory tract, which may result in severe illness and could be a fatal mistake.

SKILL SET

SQUASHING THE SQUASH VINE BORER

Many vegetable gardeners have steered clear of growing squash in recent years due to problems with squash bugs and the dreaded squash vine borer. Just as squash plants start blooming and begin to set fruit, they wilt due to squash vine borer larvae hidden inside the stems, covertly eating the plant until they're ready to leave the vine to pupate and then emerge as the adult vine borer moth. What's left behind is a mass wilted, dying squash vines. It is no surprise that squash has been genetically modified to deal with this difficult pest. Unless you purchase organic squash or grow your own, it is likely that the yellow or zucchini squash you are eating has a GMO pedigree. The adult vine borer is a moth that looks like an orange-and-black wasp. I capture and kill all that I see in the garden. They tend to be active in the early morning but they move slowly so they are easy to catch.

Hollow stem varieties of squash such as yellow and zucchini squash tend to have the most problems with borers. Pumpkins, butternut, acorn, Tatume, Trombetta, and scalloped squash will have fewer problems. They can withstand an attack from borers and still send out new growth despite the damage. Vining types of squash are better adapted to handling borer damage than bush types, but even cucumbers and melons can

be attacked by vine borers. I have experimented with a few techniques to thwart these enemies of squash plants and am pleased to report that I am now able to once again grow more squash than I know what to do with. I plant squash plants or seeds along with onions and radishes to help repel the moths from laying eggs around the squash stems. Ground-up bay leaves and trimmings from fragrant herbs like thyme, oregano, or savory can be used around the planting area to confuse the vine borer's detection of the newly planted squash.

Immediately after planting, apply a lightweight polyester row cover over the new plants until the female flowers appear. The covering must go completely to the ground and be securely fastened over garden hoops. This cover keeps the moths from laying its eggs near the young squash while allowing air, light, and water to reach the plants. The first squash blooms are all male flowers. Female flowers will have a small squash at the base of the flower. When the female flowers open, remove the row cover to allow bees to pollinate the flowers. By that time the plants are a little tougher and not quite as enticing to the moths. Some gardeners choose to do the pollination themselves by removing the petals from a male flower and touching it to open female flowers and then keeping the covers on the plants.

The vine borers will eventually kill the plants, but you will get many weeks of harvest before that occurs. When you pull up the squash plants, inspect the stems for more worms and kill them or enclose the squash vines in plastic bags and discard them in the trash to control future generations of the moths.

When you inspect your squash plants for problems, look for a tiny hole in the stem with sawdust-like frass nearby—the sign of a recent move-in by a borer. Make a cut in the stem with a sharp knife and extract the inch-long white worm. There may be more than one. Close the stem and cover the wound with some compost. The stem should heal if the worms have not done too much damage. You may also notice reddish to amber pearl-like eggs laid on leaf tops, in leaf axils, or on the stems. Remove these when you see them and crush them between your fingers.

Some gardeners use beneficial nematodes to control the borers in the soil or spray a liquid Spinosad product weekly around the base of the plants. Since the nematodes also control ants, fleas, pillbugs, and many other soil-dwelling insects pests they are a good investment. I use a shop vacuum to suck up any squash bugs and larvae that may also be lurking around the base of the squash plants.

·JUNE·

THE WATER-WISE
GARDEN

The heat is on in the Southwest and using water wisely is important whether your immediate area is in severe drought or not. Water is a limited resource and there are many ways that gardeners can harvest and utilize water in a conservative manner. Understanding how and when to water is important to success for any gardener, but it is critical to those of us who deal with daily temperatures above 90°F. And for most of us, the heat is just getting started. There are many plants that thrive in summer's temperatures, but others will need our help. While you're out there, don't forget to include wildlife in your daily routine. Keep birdbaths and toad basins filled with fresh water and make sure your bird feeders are stocked.

TO DO THIS MONTH

PLAN

- Harvesting your crops requires more time than bed preparation and planting. Daily harvesting to collect crops while small will reduce plant stress and keep them producing for a longer period. Okra, cucumbers, and squash should be harvested daily as they can grow very quickly from edible to compostable.
- Get creative with your excess harvests. Trade your pet sitter a basket of veggies for her services, butter up your boss with a basket of tomatoes, or trade your excess okra for your neighbor's excess squash. Donate extra food to the food bank.
- Most cool-season crops will be on the decline and may be attacked by insects. Remove them and plant something better adapted to the heat.
- Keep adding notes to your garden journal. Be sure to comment on the flavor of the varieties you planted as well as how much the plants produce.
- Water plants deeply to keep them healthy.

PREPARE AND MAINTAIN

- Make trellises and support structures for your tomatoes, beans, cucumbers, and peas.
- Watch for stink bugs, caterpillars, grasshoppers, and snail and slug damage.
- Mulch plants to keep them cooler and wetter.

ZONES 8–10

- Begin solarizing beds to control weeds or nematodes.
- Remove and compost the remaining cool-season vegetables.
- Plant warm-season cover crops to improve soil in unused garden beds.

SOW AND PLANT INDOORS

ZONES 7–10

- Start tomatoes, peppers, and eggplants for fall plantings.

TO DO THIS MONTH CONTINUED

SOW AND PLANT OUTDOORS

ZONE 4
- Direct seed lima beans, beets, corn, cucumbers, leaf lettuce, okra, melons, squash, sweet potatoes, rutabaga, and cilantro.
- Plant transplants of tomatoes, peppers, and eggplant after hardening off.

ZONES 5–6
- Plant bush beans, corn, and cucumbers.
- Plant sweet potato slips and Brussels sprouts and cabbage transplants.

ZONES 7–8
- Plant pole beans, bush beans, winter squash, okra, Malabar spinach, and black-eyed peas.

HARVESTING NOW

ZONES 4–6

asparagus	kale	cauliflower	beets
broccoli	lettuce	turnips	

ZONES 7–10

corn	tomatoes	potatoes	Malabar	beets
beans	peppers	eggplant	spinach	squash
cucumbers				

Life gets a little more difficult for wildlife as the warm season begins. The abundant spring blooms of wildflowers have faded and rain is less frequent. Providing food, water, and shelter for wildlife is rewarding for gardeners. Lizards, toads, and birds provide essential pest-control services as well as entertainment. Bees and butterflies have been threatened by new garden chemicals and need the help and support of gardeners everywhere.

Shallow containers of water throughout the garden provide a welcome oasis for many garden visitors. I have shallow terracotta saucers filled with a half-inch or so of water in several shady locations that usually play host to one or several toads each evening. Birds also love a shallow container of water with a surface that provides them sure footing. Many birdbaths are actually too deep for smaller birds, but you can add a stepping stone to the center to create a shallow bathing area for the small guys. Birds also appreciate shallow moving water. A dripper installed on a faucet over a tray or a small recirculating fountain will attract lots of birds. Birds will often attack tomatoes for the moisture they provide, so giving them a water source may lessen their attacks on your garden.

Keep the containers filled with fresh water and change it every two to three days to keep mosquitoes from breeding there. Mosquito Dunks are donut-shaped briquettes treated with Bti (*Bacillus thuringiensis* subsp. *israelensis*), which prevents mosquito larvae from hatching for up to thirty days. The dunks will be most effective in clean water.

Waste Not, Want Not

As droughts continue around the country, we need to be more and more careful with our use of water. Many cities have curtailed the installation of thirsty lawns. Any water I use outdoors is used for food production and a few flowers. I stopped watering my small shaded patch of Saint Augustine lawn in 2011, but it still refuses to completely die. After years of organic maintenance, it survives on rainfall alone.

Try to repurpose your water wherever you can. Collect the water when you change it in the birdbaths and use it on your plants and compost. From the house, some gardeners keep plastic buckets in the shower and transport the saved water to the garden. I keep a pitcher next to the sink to catch water used for rinsing vegetables or the coffee pot, or leftover glasses of water. That goes out to container plants several times a day to tide over the thirstier plants until the next watering day.

Watering Wisdom

Group plants according to their water needs. Rosemary, lavender, and artichokes will not require the same amount of water as squash, basil, or beans. Creating a bed with plants that like to dry out completely between watering cycles will save water and keep the plants healthier.

Plants that have protection from wind and direct sun will not require watering as frequently. Sun and wind can dry out soil very quickly. The plants in your front yard that are more exposed to those conditions may need water more frequently than those in the back yard that are surrounded by the house and fences. However, plants under the shade of trees may actually require extra watering since thirsty trees with their widespread root systems will take lots of moisture from the soil.

Watering on a cycle is wasteful and usually not quite what plants need. Unfortunately, many of us are limited to watering on certain days during drought restrictions so we water when we can. It is still a good practice to check the soil and water when the plants need it. Move back the mulch and see if the soil is actually dry before you turn on the irrigation.

Drip Irrigation

Drip irrigation systems are quite easy to install and are the most efficient means of watering for many reasons. The water is put where the plants need it, at the soil level, and little is lost to evaporation and wind compared to spray irrigation. Keeping the water off the foliage of plants limits diseases like powdery mildew and black spot. Many cities that limit watering due to drought conditions are more lenient with drip users.

If you start with a brand of drip tubing and parts when setting up your system, you should stick with that company as the emitters or fittings from one brand will probably not work with another company's products. Fitting the components together is a little like working with Tinkertoys and is quite simple once you get the hang of it. Simple, straight garden beds make it easier to design drip systems for efficient watering.

You will need to water for a longer period with drip systems as opposed to spray watering. Water for thirty minutes and wait several hours. Dig a hole several inches deep and see how far the water seeped into the soil. A deep watering will move into the soil and extend to the depth of the plant roots. Sandy soil permits the water to move deeper more quickly while clay soil tends to let the water spread laterally. Adjust the timing of your watering to get the water deep enough for the plant roots in your type of soil.

Rodents and other wild animals may chew the plastic lines for a quick drink. Keep repair couplings on hand for quick repairs. I detach and remove the lines before prepping beds for the next season's planting. It is too easy to puncture a line with a spading fork. Design your system to make each bed's drip lines easy to remove when needed.

Add a few clay saucers under emitters throughout the garden to provide water for wildlife. I notice birds taking advantage of the drip system when it is on and the saucers will ensure they will have fresh water provided for them throughout the day. Toss the water out frequently to avoid breeding mosquitoes.

In a multiple-bed system, install inline valves to shut off water to a bed that you will be digging in or that does not require as much water as the rest of the garden. Use long—at least 6 inches—U-shaped soil staples to hold water lines in place. You may fashion your own from metal clothes hangers.

Drip hose is typically sold in 100-foot or 500-foot rolls that are tightly coiled. The tubing will be easier to work with if you stretch and straighten it out before assembling lines in the garden. Enlist a helper to unwind the hose and stretch lengths of 10 to 20 feet at a time. If you are working solo, wrap the hose around a sturdy tree or post and pull to straighten it. The tubing will stretch more easily when it is warm. Place the roll on a sunny driveway, inside a hot car trunk, or under the dryer exhaust vent for a few hours to make it more pliable.

The fittings must be very snug to keep them from leaking and may require considerable hand strength to connect. Heat some water close to the boiling point and immerse the ends of the tubing in the hot water for a few minutes to soften the tubing. It will be much easier to slip the connections onto the pliable hose.

Drip emitters will sometimes clog, especially if your water is hard. A straightened paperclip is handy to clear debris from emitters for a quick fix, so I keep a few in my garden bag. Soak clogged emitters in vinegar to clean them for reuse and remember to check and replace emitters frequently. An emitter that fails to water could be disastrous for your plants. Remove end caps on drip lines and flush them several times a year to keep the emitters clog free.

When hard freezes are predicted, open the connections to the water supply and remove the end caps to allow all water to escape from the lines. When water expands as it freezes, it can break lines and connections in your drip system.

Drip tape is an alternative means of applying water in a drip system. The material is more fragile and does not last as long as a plastic drip hose with emitters. Commercial growers often prefer to use drip tape as it is less expensive initially and is more easily moved to accommodate tractors and soil moving equipment.

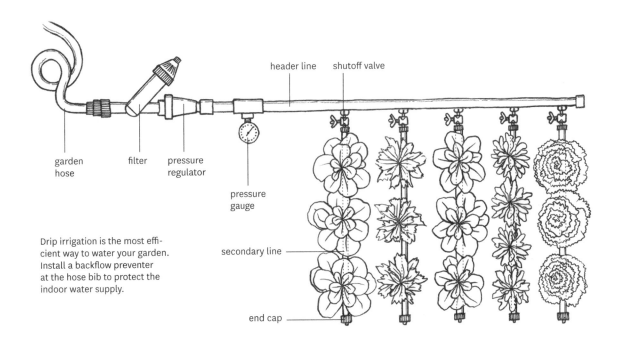

header line   shutoff valve

garden hose   filter   pressure regulator

pressure gauge

Drip irrigation is the most efficient way to water your garden. Install a backflow preventer at the hose bib to protect the indoor water supply.

secondary line

end cap

Soaker Hoses

Soaker hoses can be an efficient way to water plants deeply. Water seeps from tiny pores in the hoses. The hoses are installed in garden beds and around perennial plantings. They are often used around the foundation of homes with clay soil to keep the soil consistently moist so that the homes will not shift and crack when soil moisture fluctuates. They can also be used to water trees. Place them in the drip line of trees, not near the trunks.

Gently unwind the hoses and pin them to the ground with U-shaped soil staples to keep them in place. A thin layer of mulch may be added over the hose. Loop the hose around plants that require extra water but keep the hose several inches from the base of perennial herbs and shrubs to prevent damage. Connecting several hoses together will result in less water at the end of the line farthest from the hose connection, so avoid using more than 100 feet of hose connected together.

Although they are less expensive than drip systems initially, I have never found soaker hoses to be very long lasting. Our mineral-rich alkaline water tends to clog the pores and they ultimately water very unevenly. The hoses do not hold up well in intense heat and are destined for the trash bin in a short time. They can be useful for short-term watering needs but a well-designed drip system will be a much better investment. If animals chew through the hoses for water, repairs can be made with a hose repair coupling.

Getting the Slow Soak

If watering new fruit trees regularly is a challenge, use plastic 5-gallon buckets to get the root zone well watered. Drill several small holes near the base of the bucket and place several buckets around the drip zone of the tree and fill each with a hose. The buckets will take hours to drain and the water will deeply soak the root zone of the tree. Place a rock in each bucket if windy conditions are a concern. Add seaweed, fish emulsion, or other fertilizer as needed.

Likewise, if your compost pile is not within easy reach of a hose, you can use this same method to keep it moist. Place a bucket or two on top of the pile.

You can also buy something called Treegators, which are donut-shaped plastic bags that are placed around tree trunks or shrubs, filled with water, and then left to slowly drip-irrigate the root zone of trees. They are available in 15- and 20-gallon sizes.

Watering Myths

The following are some common misconceptions about the role of water in your garden:

"My plants need to be watered every day." Well-established garden plants should not require daily watering. In fact, giving plants a daily drink leads shallow root systems that can dry out quickly. When deep, but infrequent watering is provided, plant roots tend to go deeper in the soil in search for water. That said, newly planted seeds and transplants require water daily as their root systems are small and germinating seeds will fail if allowed to go too dry. This may also be true of container plants in the heat of summer, as they don't have extensive root systems to search out their next drink, but well-mulched containers may only need water every other day. Group container plants together to keep the temperatures more moderated.

"Plants all need an inch of water per week." Different plants will require differing amounts of water. Well-established trees may be able to go several weeks between watering, while a newly planted tree may need to be watered several times a week. Rosemary and sage don't mind being very dry between watering, but basil and chives would be happier if kept consistently moist. There is no one-size-fits-all rule for watering plants.

"My plants are wilted, so I need to water." Many garden plants will wilt in the afternoon heat to conserve water loss through their leaves. When temperatures cool down, the leaves perk up again. If the plant is still wilted after sundown, then you can start to worry about watering it. It is easy to overwater plants if you water each time you see a wilted plant.

"Morning is the best time to water plants." It is true that plants are better prepared to handle the heat of the day if they have been watered, but watering the foliage of plants that require pollination may actually be counterproductive. If you were about to sit down for a picnic and somebody suddenly doused it all with water, you wouldn't be too excited to eat—bees, butterflies, and other pollinators aren't all that different. They're not overjoyed at the prospect of a soggy meal either. Water early so that flowers and pollen are dry before insects are active, or restrict your watering to drip irrigation.

"Watering during the heat of the day can cause sunburn on plant leaves." If plants are in need of water, you can water whenever you like. The water will evaporate off of the leaves but will not damage them. A cooling spray will give the plants a little relief from the heat on a hot day. Washing dust from leaves and cleaning plants regularly is important to keep them healthy and pest free. Even with a drip system it is a good practice to give your plants the occasional shower with the hose. It's also a good time to inspect the plants closely for insects or disease. Still, there is some truth to daytime not being the most practical time to water, as more water is lost to evaporation when watering in higher temperatures.

"Native and drought-tolerant plants never need water." The native plants that you purchase have been watered daily in the garden center. They still need that daily watering until they grow the massive root systems that allow them to be drought tolerant. Planting them in well-prepared soil with a layer of mulch and some regular watering to get them through the first growing season will allow them to get a healthy root system going and then you can level off on watering. After a few seasons, you may only need to water them occasionally during prolonged dry spells, but keep in mind that even the toughest drought-tolerant plants still need an occasional drink (it is important to remember that more plants are killed by overwatering than underwatering—check the soil to see if it is dry before you water your plants, especially the drought tolerant ones).

"With sprinkler systems, you can set it and forget it." Gardeners with automatic sprinkler systems usually water much more than their plants require. It is much too easy to put everything on a timer and forget about it. It would be better to shut down the automatic cycle and water when your plants tell you they need it unless you are away for an extended trip and have no other options. Keep in mind that plants do not require the same length of watering cycle in winter as they do in summer. Set up a winter cycle and a summer cycle if your controller allows you multiple programs and inspect your sprinkler heads regularly. Until their plants start to show signs of stress, many people are unaware that their sprinkler heads are spraying in the wrong direction, clogged up, or have valves that are not working. Inspect drip irrigation lines regularly for clogged emitters and flush soaker hoses and drip lines often to keep them clean.

CATCHING RAINWATER

Since most of our rainfall seems to come all at once with long periods before the next downpour, rainwater-collection tanks are a good investment for southwestern gardeners—1000 square feet of roof space can provide 600 gallons of rainwater with just an inch of rain. And there is no better water for your plants, especially young transplants and seedlings, than chemical-free rainwater.

Large-volume tanks can be quite an investment but smaller 50- to 100-gallon tanks are more reasonable and can even be acquired for little cost or for free. Food manufacturers receive oils, syrups, and other liquids in plastic drums. These food-safe barrels (usually blue plastic) can be fitted with a hose connection and connected to your downspouts with fairly simple and readily available parts (I would avoid the use of barrels that have held petroleum products or chemicals).

When placing any barrel in the garden, make sure you have room to get a watering can positioned under the spigot. Building a sturdy table or using cinder block supports under the barrel will allow you to fill your watering can or easily attach a hose. The downspout should be positioned as low as possible on the barrel to make it possible to easily drain the water.

Trash cans or 5-gallon buckets placed under the eaves of the house or a garden shed before a rain can be a simple means of collecting many gallons of rainwater. Place a mosquito briquette in each can to kill larvae for up to a month, or use fiberglass screening secured with an elastic cord over each container.

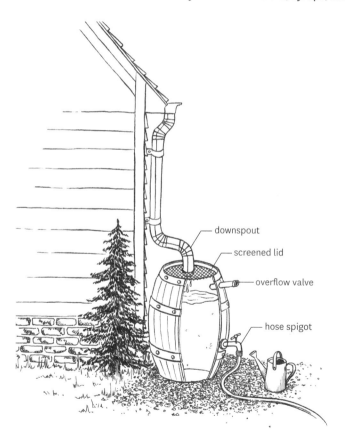

downspout

screened lid

overflow valve

hose spigot

A rain barrel can supply a steady source of chlorine-free water for new garden seedlings, indoor plants, and fertilizer mixes.

·JULY·

THE HEAT IS ON

Summer's heat can be a challenge for south-western gardeners. Much of the spring garden has finished for season and you and your plants may wilt pretty quickly. Getting out to the garden early before temperatures soar will be essential. Watering in the morning makes the garden and container plants better prepared to handle the afternoon's sizzling temperatures. Get in the habit of wearing a hat to protect your eyes, hair, and skin. The wider the brim, the better sun protection it will provide. Drink plenty of water with electrolytes when you're going to be outside for extended periods.

TO DO THIS MONTH

PLAN

- To avoid heat stress, get an early-morning start on tough garden chores like turning compost or preparing beds.
- Start planning for your fall garden.
- Make notes in your garden journal and include photos of your plants and your harvests.

PREPARE AND MAINTAIN

- Continue to hill up the soil around potato plantings.
- Water deeply to keep plants healthy.
- Remove plants that are past their prime; it is not worth wasting the water to keep them going.
- Mulch or cover crop beds where spring crops have finished.
- Compost and fertilize beds to be planted later for fall.
- Collect seeds from your healthiest plants for next year's garden.
- Prune raspberry and blackberry plants after the harvest.

SOW AND PLANT INDOORS

ZONES 4–6

- Plant broccoli, cauliflower, kale, and greens for fall production.
- Pre-sprout snow peas and sugar snap peas for better germination.

ZONES 7–8

- Plant tomatoes, eggplant, and peppers for fall gardens.
- Take cuttings from healthy tomato and basil plants and root them indoors for fall plantings.
- Start seeds of broccoli, cauliflower, and other brassicas for the fall garden.

TO DO THIS MONTH CONTINUED

SOW AND PLANT OUTDOORS

ZONE 4

- Plant transplants of broccoli, cabbage, and cauliflower.
- Sow kale and Asian green seeds for fall harvest.
- Plant a second crop of green beans and summer squash.

ZONES 5–6

- Plant dill and cilantro every month for continued harvest.

- Make a final planting of bush beans and summer squash.
- Plant carrots, kale, beets, and chard for fall harvest.

ZONES 7–10

- Plant transplants of tomatoes, peppers, and eggplant for fall.
- Sow pumpkins for halloween.
- Plant lettuce, carrots, beets, turnips, beans, and squash for fall.

HARVESTING NOW

basil	cucumbers	green beans	peppers	squash
blackberries	garlic	onions	potatoes	tomatoes

Our schedules are all different, though, and some gardeners must resort to evening hours for their summer gardening chores. Since I frequently end up doing mine in the evening, I had floodlights installed near the garden to take advantage of the later hours. A few solar lights also help to brighten up dark spots.

Mosquitoes

The longer days of summer allow us to work later, but temperatures are often still in the mid-90s at the end of the day here in south Texas and mosquitoes will attack any exposed skin within seconds of stepping outside. Mosquitoes follow the carbon dioxide trail from our breathing and can also detect sweat odors. Gardening in summer heat leads to heavy breathing and sweating so we must take steps to mask those odors, hopefully without resorting to the use of harmful chemicals. I use a number of tactics to deal with this problem.

Incense sticks are not something I ever use indoors, but having a few burning around the garden makes it very difficult for mosquitoes to find you. It's not necessary to invest in expensive garden incense—anything that smells fairly strong and I find tolerable will do the trick. Place the lighted sticks in your garden soil or pots, or use small buckets filled with sand to keep them upright and out of the reach of children and pets. I sometimes wield a water hose in one hand and an incense stick in the other while I tend to brief daily outdoor watering chores on summer evenings. Strong-smelling candles will also help to disguise your scent. My standards for indoor candles are fairly stringent—natural scents, soy wax or beeswax, and lead-free wicks—but I often get candles as gifts that don't meet my criteria. These are great for burning outside and their strong scents do a good job of beating the bugs but I find the incense tends to be more effective.

If I am out in the garden only briefly, I will grab a handful of rose-scented geranium leaves, crush them to release their oils, and rub them over exposed skin. Their scent works well to repel mosquitoes.

Look for mosquito repellents that contain lemon eucalyptus, or *Eucalyptus citriodora*. This variety of eucalyptus essential oil has been found to be as effective as DEET. I also make several home concoctions of insect-repelling formulas that smell pleasant and keep the bugs away.

DIY INSECT REPELLENT

4 ounces unscented lotion

15 drops lavender oil

15 drops lemon eucalyptus

10 drops geranium oil

½ teaspoon vanilla extract

Combine all ingredients in a small glass jar or bottle. Test the blend on a small skin area and if there is no irritation, apply liberally before going outdoors. Reapply as needed.

Vegetables That Take the Heat

Tomatoes, green beans, and cucumbers slow down to a crawl when the heat rises. Smaller-fruited cherry and paste tomatoes will tend to set fruit longer than larger tomato types. However, there are many crops that love the heat and thrive in triple-digit temperatures. Count on these summer sensations to keep growing well even when you are feeling wilted by the heat.

Okra is native to Africa and loves the heat. This member of the hibiscus family is just getting started when the heat rises and doesn't stop all summer long.

Black-eyed peas or southern peas not only provide a delicious crop, they feed the soil with nitrogen for the next season's planting.

Yard-long beans and red yard-long beans are Asian relatives of southern peas that climb much like pole beans. All summer long, they produce handfuls of beans that are 15–24 inches long (not quite a yard, despite their name). Just a few beans would be enough for a single serving. The leaves and blooms look are similar to black-eyed peas and they likewise feed the soil with nitrogen.

Sweet potatoes are morning glory relatives producing trailing vines that make a lovely ground cover. Their lush foliage suppresses weeds and requires little care other than regular deep watering until the roots are ready to harvest in fall.

Malabar spinach is a climbing, lush vine that needs a strong trellis. I trim it regularly for a nitrogen boost for the compost pile when I have more than I can eat. Keep the prolific blooms trimmed before they turn to the bright purple seeds to keep the vines in check for next season.

Swiss chard and **French sorrel** continue to produce all summer long in partial sun conditions. Both will have a stronger flavor in summer. Comfrey is not edible, but its mineral-rich leaves are a great addition to compost and fertilizer teas, and may be used as mulch. Comfrey grows best with some afternoon shade.

Eggplant and **peppers** will continue to produce in the heat of summer, especially if they are planted in a location that gives them some shade in the afternoon. The fruits will be smaller in the summer but they will grow larger again when temperatures decline.

Keep eggplant, peppers, and tomatoes blooming with a feeding of Epsom salt. Mix 2 tablespoons in a gallon of water, stir well, and pour around the base of the plants. They will respond with a flush of blooms within a few days.

If the heat has you ready to surrender for the summer, use black-eyed peas and sweet potatoes as easy-care cover crops rather than leaving the garden soil bare and open to weed invasion. The lush vines of sweet potatoes are an excellent addition of nitrogen to the compost pile in fall after the potatoes are harvested. The leaves are also edible.

Eat Your Weeds

Weeds can provide nutrition for our table and compost pile and edible flowers are a delight for the eyes and the palate. Summer is a great time to retreat indoors and explore these alternative crops.

Chickweed is a cool-season annual weed that tastes like mild spinach. It is often included in herbal remedies for the kidneys and as a blood purifier.

Chile pequin is a perennial pepper native to much of the South. The pea-sized peppers are tiny but pack a powerful punch. One or two of these tiny peppers will spice up an entire pot of chili. Often called bird peppers, they are enjoyed by many birds, especially mockingbirds, and are spread by the birds in their droppings. They grow in shady locations in the wild but will tolerate more sun if given more water. The peppers are eaten red or green and can be picked and frozen for use throughout the year.

Dandelion leaves may be eaten raw, juiced, or cooked. The leaves have been used to support liver function and as an overall tonic. Use the leaves before the plant begins to bloom for the best flavor.

Epazote is a warm-season weed that is widely used in Mexican kitchens. Its aroma is faintly oily and reminiscent of turpentine but it imparts sublime flavor to salsas, beans, and other dishes. It is a prolific self-seeder, so keep it cut back to avoid a garden takeover.

Lamb's quarter and orach are warm-season weeds that will grow very tall and produce thousands of seeds like most chenopodiums. You may want to cut the plants back before they go to seed to control them. Use the leaves in salads or cooked.

Nettles must be harvested carefully as they are well armed, but they are delicious lightly steamed or brewed for tea. They are a good source of iron and calcium and are beneficial for the immune system. Nettle tea is also used as a pest-control spray.

Poke salad is a prolific warm-season weed in the South. Its claim to fame was the catchy song "Poke Salad Annie," by Tony Jo White. I find myself singing that tune as I gather the tender young shoots in spring. The shoots are cooked in boiling water for ten minutes, rinsed and drained, then cooked again, usually with onions, garlic, and bacon. It is important to cook only the new growth in spring and to adhere to the two-step cooking process, as it can be quite toxic if not properly prepared, so tread carefully. Revered as a spring tonic, the flavor and nutrient profile is similar to spinach. The bright purple berries are beloved by birds and are used as a dye.

Purslane is a warm-season weed that is very prolific. The succulent stems are great in salads, stir-fries, and added to soups. It has a slightly sour taste and is high in minerals, vitamins A, C, and E, as well as healthy omega-3 fatty acids.

A Bounty of Basil

No summer garden would be complete without the aromatic wonder of fresh basil. The genus name, *Ocimum*, comes from the Greek word *okimon*, which appropriately enough means "smell." The most common species is *O. basilicum*, from the Greek word for "king." Basils are members of the mint family, Lamiaceae, characterized by square stems and opposite leaves on the stems. Rosemary, thyme, lavender, and oregano are also members of the mint family.

Some of my favorites are Mrs. Burns' Lemon basil, Red Rubin basil, which features smooth burgundy-colored leaves and a sweet flavor, and variegated Pesto Perpetuo, a very flavorful cultivar which rarely blooms. The large ruffled leaves of lettuce leaf basil can cover an entire slice of sandwich bread with just a single leaf. Bell pepper basil is a recent introduction and the leaves do indeed have the sweet, pungent aroma and flavor of a freshly picked bell pepper. Bell pepper basil has been a perennial for several years in my central-Texas garden.

Semi-tropical basil needs warm temperatures to thrive. Nights below 45°F will stunt its growth, so avoid planting too early. You should plan on covering basil if cool temperatures threaten it. Lots of sun—at least six to eight hours a day—will keep it looking its best. It may be grown in pots with a loose, well-draining soil mix. Frequent light fertilization with seaweed and compost tea will keep it lush and beautiful, but avoid too much fertilizer or you'll get rampant, lush growth with little flavor.

Perhaps the most important thing to remember about growing basil is that it is an annual. Its mission is to produce seeds for the next generation, so it wants to flower prolifically. Once basil begins to flower and set mature seeds, the stems get woody and the leaves get smaller and lose their flavor. As gardeners, our mission is to keep those flowers cut off before they turn to seeds to keep the plants robust and bushy. Let the plants bloom a bit since the flowers are highly attractive to bees, but avoid letting them set mature seeds. The seedpods turn brown when mature and you will find tiny black basil seeds inside the pods.

Don't be timid about trimming. Cut the stems back a third to halfway down the stem, cutting above a leaf node. It seems drastic, but this delays further flower production for a longer time. If you simply pinch the flowers, the plants produce more flowers immediately. If you are going on vacation, cut the basil back very hard, at least halfway, to avoid returning home to mature basil seed heads.

Basil flowers are great to add as fragrant filler in your flower arrangements and can last for weeks. Make fresh basil bouquets for your next outdoor gathering to help repel flying insects. Sometimes basil cuttings will begin to root in the water, creating more plants for the garden.

And, of course, you will want to make batch after batch of pesto with your basil. Pesto is the perfect way to add the richness, warmth, and freshness of summertime to foods throughout the year. I like to use ziplock bags to store pesto in the freezer. It makes it simple to break off a small portion for a recipe. You can also freeze pesto in ice cube trays, then remove from the trays and bag the cubes for easy portions.

Herbs for Summer

There's more than just basil, of course. There are many herbs that flourish with the heat of summer.

Lavender likes to be in a sunny, dry location in the garden. A raised bed is ideal in humid or wet climates. Water with drip irrigation placed well away from the base of the plants to limit fungal disease and crown rot. Like many other plants with fuzzy leaves, lavender does not tolerate its foliage being sprayed by sprinklers.

Lemon grass is root hardy in zones 8–10 but is easily grown in a container with winter protection. The lemon-flavored leaves are delightful in teas and the fibrous stems make a flavorful addition to soups, sauces, stir-fries, and marinades. The stems are usually chopped finely, ground to a paste, or used as a flavoring and then removed like bay leaves.

Lemon verbena can become a large evergreen shrub in zones 9–10 but will die back and return most years in zones 7–8. Plant it in a container and give it a warm bright location in winter and you can harvest the lemon-perfumed leaves all winter long. They are my favorite addition to the teapot and I also love them in fragrant baths and for flavoring cakes, ice cream, and cookies.

MINT

No herb garden is complete without at least one mint but they are much too invasive for me to plant directly in the garden. I grow mint in containers of 15- to 24-inch diameter. Each variety of mint is in a separate pot and they get morning sun and afternoon shade. Allow the plants an occasional bloom since the bees love the flowers, but cut them back to the soil level once or twice a year to keep the foliage tender and succulent. Whether in containers or in the ground, mint will eventually become root bound and need division. The roots get so crowded that the plants may eventually die out.

Dig out a clump of healthy foliage and roots and set it aside. Remove the overgrown roots from the bed or pot, add compost and new soil, and repot the saved plant in its new home where it will grow quite happily. It may not be wise to add mint roots to your compost pile unless you allow them to dry out completely before adding them.

Make sure you purchase a good quality mint or get cuttings from someone who has a wonderful variety. Named varieties are usually superior in flavor to something labeled simply "mint." Black Stem Peppermint, Double Mint, Chocolate Mint, Wintergreen, and Kentucky Colonel Spearmint are some of my favorites for adding to butter, vinegars, smoothies, lemonades, and cocktails.

SKILL SET

PROVIDING SHADE FOR CONTINUED HARVESTS

We gardeners gravitate toward the shade in summer's heat and if our plants could move themselves they would join us. Alas, we have to give them a helping hand. Providing shade for our plants until we get a break from triple-digit temperatures can be key to summer gardening success.

Lightweight row cover typically used for insect control provides about 15 percent shade. Double or triple it and hang it over peppers, eggplants, cucumbers, and tomatoes to keep them alive and in production. Burlap, old bed sheets, or shade cloth from home improvement stores will give 30–40 percent shade. Gradually expose the plants to full sun again when temperatures are below 90°F.

Many gardeners use ½-inch PVC pipe for hoops over the plants to prop up the row cover. Short rebar stakes are set in the edges of the bed and the pipe is bent and placed over the stakes. However, the PVC gets stained and unattractive, is difficult to store when not in use, and can become brittle and shatter with age. As an alternative, I have been using concrete reinforcing bars for hoops and find that their color blends into the garden and they are more attractive than the stark white of the PVC. They last for many years and are versatile for many garden uses. I use them for shading plants, supporting beans and peas, and for protecting plants from rabbits, deer, or pests.

PROVIDING SHADE FOR CONTINUED HARVESTS CONTINUED

Use binder clips from the office supply store or clothespins to hold deer netting or row cover onto the hoops. Spring clamps can provide a stronger grip if your garden is in a windy location.

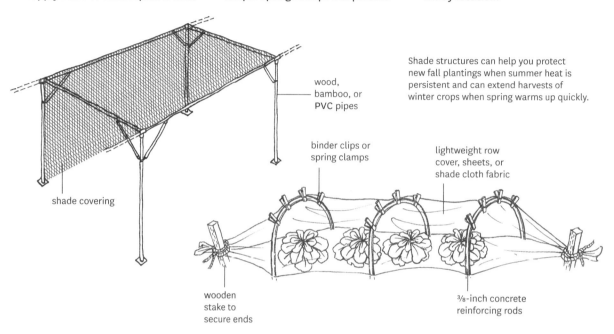

shade covering

wood, bamboo, or PVC pipes

Shade structures can help you protect new fall plantings when summer heat is persistent and can extend harvests of winter crops when spring warms up quickly.

binder clips or spring clamps

lightweight row cover, sheets, or shade cloth fabric

wooden stake to secure ends

⅜-inch concrete reinforcing rods

WORKING WITH REBAR

Concrete reinforcing bars or rebar are available at home improvement stores usually in 10-foot lengths. Choose the smaller ⅜-inch rebar as it is easier to bend and lighter than ½-inch steel. Bring gloves with you when you purchase it as it is rusty and will stain your hands.

Put the rebar on the ground and start bending the rebar in a series of small bends. It may be helpful to make marks at each 2-foot section of the rebar. Bend gently at each 2-foot mark, making an arch. For the final shaping, I put the rebar around a tree trunk or post and bend until I have the desired shape (this will mark the tree bark so don't use that favorite peach tree!).

A 10-foot length of rebar will yield an arch approximately 44–48 inches wide and 45–48 inches high. The rebar ends will be inserted about 8–10 inches into the soil so will be shorter when in use. This makes an ideal hoop size to cover kale and collard greens or young tomatoes and peppers in spring in a 4-foot-wide bed.

If your garden beds are narrower, or you want shorter hoop for covering shorter crops like lettuce, cut 12–15 inches off of the rebar with a hacksaw before bending. That will make a 36-inch-wide hoop that is about 30–34 inches tall.

The steel will develop a dark patina after a season in the garden and will no longer stain your hands with handling.

·AUGUST·

DOG DAYS

The dog days of summer are upon us and August often brings our hottest temperatures day after day. Despite the temperatures, though, August marks the end of the summer season and our focus shifts to planning and planting for fall. This is an exciting time, though! Temperatures are milder in fall, rainfall tends to be more reliable, and insects pose less of a problem. Mosquitoes disappear and even biting flies take a break. We get another show of blooms from roses and other perennials that took a summer break. There are an amazing variety of plants that grow in the cool season in the Southwest and most of those are prolific producers.

TO DO THIS MONTH

PLAN

- Be prepared for soaring temperatures. Your plants will appreciate a break from the sun as much as you do. Use row cover, shade cloth, or fabric to give your plants a respite from the sun. Take an umbrella out to the garden where you will be working.
- Update your garden journal. Note how hot the temperatures were and if there was rainfall. Make notes of the seeds you collected and herbs you harvested.
- Remove plants that are past their prime. It is not worth wasting water to keep them alive.

PREPARE AND MAINTAIN

- Cut back your basil to keep it from going to seed.
- Save seeds from your best tomatoes and pepper plants.
- Remove new tomato flowers to direct energy into the fruits already on the vines. Prune tomatoes, peppers, and eggplant to stimulate new growth.
- Fertilize to reinvigorate peppers, tomatoes, squash, and eggplants from the spring planting.
- Pinch off female flowers on pumpkin vines to direct the plant's energy toward making larger fruits.
- Colder zones will need to begin watching the weather for early frosts and be prepared to protect plants.
- Warmer zones may still take advantage of the sun's energy to solarize their soil.
- Thin runners on strawberries; weed and reapply mulch.
- Order garlic for fall planting.
- Plant oats, clover, or barley cover crops after removing garden debris.

SOW AND PLANT INDOORS

ZONES 5–6
- Start broccoli, cauliflower, Brussels sprouts, and cabbage transplants.

TO DO THIS MONTH CONTINUED

SOW AND PLANT OUTDOORS

ZONE 4

- Plant spinach in cold frames for spring harvest.
- Plant fast-growing lettuce varieties.

ZONES 5–6

- Make a final planting of bush beans and summer squash.

ZONES 7–8

- Transplant broccoli, cauliflower, collards, chard, and cabbage to the garden. Shade new plantings when temperatures are above 90°F.
- Plant tomatoes, peppers, basil, and eggplant transplants for fall and shade plants for several weeks.
- Plant seeds of corn, cucumbers, squash, and dill in the garden.

HARVESTING NOW

beans	eggplant	melons	peppers	squash
chard	Malabar	okra	potatoes	tomatoes
cucumbers	spinach	onions		

By now many of the spring-planted vegetables have ceased to produce and are ready for the compost pile. Still, some may be rejuvenated by cooler fall temperatures and can be invigorated with a light pruning, a touch of fertilizer, and a top dressing of compost. Spring-planted tomatoes and pole beans may be resuscitated with a little attention. Eggplants and peppers will have renewed vigor and produce larger fruits than they had in summer.

There is still time to plant fall beans, cucumbers, and squash, but pay attention to the days-to-harvest estimates for each. Look for varieties that have fewer days to harvest. A bush bean with 50 days to harvest makes more sense in fall than an 80-day bean if your first frost generally occurs on the first of November. You will want to have several weeks of harvest time before your first freeze date. Of course you can still stretch the harvest time by covering plants if the first frost arrives earlier than expected.

Saving Seed

August is an excellent time to focus on saving seeds for next year's garden. It's a great way to save money and improves your harvests each year. Select heirloom- or non-hybrid-type seeds for saving, as the hybrids will not always result in the same plant as they were in the prior season. If you are growing more than one squash, bean, or basil, for example, bees will transfer pollen from the various plants, resulting in seeds that will produce something far different than what you had in mind. The result may be a good one, but the plants are more likely to revert to something less than desirable. I have had good results from tomatoes that have self-sown and have

become sturdy and prolific producers with tasty fruits, but have saved seeds from hybrid squash and pumpkins that were oddly shaped and flavorless, though the plants were amazingly vigorous.

Your results will be best if you grow only one variety of a species at a time. Keep in mind that if your garden is near a neighbor's plot, that could be a source of cross-pollination. I would feel rather restricted if I had to grow only one variety of basil, squash, or tomato at a time. As a result, I tend to stick to corn, okra, or melons for seed saving as I usually only grow one variety of these at a time.

Tomatoes and corn are pollinated by wind and the pollen does not tend to travel very far (this is why it is best to plant corn in large blocks, rather than rows). So corn and tomatoes can be simple to save for seeds if the varieties are kept separated by 20 feet or more so that they do not cross-pollinate.

Some vegetables are biennial, which means that they do not produce seeds until their second year. Swiss chard, Brussels sprouts, cabbage, and beets will require a long time in the garden and they don't always survive the heat of summer in order to produce seedpods the next season. I don't have the time or space to devote to saving those iffy seed crops so I buy new seeds for them each year. One biennial plant that is easily harvested from seed is parsley. Both the curled and Italian types will go to seed rather quickly in the Southwest. Parsley planted in fall will typically go to seed at the end of the following spring (two seasons in the Southwest feels like a year to them!) and the seed is easily sown to produce more parsley.

Beans and okra are some of the easiest to save seeds from. Simply allow them to fully mature on the plant before harvesting. This should be done at the end of the season as your harvest is winding down. Leave beans and okra on the plant until the pods are turning brown and summer squash and cucumbers until they are bright yellow and the skins are turning hard—long past the time that the fruit is edible. Peppers should be fully ripe and have their full color. Watermelon and cantaloupe seeds may be saved when the fruit is eaten. Winter squash seeds are ready when the skins are hard and may be saved when you prepare the squash to eat.

If frost threatens your harvest before seeds are ready, the plants may be pulled out by the roots and hung to finish drying in a shed or garage. Beans, squash, peppers, and okra can be dried indoors in this way.

Tomato seeds are saved a bit differently. Use firm, fully ripe tomatoes. Cut the tomatoes in half and squeeze the jelly-like pulp into a jar. Add water and cover the jar loosely with a lid or a cloth with a rubber band to seal it. It will produce gases as the seeds ferment so make sure not to seal the jar tightly. Store it in a warm place (about 70°F) for a few days (you may want to do this outside as it is a bit smelly.) The liquid will ferment and the viable seeds will sink to the bottom of the container after about five days. The seeds that float will not grow. Pour off the scum at the top and spread the seeds out to dry.

Radishes are another crop that is simple to save seeds from. Leave a few radishes to bloom and produce seedpods. The pods are edible and very tasty when tender and green, but save a few for seed production. Lettuce can be allowed to go to bloom and produce seedpods; cut the lettuce plants and hang them inside a paper bag to collect the tiny seeds.

Save seeds from your prime plants for best results. Split open the vegetables and collect the hard seeds. Dry them indoors for a week or so before packaging them. Make sure the seeds are very dry before placing them in packages. Larger seeds will be easily broken in half when they are fully dry. I prefer to use paper packaging for seed saving as any moisture left within seeds can grow mildew quickly if the seeds are contained in plastic bags or containers.

I use baking sheets or plates lined with paper towels

Beans allowed to dry in the pod

corn ears hanging to dry

clean seeds with a screen

for each seed type and put the labeled seed packet on the tray so that I don't forget which seed it is. Some look very similar and it is easy to mix them up. I save envelopes from my junk mail or bills and recycle them for seeds, or reuse small glass jars for larger quantities of seeds. Label them and include the year the seed was planted and saved and where they were from originally. Store the seeds in airtight containers. Save desiccant packets from vitamin containers (or the like) and add those to your seed-storage containers.

Because seed sources were once limited, our grandparents and great-grandparents saved seeds. While we have many sources for seeds today, there are fewer and fewer companies selling seeds, and with genetic modification of seeds becoming more prevalent, we are losing access to many dependable vegetables. Some excellent varieties are being phased out, so saving seeds is our only recourse to retaining many old favorites. When you do shop for seeds, look for open-pollinated seeds or heirloom varieties from companies like Seed Savers Exchange, Johnny's Selected Seeds, Territorial Seed Company, Seeds of Change, Baker Creek Heirloom Seed Company, and Botanical Interests.

Separate good tomato seeds from the jelly-like pulp surrounding them by wet processing.

EDIBLE FLOWERS

Cooler temperatures in fall bring a wide array of edible blooms and colorful flowers add a special touch to all your foods. When you grow your own flowers organically there is no concern about chemical residues. Not all flowers are edible—in fact, some are quite poisonous—so it is vital to be certain of the plant variety. Don't pick flowers that are growing by the roadside or use flowers that may or may not have had chemicals used on them. I would not use flowers from a florist, nursery, or garden center, for example. Flowers may also aggravate some allergy conditions, so use with caution if you have numerous allergies.

Most herbs have edible flowers. Dill, fennel, mint, rosemary, and oregano blooms are all edible with less of the assertiveness of the foliage. Wash flowers by submerging them in ice water with a little salt added. Aphids and other insects will be dislodged by the salty water. Drain the flowers on towels and store them (on the damp towels) in a tightly sealed container. If the flowers become wilted, refresh them by submerging them in ice water again.

Anise hyssop. The lavender blooms have a delicate licorice flavor and are a nice addition to salads and dips. Bees love the blooms also.

Arugula blooms have a milder version of the peppery flavor of the leaves. Sprinkle them in salads or add to vinegars.

Borage has beautiful blue or lavender star-shaped flowers with a mild cucumber flavor. Top an appetizer with a beautiful blossom or add to salads.

Calendula petals come in shades of yellow, orange, and pink and are a bright and colorful addition to salads and herb butters. Pull the petals off the inedible center disk.

Carnations. The petals have a very sweet flavor. Trim off the bitter-tasting white bases.

Chive flowers have a peppery, radish-like flavor and I love to add them to tuna salad or deviled eggs. Place the tight flower buds in rice wine vinegar to make delicious onion-flavored vinegar for salad dressings and marinades.

Daylily. Use the blooms in stir-fries, as a garnish for soup, to top a cake, or filled with soft cheese. The pale yellow or orange blooms have the best flavor. The petals may be added to salads or used as garnish.

Lavender (from *Lavandula angustifolia*, or *L. intermedia*) is delightful in rich chocolate brownies, cakes, or sauces, or in herb seasoning mixtures for meats and vegetables and as a sweet addition to lemonade. Other types of lavender are not nearly as flavorful.

Nasturtium. This brightly colored peppery bloom is one of the most popular of the edible flowers. Chop and add blooms to salads, fill with an herb-cheese blend, use as garnish, and use the flower buds like capers.

Pansies and violas come in an array of colors and each has a subtly different flavor. I love to use the blossoms to decorate cakes or cupcakes and in flower ice cubes. Use them in herb butter and salads.

Rose petals make a nice addition to herb vinegars, salads, cakes, and drinks. Add to honey, butter, or preserves and use in sorbet.

Rosemary blooms have the flavor of the leaves, just milder. The blooms are a nice garnish for dishes that incorporate the herb leaves. A potato-and-egg frittata with a sprinkling of the blooms is a personal favorite.

Squash blossoms. Use the male blossoms just as they open (female flowers will have a small fruit just below the bloom; they are edible also, but why waste the squash?). Add to quesadillas, soups, or stuff with cheese.

SOLARIZE YOUR SOIL

Digging a new garden bed in triple-digit heat is no picnic. Take advantage of summer's heat to kill weeds in a future garden location. In four to six weeks the sun's rays will kill disease pathogens, seeds, and tough perennial weeds without a lot of digging. Mow grass or weeds as low as possible and remove any large rocks or twigs. Rake the soil surface to level it and water well. The water should penetrate the soil deeply, as wet soil transfers the sun's heat more efficiently. Several hours after watering, use a trowel to examine how deeply the water has penetrated. Ideally the water should move 10 to 12 inches deep in the soil (if you even have that much soil!).

Cover the area, extending a foot or so beyond the future garden's border, with a 4- to 6-mil clear plastic. The plastic should be in direct contact with the soil. Air trapped under the plastic will inhibit heat transfer. Use soil, rocks, or boards on the edges of the plastic. Check carefully for air bubbles and eliminate them. Soil temperatures may rise to 140°F under the plastic. Black plastic may be used for winter solarization, as it will transfer more heat in cooler temperatures than clear plastic.

For nutgrass or Bermuda control, leave the plastic down for at least six weeks. Many soil insects will be killed by solarization also, although mobile pests like root-knot nematodes may simply move to escape the heat. You will gain some temporary control of nematodes with solarization.

The solarized soil will likely be dry, hard, and compacted after the plastic is removed. Inoculate it with a thin layer of dry molasses to stimulate microbe reproduction, cover with a few inches of compost and water it in. Several days later, turn the soil and begin making new garden beds. The cooked roots and organic matter in the solarized soil will become quickly available to the newly planted garden.

THE PROMISE
OF FALL

Temperatures are starting to decline a bit and some southwestern gardeners can expect their first frost this month. Those gardeners will want to begin their final harvests before frosts can damage vegetables. Fall planting begins in earnest for those in more moderate zones. Choosing which plants to eliminate so that beds are free for fall and winter selections is always a challenge. We are sometimes forced to pull up perfectly productive summer plants so that our fall plantings will have time to get established before really cold weather begins. Soil temperatures may still be very high from summer's heat. Cool them down with some shade to allow fall and winter seeds to germinate.

TO DO THIS MONTH

PLAN

- Complete entries in your garden journal and make notes about harvests, weather, and your failures and successes.

PREPARE AND MAINTAIN

- Harvest the garden before a heavy frost or freeze. Pull tomato and pepper plants and hang them in a sheltered spot. The fruit attached will continue to mature and ripen.
- Green tomatoes may be collected and ripened indoors. Dice and freeze or dehydrate peppers to savor all winter long.
- Basil goes downhill rapidly when nights drop below 50°F. Harvest it and freeze or make herbal oils and butters. The flavor is not well preserved by drying.
- Gather all available leaves and use your spent garden plants and trimmings as compost material.
- Gather herbs for freezing and drying.
- Collect seeds from your plants for next year's garden.
- Cover crop the garden in colder climates with fast-growing winter rye.
- Warmer zones may still need to shade soil for several weeks to lower soil temperatures for fall crops. Water soil deeply to cool it several days in advance of planting.

SOW AND PLANT OUTDOORS

ZONE 4
- Plant spinach in cold frames for overwintering.
- Plant garlic and shallots.

ZONES 5–6
- Plant spinach and kale under row cover.
- Plant garlic.

ZONES 7–10
- Plant greens, spinach, radishes, and lettuce for salads. Plant beets, turnips, kohlrabi, kale, carrots, and parsley.

- Plant broccoli, cauliflower, kale, and bok choy transplants.

ZONE 10
- Still time to get in another planting of squash, cucumbers, and okra.
- Make the final plantings of tomatoes and peppers.
- Plant lettuce, spinach, and other greens.

HARVESTING NOW

ZONE 4

beets	greens	parsnips
carrots	late apples	turnips

Pears and persimmons are ripening. Pick them and ripen indoors to protect the fruit but leave a few for birds and wildlife.

ZONES 5–10

basil	cucumbers	lettuce	sweet	winter
beans	eggplant	peppers	potatoes	squash
beets	greens	squash	tomatoes	

Weeds may have taken over your garden and many gardeners give up when faced with an apparently insurmountable battle with weeds. The type of weeds that we have can tell us a lot about our soil and there are aids to make the war winnable. If you keep the weeds controlled before they can reseed, each year your garden will be less and less troubled by weeds and you will harvest more desirable crops.

Cooler temperatures in fall also mean that deer will be entering their mating season soon and will be trying to fatten up for the winter. If you are in deer country that probably means they are casting their eyes on your vegetable garden as their all you can eat buffet. A tall, sturdy fence is your best defense but there are other means of controlling these four-legged pests.

Weed Wisdom

A weed is an unloved plant is a common refrain. Mint, passion vine, comfrey, bamboo, and equisetum can be valuable plants in the right location, but many gardeners rue the day those useful but invasive perennial plants were added to their landscape and might consider them weeds.

Weeds are spread by birds, animals, wind, and water and often come with garden plants—a weed free garden is quite unlikely. Animal manures can contain many viable weed seeds so it is best to compost the manure first to cook the weed seeds.

Controlling weeds when they are small is generally easier but you will need to identify them in their seedling stage. If you don't get them while they are small, as least don't allow them to go to seeding stage. The old adage "one season of seeds is seven seasons of weeds" is

worth remembering. Weeds use water and nutrients that your plants need and they can compete for space with your vegetables' roots and shade out desirable plants.

Weeds for Beneficial Insects

Despite the bad rap that most weeds get, there are some that feed beneficial insects or birds and are worth keeping. Members of the milkweed family provide important larval food sources for monarch butterflies and are often covered with aphids, which attract ladybugs. Sow thistle also attracts aphids and becomes a nursery crop for building a good population of ladybugs in the early spring garden. Dill, yarrow, and wild carrot may play host to the Braconid wasp, which injects its eggs into host insects like the tomato hornworm. Ground beetles are voracious caterpillar eaters in their larval and adult forms. The adult form is attracted by white clover.

If you notice that a weedy plant is playing host to beneficial insects in the garden, try to control its flowering. I will snap off the flowering heads of sow thistle without disturbing the aphids and ladybugs that inhabit them. Allow some of these weeds to flourish in areas surrounding your garden. Providing habitat for birds and bugs is an essential part of a healthy ecosystem.

What Weeds Tell You About Your Soil

Soil is mysterious. We are not really sure what nutrients are available to our plants just by looking at the soil, but the weeds that grow in our garden can provide many clues. Weeds are opportunistic plants that grow where conditions are favorable for them and they may tell you what your soil is lacking. I would prefer to start a new garden in an area that has healthy, abundant weeds rather than one that had only one or two weed types or was lacking in any plant growth.

Hard, compacted soil will tend to favor weeds with deep taproots like sow thistle, dandelions, and thistles. The roots of these plants will penetrate the hardened soils, break it up, and make minerals deep in the soil available to plants on the surface as the tops die back. Wet or poorly draining soil may harbor bindweed, nutgrass, equisetum or horsetail, sheep sorrel, or dock. Mullein, ox-eye daisies, sandburs, and clover are common in soil that is deficient in nitrogen.

As you continue to build your soil, add organic material, and increase oxygen levels in the soil you will find that the number of weeds you are dealing with will decline. Purslane, chickweed, lamb's quarter, henbit, and pigweed are often found in well-balanced, healthy soil. So congratulate yourself and keep pulling (or eat them)!

ANNUAL SEED PRODUCTION OF WEEDS

WEED TYPE	NUMBER OF SEEDS PER PLANT
dandelion	15,000
dock, curled	29,500
evening primrose	118,500
mullein	223,200
purslane	1,800,000
shepherd's purse	150,000
sunflower, common	7200
thistle, sow	9750

Seeds can remain viable in the soil for quite a long time, but most will fail to germinate after five years. If you can keep more seeds from being added to the seed bank, you will eventually gain control. Knowing how prolific weeds are will help you stay more focused on controlling them.

Tips and Techniques for Landscaping with Deer

As difficult as it is to imagine today, there was once a time when deer were becoming scarce due to overhunting. Since then, however, control of natural predators and stricter hunting laws have created a deer population explosion. Many areas have a population between three to five times greater than that which would be considered normal.

The problems with deer extend beyond the damage they do to suburban landscapes. When native habitats are overpopulated with deer there are severe impacts to the vegetation from the browsing activity of deer and the rubbing of the antlers of the male deer. In some areas there is little vegetation between the ground and about 5 feet high, which is the reach for most deer. This in turn reduces habitat for many other woodland creatures including rabbits, lizards, snakes, and many birds.

Deer populations in a natural cycle are affected by weather extremes. In very cold or dry periods, deer starve and will stop reproducing or will abort or absorb the fetus. Up to half the population of deer can be lost at one time. When conditions are good, does will have three fawns instead of one or two, and juvenile does will bear young by their first spring. Populations may double in one year. Our role in this is simple: the most important thing that we can do to control deer populations is not to feed them. Corn, hay, and other food supplements provided by humans give sufficient nutrient levels to keep birth rates artificially high in all seasons, despite drought.

There are a few things we should remember about deer. No plant is truly deer proof. If deer are hungry they will eat anything. Deer that have died from starvation have been found with full stomachs of twigs and dead leaves. Your fruit trees and vegetable garden, even the rose bushes, look like a scrumptious salad bar to a herd of deer.

Deer most often browse just the tips of plants. New growth of even deer-resistant plants often lacks the strong flavor of the mature plant, so they may be browsed. Plants in nurseries and garden centers have been watered and fed to grow quickly (making them taste milder than they typically would), so even "deer-proof" plants will be browsed when newly planted. Keep new beds protected by netting, sprays, or electric wires. When "deer-proof" plants are continually overwatered or overfed, even with natural fertilizers, they will be tastier to deer. Water only as much as the plants truly need. Observe your neighbor's yard to see what the deer are not eating and plant the same things.

Deer are creatures of habit. When they experience foods that do not make them sick, they will eat them again. When they enter an area and are not bothered, they will go there again. Young deer learn the food-trail systems from their mothers. Deer trails are scented by glands in the feet so that other deer recognize a safe route. Deer rely heavily on their keen sense of smell, excellent hearing, and 270-degree visual field. As a prey species, their main goal is to not get eaten.

Water provided for birds or other animals may become an important source for the deer in your area and may bring them to your garden. Consider moving water supplies to protected areas.

Fences and Netting

Deer won't tend to jump where they can't see, so a 6-foot wood privacy fence will keep most deer out. For wire or chain-link fences to work they need to be at least 7½ feet, though 8 feet is better. Wire strands can be run along the top of the fence to extend the height. A pregnant doe can jump a 6-foot fence from a standing position.

Deer jump high, but not wide. Two shorter fences spaced 4 feet apart are expensive, but can work if local codes don't allow a higher fence. A shrub line inside the fence or vines to obscure the view inside the fence can make a single, lower fence effective.

Electric fences can be difficult to manage, dangerous for children and pets, and easily jumped. A baited electric fence can be effective. Spread peanut butter at intervals on a 30-inch-high wire. Deer taste the peanut butter and get a shock. They will usually avoid an area after being shocked.

Black polypropylene fences are less expensive to install and barely visible from a distance. They should be secured to the ground at intervals to prevent deer from digging under. Support stakes can be placed 12 feet apart.

Deer netting can be placed over plants which are very attractive to deer such as vegetables. The netting comes in many sizes: 7 ft. × 100 ft., 14 ft. × 14 ft., 4 ft. × 50 ft., and so on. The netting should be held up over the plant material by PVC pipe, stakes, or rebar. Deer will push it down and eat the plants through the netting if it is laid on top of the plants. You can fashion rebar hoops from ⅜-inch rebar and pin the netting down on each side with U-shaped soil staples. The netting can also be used to make fences around tomatoes or peppers or larger vegetables.

Netting should be installed fairly taut so that deer cannot become entangled in it and break their legs. If handled with some care the netting should last for several planting seasons. I don't spray the edible foliage of plants like kale or lettuce. Instead, those are protected with netting and hoops.

Repellants and Deterrents

Commonly used deterrents include soap, garlic, hot pepper wax, predator urine, blood meal, or rotten eggs to mask the flavor of normally desirable plants and essentially train the deer not to feed in an area. These sprays vary in the amount of time they stay on the plants and usually need to be reapplied after heavy rains. All have varying degrees of effectiveness depending on the deer population and amount of natural forage present. Deer Off, Hinder, and Liquid Fence are all readily available formulas. Deterrents must be applied at least weekly, reapplied after a rain, and applied to all newly planted material. Avoid sprays that contain Thiram, a toxic product. It is not safe on edible crops, so make sure to carefully read the labels of any products you are considering.

The repellent sprays work well, but their smell is not pleasant. I Must Garden is another product that has a mint- and cinnamon-scented repellent that does not smell horrible and works just as well. Keep all new growth treated to prevent browsing.

I've also had success with making my own repellants at home. Mix 2 tablespoons of hot pepper sauce,

1 tablespoon liquid dish soap, and 1 teaspoon garlic powder with a gallon of water. Be careful though, as this mixture may burn tender plants.

Some gardeners have had success with trying white plastic bags to posts or other garden structures. The effect is thought to mimic the white flash of the deer's tail when in distress. Move the bags around periodically to keep this working. Aluminum pie tins that clang may also frightened the deer (though they may annoy the neighbors as well!). Water sprays or floodlights that turn on with motion detectors will work if they are moved around with some frequency. Radios that turn on with motion lose their effectiveness quickly. Motion-controlled sprinklers can act as deterrents if moved around frequently. Make sure your house guests know about it if they roam the garden in the evening and be careful not to soak the neighbors.

Dogs can be a valuable deterrent, but not all breeds work equally well. Dogs with a strong herding or guarding instinct like Doberman pinschers, Great Pyrenees, Rottweilers, collies, border collies, and German shepherds will probably be more successful. But a Jack Russell terrier might do the job with great gusto! Dogs' personalities can vary greatly so there is no guarantee that your Doberman won't be greeting the deer herd at the gate with a wagging tail while your poodle may chase them for miles. A dog tied to a chain will not be effective because the deer soon learn the limits of the chain. Deer can easily injure a dog so make sure your dog is not in danger of being kicked by deer.

All Seasons Brand Deer Repellant has a plastic cup filled with blood meal that is vented on the bottom to release the scent and sealed on top to protect from the elements. They have to be installed fairly close to the plants and it takes quite a few to work well, but they have been fairly successful for me, are easy to install and last for up to four months. They can be hung on a string or installed on the stakes supplied in the package.

For more information about gardening in deer habitat, see the further reading section.

SKILL SET

WEAPONS IN THE WAR ON WEEDS

Struggles with weeds can discourage many new gardeners. Hoeing weeds is most effective for plants that do not have taproots and is best done before the weeds start to bloom. This works well for chickweed, henbit, and pigweed. Repeatedly cutting the tops from even perennial weeds will eventually discourage them. If all these fail, then pull the weeds. If you don't have time to dig out deep-rooted weeds, at least snap off the seed heads to avoid a seven-year curse. If a bed is really out of control, mow or use a weedeater to control seed production in the short term.

Pull weeds when the soil is damp to avoid breaking off deep-rooted plants. A broken-off weed is invigorated and becomes even harder to extract the next time. Use pliers to pull out pecan tree sprouts, oak, elm, or hackberry seedlings. Grab the seedling near the soil line and pull straight up to extract the entire root.

Plant densely so that your vegetables are "living mulch" to block sunlight from the soil and limit the germination of weed seeds. Plant multiple crops in beds to discourage weeds. Nature abhors a vacuum—soil that is open and available will find a weed seed to fill it. Plant broccoli transplants with lettuce and radish seeds between the transplants. The lettuce and radishes will provide early harvests before the broccoli fills in the bed and they prevent other weeds from gaining a foothold.

Newspaper can smother your weeds. Use only the newsprint, not the shiny ad inserts. Lay eight to ten sheets over dampened soil and overlap edges with more paper. Cover the entire surface of the bed and then water the paper well before covering the paper completely with shredded hardwood mulch, leaves, or compost. This technique will discourage spurge, pigweed, and many other weeds but is not always successful with nut sedge or Bermuda grass. Solarization is a more dependable means of control for these persistent weeds, or you may reapply the newspaper mulch as weeds reappear.

Keeping soil covered with several inches of organic mulch keeps weed seeds from getting the sunlight they need to germinate. Mulching is a year-round task in the Southwest as the sun cooks organic material rather quickly. As the mulch degrades, it feeds the soil and adds organic material. Keep mulch away from tender plant stems and tree trunks.

Cover crops not only improve the soil, they crowd out weeds to make next season's garden more successful. Elbon or cereal rye has a fibrous root system and grows tall and thick enough to thwart any chance of cool-season weeds getting a foothold in the garden. It can be mowed or cut and collected and added to fall leaves to make excellent compost for the spring garden. Cut down the rye before it goes to seed and till it into the soil, allowing it to decompose for several weeks. Rye increases the organic matter and microbe activity in the soil along with the biochemical weed control.

Buckwheat, sweet potatoes, or black-eyed peas can do the same for the summer garden if you choose to cut back on gardening in the hottest part of the year. They will prevent summer weed seeds from gaining a foothold in the garden by covering the soil surface.

Vinegar may be sprayed on plants as a natural herbicide. A 9 percent pickling vinegar with added orange oil and soap will kill everything it is sprayed on. Hard-to-kill plants like poison ivy, bindweed, or nut sedge may require several applications to die completely. The mix should be combined in a pump sprayer and used immediately after mixing. It is most effective on a hot sunny day when no rain is expected. Avoid spraying on windy days as it will burn your skin and any other plants it comes in contact with.

ORGANIC HERBICIDE RECIPE

1 gallon 9 percent vinegar
¼ cup orange oil
2 tablespoons molasses
2 tablespoons soap

Note that there is no water in this formula. Mix everything in a pump sprayer. Coat all the gaskets of your sprayer with petroleum jelly before using this to minimize damage to the sprayer. Use the mix immediately and wash the sprayer well after use. Fill the sprayer with clear water, pressurize again, and spray to clean out all of the spray residue. Wear gloves and long sleeves to protect your skin.

·OCTOBER·

PREPARE FOR THE COMING COLD

Tree leaves are changing color, pumpkins are ready to harvest, and our gardens are full of the lingering crops of summer as well as the beginnings of our fall plantings. Frosts and freezes are just around the corner if they have not already visited your garden. We can prepare for them and manage to keep our gardens alive with cold frames, row covers, and mulching. Now is a great time to wander around the neighborhood collecting all the leaves from your neighbors' leaf piles. They are an important element in the gardener's gold you will be cultivating as compost and leaf mold.

TO DO THIS MONTH

PLAN

- What plant did you have too much of? Which crop left you wishing for more? Make notes about your harvests—and what you and your family liked and disliked—so that you'll have a garden better tailored to your kitchen next year.

PREPARE AND MAINTAIN

- Continue to collect all available leaves for compost and mulch. A gardener can never have too many!
- Mulch all bare soil to reduce cool-season weed germination.
- Thin last month's plantings of carrots, beets, greens, or lettuce.
- Gardeners in cooler zones should mulch their asparagus and strawberries well.

SOW AND PLANT OUTDOORS

ZONES 4–6

- Sow spinach and parsnips in a cold frame for overwintering.
- Plant garlic and shallots.

ZONES 7–10

- Sow spinach, lettuce, Chinese cabbage, bok choy, radishes, turnips, mâche, mustard, beets, carrots, and cress from seed.
- Plant garlic, leeks, onions, and shallots.
- Set out strawberry plants and mulch them well.
- Plant cover crops like elbon rye, vetch, Austrian peas, or clover to improve soil, reduce weeds, and add to compost all winter long.
- Fall is the best time to plant trees and shrubs in the south.

ZONES 9–10

- Make final plantings of tomatoes, peppers, and eggplant.

HARVESTING NOW

ZONES 4–6

Brussels sprouts	cabbage carrots	kale lettuce	parsnips spinach

- Begin digging sweet potatoes when the foliage starts to decline. Cure the potatoes for several weeks out of sunlight to ensure long-term storage.
- Harvest winter squash when the skins are very hard. The skin should resist when you scratch it with your fingernail.

ZONES 7–10

beans bok choy	broccoli eggplant	kale lettuce	peppers radishes	squash tomatoes

October weather is perfect for gardening and there is much to be harvested in the warmer zones of the Southwest. We typically begin to see more rainfall and can relax a bit with watering chores, but remember that damp soil will protect crops from frost better than if it were dry. Trying to get soil sufficiently moist just before freezing temperatures will not be as effective since the wet soil does not have time to warm up.

Warmer-than-normal fall temperatures can make getting your cool-season vegetables started more difficult. Cover beds with shade cloth, burlap, sheets, or lightweight row cover to filter sunlight and reduce soil temperatures so that fall lettuce and cilantro will not bolt. Red-leaved lettuce and Romaine types tend to be more likely to bolt in warm temperatures so I plant those a bit later than types like Salad Bowl or Buttercrunch.

Mulching beds before temperatures cool the soil will also keep plants happier. Mulch holds warmth around the plants and keeps the soil from drying out. Cool-season weeds like chickweed, henbit, and pigweed may start to appear, so use a stirrup hoe to clear them out before they are large and renew mulch to keep more weed seeds from germinating.

We are beginning to harvest the fall vegetables and herbs and may still have remnants of the summer garden that are producing. Fall-planted kale, broccoli, and lettuce will be sweeter with the cooler temperatures of fall.

The first freeze is on its way, but even nights below 45°F can damage any tomatoes, peppers, or basil you might still be harvesting. Spun polyester row cover is a lightweight and effective means of protecting any tender plants. It comes in a number of weights and can protect plants from 5° to 35°, depending on its thickness. You can use sheet or blankets to protect plants but they take a long time to dry if they get damp in the garden and then are likely to mildew and look unsightly. I have pieces of row cover cut to fit each garden bed and I label the pieces with the sizes on the corner of the sheet since my garden beds are different sizes. As I remove the row cover, it gets folded and stored in covered plastic garbage cans. The cans are easy to store out of the way and are brought out again when cold temperatures threaten.

It is important to include the soil in the covering for plants. When we put a blanket over our body, the blanket holds in the heat that our body produces. Plants do not generate their own heat but must rely on the warmth of the soil to keep them warm. Wrapping a plant top like a lollipop does little to keep it warm. Wet soil generates heat more efficiently than dry soil so a deep watering before a freeze is helpful.

Row cover can be floated over the top of the plants but will insulate better if suspended over the plants. See the July chapter for more instructions on building hoops from PVC or rebar for your row covers.

A Bounty of Leaves

My friends have often joked that I should have an "I Brake for Leaves" bumper sticker on my car. It doesn't matter where I'm off to, or what I am wearing, if I see any bags of leaves left at the curb I will pack my truck to capacity. A gardener can never have too many leaves! It is a sad thing to see leaves set at the curbside destined for the landfill, though many cities have required that leaves and other compostable materials be put in paper bags so that they may be composted rather than go in the trash. In some cities the landfills are taking in up to 50 percent or more of compostable materials, especially in the fall. The leaves are a great source of carbon material for composting and can be used for mulching the garden. If the leaves are set out in paper bags I use them first as the bags will break down. The empty paper bags may be used under wood chips or leaf mulch or torn and added to the compost pile, or you can empty them into wire fencing rings to store leaves for future compost batches.

I have collected many large black planting containers that were used for trees. These 30- to 50-gallon containers have drainage holes and can be filled with leaves and top dressed with a little garden soil or compost and stored where they're not in the way. The leaves will break down and become crumbly leaf mold and the built-in handles on the pots make them easy to move around the garden.

Plastic bags of leaves can be stockpiled in an out-of-the-way area. Add some water to each bag to enhance the decomposition of the leaves. After several months they will become a crumbly leaf mold that makes great mulch or it can be dug into beds to increase organic material. If you need a wind break around your garden, the bags of leaves may be used to block cold winds from the northwest side of the garden or used to block prevailing winds.

SKILL SET

COLD FRAMES

For gardeners who must deal with colder temperatures a cold frame is a sensible addition to the garden. It is simply a box that sits over the garden bed to hold heat around plants. They can be constructed with recycled materials like old windows. When the temperature inside the cold frame reaches 65°F, open the frame to allow heat to escape. Close it again at night to hold the heat inside. You may want to keep a thermometer inside to keep an eye on the temperature so that your cold frame doesn't become an oven on warm days.

Be sure to remove the top from the cold frame in zones with extremely cold winters. Cold air and heavy snow can break the glass.

For a quick and easy cold frame that requires no carpentry skills, use greenhouse polycarbonate panels. The panels come in 8- to 12-foot lengths and various widths. Place two stakes side by side in the garden bed, allowing enough space to slide the plastic panel between the stakes. Add additional stakes at each corner

A cold frame will protect new seedlings or extend the harvest of tender crops in cold-winter areas.

and several feet apart along the sides. Slide the panel between the stakes on one side and bend it over the bed to stakes on the other side. Add hooks to the outside stakes at the soil line and tie the twine on the hooks and over the frame to prevent the frame from taking flight during high winds. Close the ends of the frame with fabric or additional plastic for colder nights and open them during the day to allow heat to escape.

Provide extra heat for your cold frame by placing 1-gallon plastic jugs inside filled with water. Daytime heating will warm up the water and allow it to radiate heat in the evening to protect plants.

·NOVEMBER·

A TIME
TO CELEBRATE
THE HARVEST

This is a month to celebrate our bounty and continue to plan and plant for abundant harvests to come. The days grow shorter and winter's chill is evident. Keeping an eye on the weather becomes a daily (even twice daily) task for gardeners. Temperatures can change drastically now so we should be prepared with row covers, cold frames, and hoops to protect the garden. The fall garden has really started to produce by this point and successive plantings of radishes, kohlrabi, and beets should provide a steady supply in the kitchen. These crops won't store well in the garden. They will tend to be tough and woody if left outside too long. Radishes will have a hotter flavor if left too long before harvesting. Label all crops with the date planted so that you know which need to be harvested next.

TO DO THIS MONTH

PLAN

- Assess garden successes and failures and make notes of them in your journal. Make notes of seeds that you have saved for next year's garden. Note when you have your first freeze or frost.

- Update your garden planting plan for the year.

PREPARE AND MAINTAIN

- Water deeply before a freeze. Wet soil protects plants from cold more efficiently than dry soil.
- Be prepared to protect tender plants with row cover when the temperature drops.
- Check stored onions, potatoes, and garlic for spoilage.
- Clean, sharpen, and store tools for winter in colder climates.

- Clean up plant debris to eliminate pest and disease problems that may overwinter in the garden.
- Turn the compost piles.
- Thin plantings of lettuce, greens, beets, and carrots from last month.
- Mulch all exposed soil.

SOW AND PLANT INDOORS

ZONES 4–6
- Plant parsley and lettuce in pots to enjoy indoors in winter.

ZONES 7–9
- Start seeds of kale, lettuce, broccoli, cabbage, and cauliflower.

ZONE 10
- Start seeds of tomatoes, peppers, and eggplant.

TO DO THIS MONTH CONTINUED

SOW AND PLANT OUTDOORS

ZONES 5-6

- Plant garlic and shallots, and mulch well.

ZONES 7-10

- Set out strawberry transplants or divide rooted runners and plant them.
- Plant garlic, shallots, onions, fava beans, sugar snap peas, leeks, and kale.

HARVESTING NOW

ZONES 4-7

Brussels sprouts	cabbage carrots	kale lettuce	parsnips spinach

- Dig root crops before soil freezes.

ZONES 8-9

arugula	collards	lettuce	pumpkins	sweet
bok choy	kale	mustard	radishes	potatoes
broccoli	kohlrabi	greens	squash	

- Harvest eggplant, tomatoes, and peppers before freezing temperatures.

ZONE 10

beans	cucumbers	lettuce
carrots	kale	peas

If leaves on kale, chard, collards, and other greens start to grow large or look damaged by insects or cold, trim them off, chop them coarsely, and put them in the compost pile. Your compost will appreciate the nitrogen boost from the fresh leaves. Consistent harvest keeps the plants in production and delays blooming.

In milder climate zones 8–10 you may be able to overwinter many peppers and eggplants if the winter is a mild one. Once they are damaged by frost, leave the stems long and apply mulch around their base. In spring, cut the old stalks down and pull back the mulch. You may see new green sprouts coming up around the base of the plants. These successive-season plants are often much hardier and earlier to produce. If they don't return, simply pull up the old plants and prepare the soil for a new planting. If you have grown them in containers, move them to a warm location for the winter. They may not produce much in winter but will give you a head start next spring when you cut them back, feed them, and move them back outdoors. Gardeners in this region may also still be harvesting tomatoes in November and December if the plants are protected from occasional cold spells.

Continue to keep an eye on the forecast. If it is already 40°F when the sun goes down then I am more concerned about the chance of a freeze. Cloudy nights will tend to be warmer as the clouds act like a blanket in the atmosphere. The coldest nights will be clear. Cold fronts are generally predicted several days in advance, but I check the forecast several times throughout the day. You may want to set up a weather-alert application on your phone or computer that will warn you of changes in the weather.

Mulch and More Mulch

As far as I'm concerned, mulching is second only to composting in terms of how vital it is for the success of your gardens. It keeps plants cooler in summer, warmer in winter, and breaks down to increase organic material and feed soil microbes and block the germination of weed seeds. Beyond those benefits, I find that a well-mulched garden just looks better. Is your garden sporting a nice layer of mulch this season?

Mulch protects plants from soilborne diseases also by protecting them from direct soil contact. Be careful, though, as mulch can create problems for younger plants that are still tender as it can harbor insects that will attack the plants. Mulch piled too high around tree trunks or plant roots can cause damage and lead to diseases. Keep mulch a few inches from the bases of trees, shrubs, and vegetable plants.

Almost any organic material may be used as mulch. As you might have guessed by now, leaves are my favorite mulch material since they are abundant and free. There are occasional bits of trash, nuts, and weed seeds that come along with them but they are still great for the price. If you want more finely textured mulch, grind the leaves in a trash can with a weedeater until they are the desired texture. You could also mow over the leaves to grind them up. Leaves break down quickly so that they can be incorporated into the soil with the next planting after a season of acting as mulch. Some gardeners are concerned that certain leaves like oak leaves will be too acidic and alter soil pH, but this is not something that we need to worry about. The thick cuticle on oak leaves does make them slow to break down, though, so grinding or mowing them will accelerate their decomposition.

A coarsely shredded mulch texture is best and tends to settle closely to the plant and stay in place. Large chunks of mulch materials can wash away from plants, and finely shredded mulch can pack too tightly and limit water and air flow to plant roots. Stir mulch occasionally with a rake or garden fork to keep it loose and keep water flowing through it. Shredded native hardwood mulch is available from many tree trimmers for free and has green nitrogen-rich foliage shredded with the wood so that the mulch breaks down quickly into nutrient-rich compost.

Pine needles are a long-lasting and tidy-looking mulch and insects do not like crawling around on them. They are ideal for mulching strawberry plants since they inhibit insect damage on the berries. They also tend to be mildly acidic so can be beneficial for alkaline soils. Pine needles are sold in compressed bales in some garden centers.

In terms of hay, alfalfa hay looks a bit untidy but adds valuable nitrogen. It is tightly compressed and can be difficult to spread, but it is the only hay I would recommend using unless you are certain it was organically grown. Broadleaf herbicides used in hay can be very persistent and will kill your garden plants and persist in the soil for many years. Some alfalfa is now genetically modified so look for organic, non-GMO alfalfa.

Grass clippings make excellent mulch, but do not pile green clippings too thickly. The grass will form thick mats that will block air and water passage to the soil. Planting cereal or elbon rye as a winter cover crop allows you to chop back the abundant grassy tops throughout the cool season and use them as mulch. Sheet composting is a method that uses grass layered with leaves turned into bare garden soil and watered

deeply. It's an effective way of rapidly improving your soil. I use many drought-tolerant native grasses and lemon grass in the landscape. When I cut the old foliage back in late winter I use the trimmings, which break down into a finely textured and attractive mulch, in perennial beds.

Don't forget to include your container plants in your mulching chores. A layer of compost and shredded mulch will extend the time between watering for containers and protect them from temperature extremes. Don't bring mulch layers all the way to the top edge of a container. Make sure to leave some space at the top of the pot so that there is room to water the container adequately.

Companion Planting

As you might have discovered, some plants make great neighbors for other plants. Companion planting is an ancient practice that probably came about from centuries of observant gardeners finding out which combinations worked for them. We know that plants and insects have evolved together and have close relationships that allow them to succeed when grown together. Planting many diverse plants within the garden can confuse garden pests and protect plants. Large-scale plantings of one vegetable can actually attract more pests as they can detect them more easily with their antennae.

The "Three Sisters" companion planting technique used by American Indians is a great example of this. I was taught this method when I was a child. Beans, squash, and corn are planted together for the mutual benefit of all three crops. The beans use the corn stalks for support and provide nitrogen for the hungry corn plants. The squash plants cover the soil and act as living mulch, keeping the soil shaded, moist, and free of weeds.

Some plants repel insect pests while others attract beneficial insects. Plants can attract and trap harmful insects to give other plants a break from attacks. Allowing parsley, fennel, and dill to bloom attracts ladybugs, lacewings, and beneficial wasps which feed on their nectar.

Leeks are a good companion for roses. Leeks are planted around the base of rose bushes. The leeks discourage many pests and diseases that roses are prone to and the leeks are dormant when the roses are in their full growth. Leeks grow lush in fall and winter when the roses are dormant. Keep the leeks at least a foot away from the rose trunks so that the rose's roots will not be disturbed as the leeks are dug and divided.

Many companion techniques match larger, slower-growing plants with faster and smaller crops to grow more food in small gardens. Here's an example of fall companion planting that works well for me: I plant broccoli and cauliflower transplants in wide raised beds in multiple rows about 18 inches apart. I sow radish and lettuce seeds between the transplants and plug in green onion sets. The seeded crops grow quickly and have shallow root systems compared to the deeper-rooted brassicas. The lettuce can be thinned and eaten rather quickly and the radishes and green onions grow very fast and are harvested long before the broccoli is large enough to shade the seedlings. The thickly planted vegetables prevent weeds from gaining a chance to sprout and provide a number of crops from one planting space.

Fast-growing radishes are also an excellent companion to slower-growing, more delicate carrot seedlings. The radish roots assist the carrots in breaking through the soil and since they will be harvested much sooner than the carrots, they won't compete when the carrots need space.

African and French marigolds, castor beans, and Elbon rye have been shown to eliminate root-knot nematodes from soil. Elbon rye is generally used as a cool-season cover crop and tilled into the soil while the marigolds and castor beans can be interplanted with susceptible plants. Castor beans grow to be very large (up to 12 feet tall) and can shade plantings. Be careful, though, as all parts of the castor bean are poisonous, especially the bean seeds, which are the source of ricin, used as a poisonous gas. Cut and discard the seedpods to control their spread and keep them away from pets and children. The large richly patterned red leaves are a beautiful addition to the garden and can be used to great effect in floral arrangements. Mustard, leeks, and onions are also nematode-repellant crops.

HERBS FOR WINTER

Heat-loving **basil** starts to fade when night temperatures dip below 50°F, but it can be replaced during the winter months with these tasty winter herbs in the milder parts of the Southwest.

Chervil. This herb has a delicate licorice flavor and is the perfect partner for eggs. It thrives in winter temperatures and often sets seed, so it will come back each winter.

Chamomile. This plant needs the cooler weather of winter to thrive. In early spring it will produce tall white and yellow blooms that may be cut and dried for baths and tea. It readily self-sows and appreciates some afternoon shade.

Cilantro. It's unfortunate that cilantro won't grow in most of the Southwest in the summer, when many of us are harvesting tomatoes, but at least it's available in the grocery store. Replace the basil beds with cilantro for the winter garden. Cilantro will begin to put bloom spikes on when temperatures are warm. The foliage will be more fern-like and become bitter as blooms appear. Keep harvesting regularly to delay blooming. The seeds of cilantro are known as coriander and are a flavorful addition to meats, marinades, sauces, and drinks.

Dill and fennel. The feathery foliage and rich yellow umbrella shaped flowers of these plants make an attractive addition to the winter garden. I save seeds harvested in early spring and scatter them over the shadier portions of the garden. The plants will often be eaten by black, yellow, and green caterpillars—the larval stage of beautiful swallowtail butterflies. If the caterpillars are eating more dill than I care to share, they are carefully moved to the fennel. Fennel has more abundant foliage and I tend to use it less than dill. Both fennel and dill will attract aphids along their stems as they begin to bloom. Don't reach for the spray though. If you wait patiently you will notice ladybugs and their black alligator-shaped larva munching on the aphids.

Bouquet dill is a shorter form that blooms quickly and produces large seed heads. It grows to about 3 feet when blooming. Fernleaf dill is short, about 20 inches tall, and slower to bloom. It is the best choice for cooks who want lots of dill foliage.

Fennel bulbs are a crunchy, sweet licorice-flavored vegetable that add zest to winter salads and stir-fries. The green fennel seeds are a tasty way to settle stomach troubles or add zip to a sauce. Allow some of the seeds to dry and save them for the next fall garden. Zeta Fino and Florence are bulbing types of fennel. Cut the bulbs just under the swollen base and new bulbs will appear. Common fennel and the smoky foliage of bronze fennel are used for their foliage and seeds but do not produce the delicious bulbs.

Parsley. Both Italian and Curled parsley are more than just a garnish. They are good sources of vitamin C, iron, and chlorophyll. They are natural diuretics as well and are good for anemia. Use parsley as a border plant or plant it in containers. Its carrot-like roots will require a deep container of at least 10 to 12 inches. The leaves are an important food for swallowtail butterfly larvae. If there are too many of these green-, black-, and yellow-striped worms on my parsley, they also get moved to the fennel.

Sorrel is actually grown as a perennial in many areas in the Southwest. The flavor is very strong in the warmer months but it has a nice lemony zip in the cool season. I cut all the foliage back and compost it at the end of summer to allow fresh new foliage to appear. The leaves are a nice addition to salads, while sorrel and potato soup and sorrel sauce for fish and pasta are staples in my winter kitchen. This herb appreciates afternoon shade, regular watering, and rich soil.

HOLIDAY HERB BUNDLES

An assortment of herbs from the garden tied together in a pretty bundle can make an attractive decoration in the kitchen and a welcome gift for your holiday hosts. A bundle with rosemary, thyme, sage, and marjoram placed inside a turkey with added salt, peppercorns, and an onion will infuse the turkey with amazing flavor. Tie them with a ribbon and enjoy the fragrance indoors until you're ready to cook with them.

Gather five to seven stems of each herb together and tie the entire bundle tightly with a rubber band. The herbs will shrink as they dry, so tying them tightly is essential. Tie a loop in the ribbon for hanging the bundle and then wrap the ribbon to hide the rubber band. Add a cluster of flowers that dry well for a pop of color near the top of the bundle. Rose buds, marigolds, gomphrena, and strawflowers are bright accents that dry well and hold their color.

Hang your herb swag in a well-ventilated location out of direct sunlight. Pinch off herbs as needed or remove the flowers, rubber bands, and ribbon and use the entire bundle.

·DECEMBER·

GIFTS OF THE GARDEN

Many gardeners are preoccupied with other duties during the holiday season. December is a good time to let things wind down a bit and simply maintain what is growing without expanding the plantings. Days are shorter and we have less time for garden maintenance. We may have some of the coldest temperatures of the year, but may also have warm sunny days that permit us to harvest more of our garden's bounty. But there is still much we can do. Wrap up the year by inspiring others with your gardening successes—give the gift of garden tools, seeds, or a garden book to get someone hooked on gardening. Bring some of your garden indoors to decorate and share your bounty with friends. Consider adding cover crops to your garden if you need to improve

CONTINUED ON PAGE 156

TO DO THIS MONTH

PLAN

- Begin thinking about the next season's garden and inventory and order seeds for the coming year.

- Make notes in your garden journal about the year's successes and failures and make goals for the coming year. Record significant weather events.

PREPARE AND MAINTAIN

- Monitor stored onions, garlic, tomatoes, and peppers to check for spoilage.
- Cover crops as needed to protect from cold.
- Hill up leeks to blanch them.
- Start planning for next season's garden.
- Gardeners in milder climates can begin building new beds and improving soil for the spring season.

- Continue to collect leaves and make compost when the weather allows.
- Plant cover crops after harvesting final plantings.
- Cut back asparagus fronds after they have frozen and mulch the bed to prepare for spring harvests.

SOW AND PLANT INDOORS

ZONES 4–7
- Start seeds of salad greens and herbs in a sunny window or under grow lights for fresh salads.

ZONES 8–10
- Start seeds for broccoli, cabbage, Brussels sprouts, cauliflower, and English peas.

SOW AND PLANT OUTDOORS

ZONES 8–10

- Continue to plant carrots, beets, onions from seeds, chives, parsley, lettuce, kohlrabi, mustard greens, and radishes.

HARVESTING NOW

ZONES 6–7

kale	leeks	spinach

ZONES 8–10

beets	Brussels	carrots	greens	lettuce
bok choy	sprouts	cauliflower	kale	spinach
broccoli	cabbage	green onions		

the soil or get weeds under control. They are an inexpensive and effective means of building garden soil. Composting now will give you gardener's gold for the coming spring garden season so collect all the leaves, grass clippings, garden debris and vegetable trimmings you can to improve your soil for the next year. Keep the pile covered to maintain moisture and warmth in colder zones.

Take the time to evaluate your garden year and study your successes and failures. Make plans now for an even better garden in the coming year.

Many of our plants will perform double duty to decorate our homes and provide fragrance and beauty indoors. Sage, bay laurel, and rosemary can be added to real or artificial greenery for mantels or in holiday garlands and wreaths. Bundles of dried herbs can be added to the fireplace as fire starters that make the house smell fragrant.

Dry basil seed heads in bunches and use them for fragrant decorations on wreath or holiday trees. They can be sprayed with metallic spray paint for even more pizazz. Curled parsley and scented geraniums make frilly collars for indoor flower arrangements. Tie a small bundle of catnip, bay laurel, or rosemary onto a gift bag for an added treat.

Add a few sprigs of rosemary, basil, or jalapenos to some high-quality vodka for an infusion. Refrigerate the vodka and taste daily to determine if the desired flavor level has been achieved. Most will be ready within several days to a week. Once it is to your liking, strain the flavoring agents out and discard. Keep the infused spirit for up to two months in the refrigerator. Provide the recipient with some recipes for using the vodka. Rosemary-infused vodka paired with grapefruit juice and a splash of sparkling water is a delicious combination.

Crushed dried herbs mixed with baking soda and essential oils to make a fragrant carpet deodorizer to make your home smell fresh and welcoming. Change the herbs, spices, and oils to suit your taste. I make a great blend with dried rosemary and cinnamon powder and orange essential oil.

Gifts for the Gardener

If you have a gardener on your gift list, here are some items that are sure to please everyone from the beginning gardener to the seasoned veteran.

A good pair of pruners: splurge for a brand that will last a lifetime, or get the lefty in your life some left-handed shears. My Felco shears are the first tool I grab when I head to the garden.

Garden support: a set of high-quality tomato cages from the Texas Tomato Cage Company is sure to please a tomato lover. These sturdy supports are made from galvanized metal so they do not rust, and they fold flat for easy, compact storage when not in use.

A subscription to a favorite gardening magazine.

A gallon of organic liquid fertilizer or a container of seaweed powder.

A good quality pump or hose end sprayer.

Some of your favorite gardening **books**.

A salad spinner for washing lettuce and herbs.

A beautiful **pot**.

Wind chimes or other garden "jewelry."

A garden **tool bag**.

A high-quality **garden fork or shovel**.

A truckload of compost: don't laugh! I got that for my birthday once and I was thrilled with it! A sign that said "Happy Birthday" was stuck in the top of the pile.

A potted amaryllis or a basket of bulbs for the garden or a container. Include planting and care instructions and chill bulbs that require chilling like hyacinths, tulips, and paper white narcissus. I find that paper whites will grow shorter and not be as lanky if they are refrigerated for at least four weeks at 40°F.

Herbs, preserves, oils, vinegar, potpourri, swags, and dried herbs for use in teas or in cooking. A lovely teapot and an assortment of dried mint, chamomile flowers, and dried lemon verbena will provide many delightful cups of tea for the recipient.

Coping with the Cold

December, January, and February bring our best chances for hard freezes, sleet, and snow. Your garden should be well mulched and have hoops and row covers or a cold frame to protect plants from extreme cold. Sometimes plants will still freeze despite your precautions. Avoid harvesting plants while they are still frozen. They will immediately wilt and turn to mush when you bring them inside. If they thaw gradually outdoors they may have a few damaged leaves but will recover more quickly if left undisturbed when frozen. If the plants are damaged by cold don't pull them out too quickly. Damaged leaves can often be trimmed away and the plants can be rebound more quickly than new plants would grow.

When severe cold is predicted, harvest greens, broccoli, and lettuce in advance. They will store fresh from the garden for at least a week until temperatures change.

Enjoying the Green Harvest

Leaf lettuce should be cut frequently to keep it producing new succulent leaves and to delay the formation of seed heads. Properly washed and drained lettuce can last for several weeks in the refrigerator. A salad spinner is a worthwhile investment because it will wash and store lettuce, herbs, and greens and will keep them crisp and tasty for a long time. The salad spinner has a colander that fits inside a bowl. Add water to the bowl and swish the lettuce around. Pull the lettuce from the water so that any sand or insects are left in the water and add the lettuce to the colander, allowing it to drain. When most of the water has drained off put the colander in the bowl and spin the lettuce a few times to remove more water. Pour off the water and continue until only a small amount of water remains beneath the colander. That water will keep the lettuce crisp, but since it is not touching the lettuce leaves directly, they will not turn to mush. Tightly cover and keep the bowl in the coldest part of the refrigerator. I wash enough lettuce for a several day's salads at one time and store it. That makes putting together a salad much faster. Grated radishes, kohlrabi, and beets are tasty and nutritious salad toppings. If you have had luck with your fall tomato crop you may have a few of those to add also.

An alternative method for storing lettuce is placing it in a large bowl above an overturned saucer or small plate. The plate allows excess water to drain away from the lettuce but the small amount of water underneath keeps the humidity up so that the lettuce stays crisp. Waterlogged lettuce will turn to mush quickly so be sure to drain it well.

Lettuce, greens, or broccoli can sometimes be hosts to thousands of tiny aphids or small caterpillars, which are not the most appetizing addition to your salads. To enjoy your harvest, sans insects, add some salt to the water that you are using to rinse the vegetables—about a tablespoon to a quart of water—and swish the vegetables in the salted water for several minutes. Lift the greens from the water and the critters should remain at the bottom of the bowl. Rinse until all the invaders are gone.

Sorrel, arugula, endive, mâche, fennel, bok choy, and cress are also tasty additions to the salad bowl. Add parsley, green onions, chives, thinly sliced turnips, mint, and cilantro to make your daily winter salads anything but boring. I seldom buy lettuce from the grocery store as the flavor is rather bland and it does not last more than a few days in the refrigerator. As a result, I usually enjoy daily salads only when lettuce is in season. Add tuna, artichoke hearts, cooked beans, olives, boiled eggs, chicken, cheese, or other proteins to make it a meal.

A well-stocked pantry with a variety of oils and vinegars to make salad dressings will truly enhance your salad. Most store-bought dressings are full of sugar, salt and chemicals and simple vinaigrette is easy to master. I have an Oster blender and the blender blade fits on a standard quart canning jar. I place all my ingredients in the jar, give it a whirl and then screw on a lid to store the remainder for the next few days' salads. Each time I make the dressing, I vary the ingredients so it never gets boring.

COVER CROPS

Maybe you don't require as much of your garden in winter as in summer when space-hungry tomatoes, squash, pumpkins, and corn are growing. You may choose not to deal with the uncertainty of cold fronts and covering and uncovering the garden all winter long, but don't let your garden sit empty for the season. Grow a cover crop to increase fertility in your soil, prevent soil erosion, suppress weed growth, and improve the texture of your soil. Plant yields following cover crops will be much higher due to the increased fertility and microbe life in the soil. Worms and beneficial soil organisms thrive in the root zone of cover crops and will stick around when you plant your next crop. Cover crops typically grow so thickly that they shade the soil and don't allow weeds to grow.

Seeds for cover crops are fairly inexpensive and you may be able to buy them by the pound at your local garden center or feed store so that you buy only what you require. They are also available online and via mail order through seed companies. Avoid purchasing any seeds that are dyed bright colors. That bright green, yellow, or pink color usually means that the seed has been given a chemical bath that you don't want to include in your garden. Plan to plant your cover crops several weeks before the first freeze so that they get established before soil temperatures are cool. Cover crops are often referred to as green manure since they are a rich source of nitrogen for the soil.

Water the soil before you add seeds and barely cover the seeds with soil. Smaller cover-crop seeds may be pressed into the soil and left uncovered. Water lightly every day until the seeds germinate and then water regularly to ensure the crops grow full and lush. Grass-type cover crops will appreciate an application of seaweed or fish emulsion during the growing season but legume types will not require feeding. Birds love many of these seeds, so you may need to cover them with row cover to keep them from being eaten. Once the seeds have germinated and reached several inches in height they will be less attractive to birds.

SKILL SET

COOL SEASON COVER CROPS

Vetch attracts beneficial insects in spring. Cut the tops back and leave the nitrogen-rich roots in place to provide for nitrogen-hungry crops like corn, tomatoes, and okra in spring. Dig a hole in the planting bed and add a little compost and your transplant or seeds. Vetch will produce more nitrogen if it is inoculated with rhizobium bacteria before planting. Wet the seeds and sprinkle the black powder over them just before planting. Don't be alarmed if you see vetch tendrils thick with aphids in early spring. Those aphids will attract a healthy population of ladybugs for your garden all year by providing a food source for their young. The beneficial beetles lay eggs where there is a good supply of aphids for the newly hatched and hungry larvae to consume. I have seen sparrows and wrens methodically cleaning the aphids from vetch stems by swiping them through their beaks. Bees are also attracted to the blooms of vetch. You are feeding your soil and a lot more!

Elbon or cereal rye is one of the best for crowding out cool-season weeds like henbit, chickweed, and pigweed. Elbon will grow very tall, up to 2 feet, and may be cut to the ground several times during the growing season. The nitrogen-rich tops are perfect for adding to your saved leaves to make rich compost all winter long. The roots of elbon rye trap root-knot nematodes and kill them so you can plant crops like okra, tomatoes, and peppers with fewer problems from nematodes for a season. Don't let it produce seed heads; cut it close to the ground with shears or a string trimmer several weeks before spring planting time to weaken it and leave the roots in the soil. Leave the last cutting of the green tops on the soil to provide nitrogen for the next crop. Dig holes for transplants or seeds right into the root zone. You may also use your garden fork to dig up and disturb the roots several weeks before you wish to plant. This will give the roots time to fully decompose and for the soil to be ready for the next planting. Use ¾–1 pound of seeds per 100 square feet of space.

Red clover has red flowers loved by butterflies and used in medicinal teas. It is a legume, so it adds nitrogen to the soil. Cut the plants back when about half of the cover crop begins to bloom. I leave a few plants around the edges for blooms for wildlife and to collect and dry for tea. Cut the tops back a few weeks before you wish to plant in spring let them dry for a few days and then turn them into the soil with a spading fork. Plant 1 pound per 1000 square feet. It combines well with oats, but plant at a reduced rate if combining the two crops.

Oats are fast growing and combine well with vetch. Plant 1–2 pounds per 1000 square feet. Plant at the reduced rate when growing in combination with other crops. Don't allow the tops to produce seed heads; cut them back when seed heads begin to form.

Mustard greens are a cool-season cover crop that will help kill nematodes in the soil when the plants are tilled in and they add lots of organic matter. Plant ½–1 pound per 1000 square feet.

Turnips provide edible greens and roots and are a valuable cool-season cover crop. Plant 3 ounces per 1000 square feet.

Austrian field peas are ideal for dense or poorly drained soil. Plant 2–4 pounds per 1000 square feet.

SKILL SET

SUMMER COVER CROPS

Buckwheat is a summer cover crop that provides food for bees and other beneficial insects. Plant 2–3 pounds per 1000 square feet and cut the plants back after they bloom to control seeding. Cut back different areas at a time so that there are always blooms present.

Southern peas, black-eyed peas, or cowpeas are legumes that thrive in summer and add nitrogen to the soil. Plant 2–3 pounds per 1000 square feet and inoculate seeds with bacteria to improve nitrogen fixation.

EDIBLES
A TO Z

PLANTING AND HARVESTING CHART
ZONES 4 & 5

Planting
Harvesting

These charts provide approximate dates for planting and harvesting crops sown outdoors by seed or transplants without additional protection. Exact planting dates will vary depending on your garden's microclimate and the uncertainties of each season's weather. More specific planting information is included with each vegetable's profile. Gardeners who choose to utilize row covers, cold frames, and shade coverings will be able to extend both planting and harvesting dates several weeks on either side of the ranges.

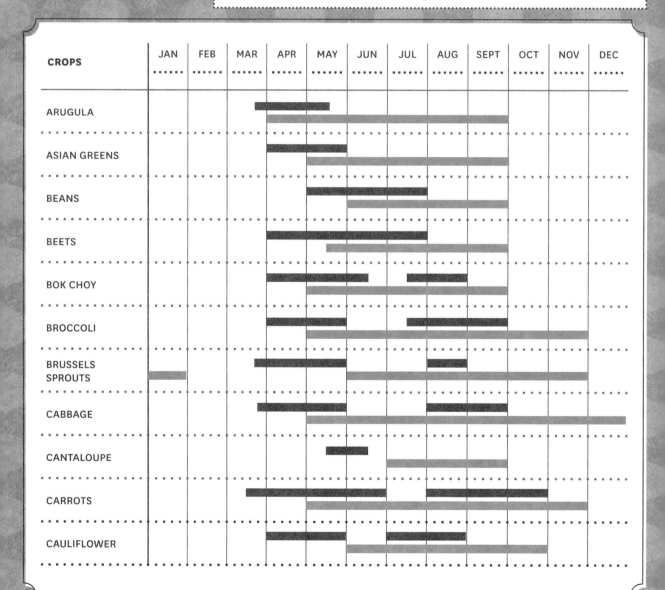

CROPS	JAN	FEB	MAR	APR	MAY	JUN	JUL	AUG	SEPT	OCT	NOV	DEC
ARUGULA												
ASIAN GREENS												
BEANS												
BEETS												
BOK CHOY												
BROCCOLI												
BRUSSELS SPROUTS												
CABBAGE												
CANTALOUPE												
CARROTS												
CAULIFLOWER												

CROPS

CROPS	JAN	FEB	MAR	APR	MAY	JUN	JUL	AUG	SEPT	OCT	NOV	DEC
COLLARDS				■	■	■	▭	▭				
CORN					■	▭	▭	▭	▭			
CUCUMBERS					■	▭	▭	▭				
EGGPLANT					■	▭	▭	▭	▭			
GARLIC						▭	▭	▭	■	■	■	
KALE			■	■	■	▭	▭■	▭■	▭■	▭	▭	▭
KOHLRABI				■	■	▭	▭					
LEEKS				■	■	▭	▭	▭				
LETTUCE AND SALAD GREENS				■	■	■	■	▭	▭	▭	▭	▭
OKRA					■	■	▭	▭				
ONIONS		■	■	■	■	▭	▭■	▭■	■	■	■	
PEAS		■	■	■	■▭	▭	▭	▭	▭	▭	▭	
PEPPERS					■		▭	▭	▭	▭		
POTATOES			■	■	■	■			▭	▭		
PURSLANE						■	■▭	■▭				

(■ = planting period; ▭ = harvest period)

- ▬ Planting
- ▬ Harvesting

CROPS	JAN	FEB	MAR	APR	MAY	JUN	JUL	AUG	SEPT	OCT	NOV	DEC
RADISHES		Planting	Planting	Planting · Harvesting	Harvesting	Harvesting	Harvesting	Planting	Planting · Harvesting	Harvesting	Harvesting	
SOUTHERN PEAS	NOT RECOMMENDED FOR THIS REGION											
SPINACH		Planting	Planting	Harvesting	Harvesting	Harvesting	Harvesting	Planting	Planting	Harvesting	Harvesting	
SUMMER SQUASH					Planting	Planting · Harvesting	Harvesting	Harvesting	Harvesting			
SWEET POTATOES						Planting				Harvesting		
SWISS CHARD				Planting	Planting · Harvesting	Harvesting	Harvesting	Harvesting	Harvesting	Harvesting	Harvesting	Harvesting
TOMATOES (TRANSPLANTS)					Planting		Harvesting	Harvesting	Harvesting			
TURNIPS				Planting	Planting · Harvesting	Harvesting	Harvesting	Planting	Harvesting	Harvesting	Harvesting	
WATERMELONS					Planting			Harvesting	Harvesting			
WINTER SQUASH AND PUMPKINS					Planting	Planting · Harvesting	Harvesting	Harvesting	Harvesting			

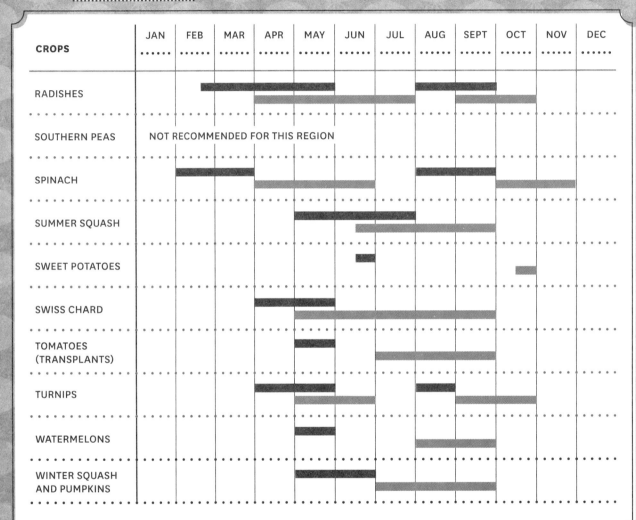

PLANTING AND HARVESTING CHART
ZONES 6 & 7

Planting
Harvesting

These charts provide approximate dates for planting and harvesting crops sown outdoors by seed or transplants without additional protection. Exact planting dates will vary depending on your garden's microclimate and the uncertainties of each season's weather. More specific planting information is included with each vegetable's profile. Gardeners who choose to utilize row covers, cold frames, and shade coverings will be able to extend both planting and harvesting dates several weeks on either side of the ranges.

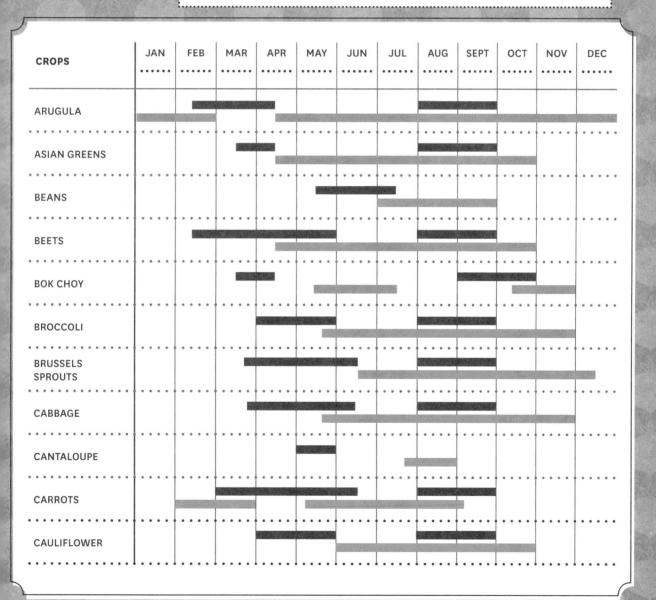

CROPS	JAN	FEB	MAR	APR	MAY	JUN	JUL	AUG	SEPT	OCT	NOV	DEC
ARUGULA												
ASIAN GREENS												
BEANS												
BEETS												
BOK CHOY												
BROCCOLI												
BRUSSELS SPROUTS												
CABBAGE												
CANTALOUPE												
CARROTS												
CAULIFLOWER												

167

Planting
Harvesting

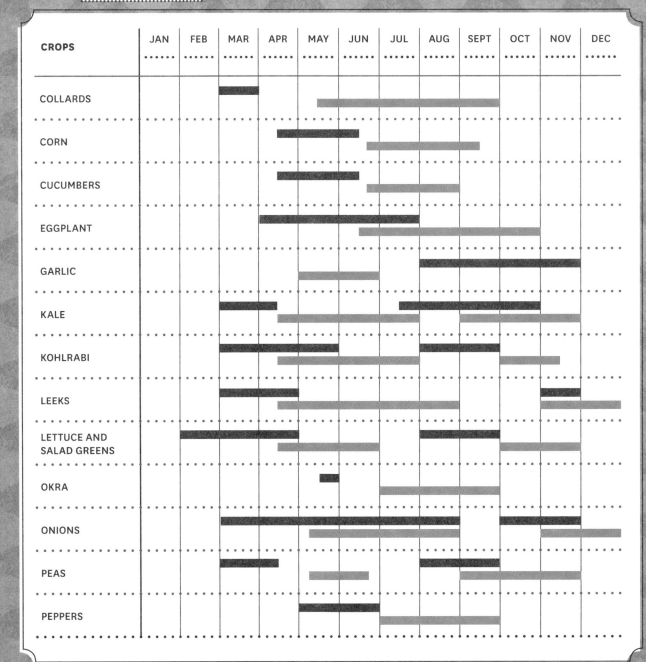

CROPS	JAN	FEB	MAR	APR	MAY	JUN	JUL	AUG	SEPT	OCT	NOV	DEC
COLLARDS			■			▬	▬	▬	▬			
CORN				■	■		▬	▬				
CUCUMBERS				■	■		▬	▬				
EGGPLANT				■	■	■	■		▬			
GARLIC					▬	▬		■	■	■	■	■
KALE			■	■	▬	▬		■	■	▬		
KOHLRABI			■	■	■	▬		■	■	▬	▬	
LEEKS			■	■	▬	▬	▬	▬	▬		■ ▬	▬
LETTUCE AND SALAD GREENS		■	■	■	▬	▬		■	■	▬		
OKRA					■		▬	▬	▬			
ONIONS			■	■	■	▬	▬	▬		■	■ ▬	▬
PEAS			■	■	▬	▬		■	■	▬	▬	
PEPPERS					■	■	▬	▬	▬			

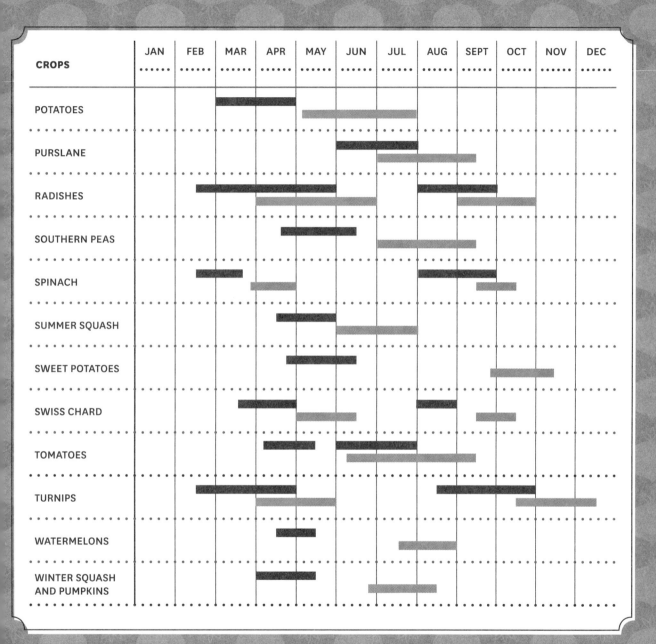

CROPS	JAN	FEB	MAR	APR	MAY	JUN	JUL	AUG	SEPT	OCT	NOV	DEC
POTATOES			■	■	░	░	░					
PURSLANE						■	■	░	░			
RADISHES			■	■	░	░		■	■	░		
SOUTHERN PEAS				■	░	░	░					
SPINACH		■	░	░				■	░	░		
SUMMER SQUASH				■	░	░						
SWEET POTATOES				■	■				░	░	░	
SWISS CHARD			■	■	░	░		■	░	░		
TOMATOES				■	░	■	░	░				
TURNIPS			■	■	░	░		■	■	░	░	
WATERMELONS				■			░	░				
WINTER SQUASH AND PUMPKINS				■		░	░					

169

PLANTING AND HARVESTING CHART
ZONES 8 & 9

■ Planting
■ Harvesting

These charts provide approximate dates for planting and harvesting crops sown outdoors by seed or transplants without additional protection. Exact planting dates will vary depending on your garden's microclimate and the uncertainties of each season's weather. More specific planting information is included with each vegetable's profile. Gardeners who choose to utilize row covers, cold frames, and shade coverings will be able to extend both planting and harvesting dates several weeks on either side of the ranges.

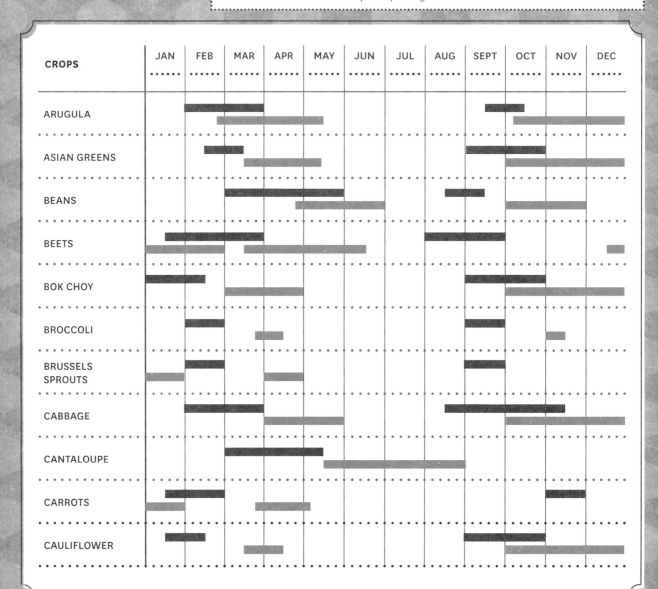

CROPS	JAN	FEB	MAR	APR	MAY	JUN	JUL	AUG	SEPT	OCT	NOV	DEC
ARUGULA												
ASIAN GREENS												
BEANS												
BEETS												
BOK CHOY												
BROCCOLI												
BRUSSELS SPROUTS												
CABBAGE												
CANTALOUPE												
CARROTS												
CAULIFLOWER												

CROPS

Crop	JAN	FEB	MAR	APR	MAY	JUN	JUL	AUG	SEPT	OCT	NOV	DEC
COLLARDS	○	●○	●○	○						●	●○	○
CORN			●	●	●○	●○	○	●		○	○	
CUCUMBERS			●	●	●○	●○	○		●		○	
EGGPLANT				●	●	●	○	○	○	○		
GARLIC	○	○								●	●	
KALE	○	●○	●	○	○				●	●	●○	●○
KOHLRABI		●	●	●○	○				●	●○	●○	○
LEEKS	○	○	○	○	○				●	●○	●○	○
LETTUCE AND SALAD GREENS	●○	●○	○	○	○				●	●○	●○	○
OKRA				●	●○	○	○	○	○	○		
ONIONS	●	●○	○	○	○						●	●
PEAS	○	●○	●	○	○		●	●	●	●○	●○	○
PEPPERS			●	●	●○	●○	●○	○	○	○	○	○
POTATOES		●			○							
PURSLANE					●○	●	●○	○	○			

Planting
Harvesting

CROPS	JAN	FEB	MAR	APR	MAY	JUN	JUL	AUG	SEPT	OCT	NOV	DEC
RADISHES	■■■	■■■	■■■	■					■■■	■■■	■■■	■
	───	───	───	─						───	───	───
SOUTHERN PEAS			■■	■■		───	───	───				
SPINACH	■■	■	───	───					■■	■■	■■	
										───	───	
SUMMER SQUASH		■■	■		───	───	───	───	■			
SWEET POTATOES			■■	■■			───	───	───			
SWISS CHARD	■■	■■	■							■		
			───	───							─	───
TOMATOES		■■	■■		───	───	■		───	───	───	
TURNIPS	■■	■■	■■								■■	■
			───	───								─
WATERMELONS			■■	■		───	───	───				
WINTER SQUASH AND PUMPKINS			■■	■	───	───	───	───	───	───	───	

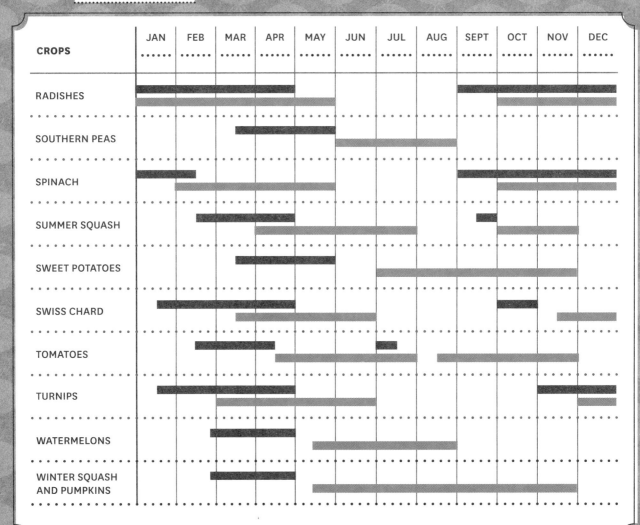

PLANTING AND HARVESTING CHART
ZONE 10

Planting
Harvesting

These charts provide approximate dates for planting and harvesting crops sown outdoors by seed or transplants without additional protection. Exact planting dates will vary depending on your garden's microclimate and the uncertainties of each season's weather. More specific planting information is included with each vegetable's profile. Gardeners who choose to utilize row covers, cold frames, and shade coverings will be able to extend both planting and harvesting dates several weeks on either side of the ranges.

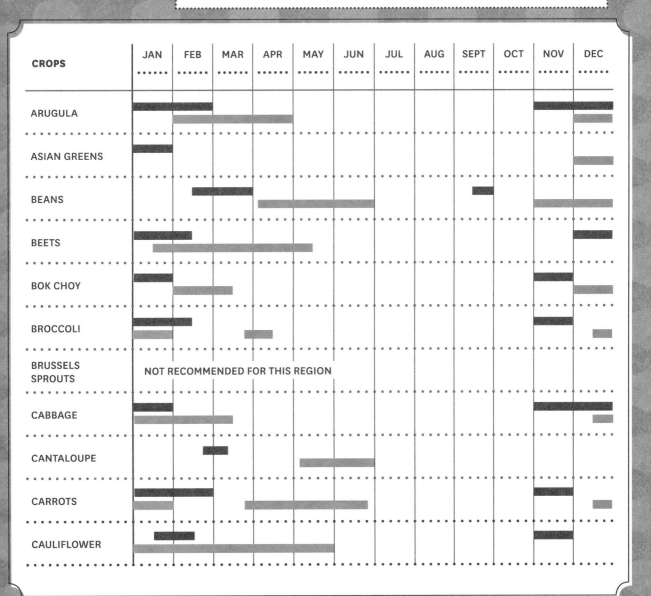

CROPS	JAN	FEB	MAR	APR	MAY	JUN	JUL	AUG	SEPT	OCT	NOV	DEC
ARUGULA												
ASIAN GREENS												
BEANS												
BEETS												
BOK CHOY												
BROCCOLI												
BRUSSELS SPROUTS	NOT RECOMMENDED FOR THIS REGION											
CABBAGE												
CANTALOUPE												
CARROTS												
CAULIFLOWER												

173

Legend:
- ■ Planting
- ■ Harvesting

CROPS	JAN	FEB	MAR	APR	MAY	JUN	JUL	AUG	SEPT	OCT	NOV	DEC
COLLARDS	■ Planting Jan–Mar											■ Planting Dec
	■ Harvesting Jan–Jun											
CORN		■ Planting Feb–Mar							■ Planting Sept			■ Harvesting Dec
	■ Harvesting Jan				■ Harvesting May–Jun						
CUCUMBERS		■ Planting Feb–Mar								■ Planting Oct		
	■ Harvesting Jan			■ Harvesting Apr–Jun						■ Harvesting Oct–Dec	
EGGPLANT		■ Planting Feb–Mar						■ Planting Aug				
				■ Harvesting Apr–Jun					■ Harvesting Sept–Nov		
GARLIC	■ Planting Jan											■ Planting Dec
				■ Harvesting Apr–Jun								
KALE	■ Planting Jan–Mar										■ Planting Nov–Dec	
	■ Harvesting Jan–Apr											
KOHLRABI	■ Planting Jan–Feb										■ Planting Nov–Dec	
	■ Harvesting Jan–Apr											■ Harvesting Dec
LEEKS	■ Planting Jan–Feb										■ Planting Nov–Dec	
	■ Harvesting Jan–Apr											■ Harvesting Dec
LETTUCE AND SALAD GREENS	■ Planting Jan–Mar											■ Planting Dec
	■ Harvesting Jan–Apr											
OKRA			■ Planting Mar–May									
				■ Harvesting May–Aug							
ONIONS	■ Planting Jan										■ Planting Nov–Dec	
		■ Harvesting Feb–May									
PEAS	NOT RECOMMENDED FOR THIS REGION											
PEPPERS			■ Planting Mar–Apr					■ Planting Aug				
					■ Harvesting May–Aug				■ Harvesting Sept–Nov		

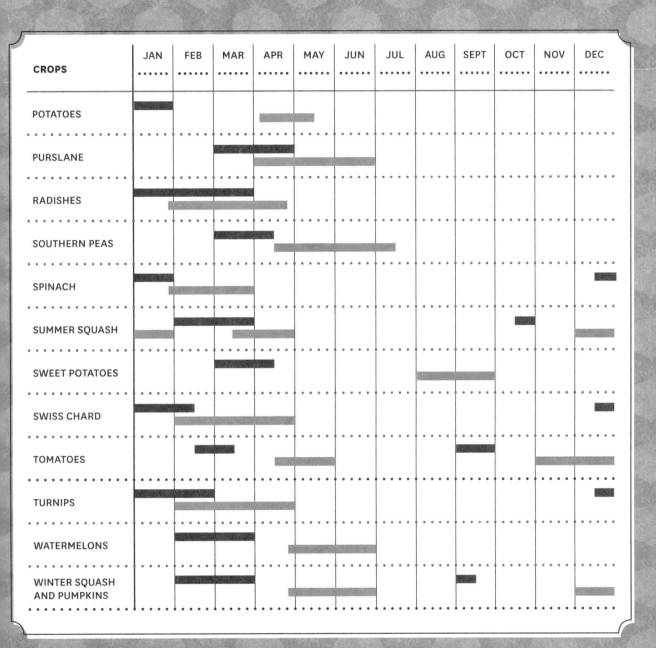

CROPS	JAN	FEB	MAR	APR	MAY	JUN	JUL	AUG	SEPT	OCT	NOV	DEC
POTATOES	▬			▬								
PURSLANE			▬	▬	▬	▬						
RADISHES	▬	▬	▬									
SOUTHERN PEAS			▬	▬	▬	▬						
SPINACH	▬	▬										▬
SUMMER SQUASH	▬	▬	▬							▬		▬
SWEET POTATOES			▬	▬				▬	▬			
SWISS CHARD	▬	▬	▬						▬			▬
TOMATOES		▬	▬		▬	▬			▬		▬	▬
TURNIPS	▬	▬	▬									▬
WATERMELONS		▬	▬		▬	▬						
WINTER SQUASH AND PUMPKINS		▬	▬		▬	▬		▬				▬

175

Artichokes

Globe artichokes are a member of the thistle family. Their velvety gray foliage and tall sturdy stems make them an attractive landscape addition. The edible part of the plant is the flower bud. I can't resist allowing a few of the buds to form the gorgeous complex thistle flowers to make beautiful fresh and dried flower arrangements.

GROWING Artichokes are purchased as bare root plants in winter and in 4-inch pots or 1-gallon containers in spring. Since they are thistles, they aren't terribly picky about soil, but a well-drained soil or a large container (at least 24 inches wide) would work best. The plants like full sun, but can tolerate up to half a day of shade in the Southwest. They will be 3–4 feet tall at bloom stage and are almost as wide as they are tall. They do not perform well in heavy clay or wet soils unless planted in raised beds to provide excellent drainage. A plant that produces blooms will die to the ground afterward, but will produce offshoots at the base of the plant called pups. Artichokes are not cold tolerant so are best grown in zones 8–10.

Artichokes have few pest problems and many beneficial insects will feed on the prolific pollen of the artichoke blooms. Aphids sometimes appear on the leaves, but I don't treat them. The aphids attract ladybugs and lacewings to my garden and these insects will then lay eggs where their young will have a plentiful diet of aphids, thus providing a bountiful crop of beneficial insects in early spring.

Another insect that likes artichokes and their close relative cardoon is the lygus or leaf-footed bug (a type of stink bug), a serious pest on tomatoes, peppers, and eggplant. These bugs love to hang out on the artichokes and cardoon and will mate and lay eggs there also. The bright red nymphs of the lygus bug cluster on the stems and

flowers of artichokes. I keep a spray bottle filled with soapy water near the artichokes and spray the lygus bug adults until they are unable to fly off and then quickly dispatch their non-flying descendants. Using artichokes as a trap crop for both beneficial ladybugs and the lygus bug has reduced the number of problem pests in the garden. The soap spray doesn't seem to harm the artichokes at all, and since the bloom stalk dies after it blooms, it would not really matter even if it did.

HARVESTING Harvest the artichoke buds when they are about 3 inches across. Cut several inches of the stem below the bud as it is also edible. The buds are usually steamed and then eaten. The bottom of the bud, called the choke, is the most delicious portion. You will generally harvest five to nine buds on each artichoke stem.

Cardoon is a wild perennial variety of artichoke with similar leaves and smaller flowers, but still very attractive. The cardoon's bloom buds are not eaten, but the fleshy midrib of its leaves can be peeled like celery and cooked. It has a bitter, chicory-type flavor and is often served in soups or casseroles with white beans. It is more cold tolerant than artichokes and the foliage is attractive most of the year.

VARIETIES **Green Globe** is a large softball-sized fruit that is perennial in zones 7–10. **Imperial Star** and **Tempo** are best grown as annuals in zones 1–6. Elongated artichokes have six to eight main buds, smaller than Globe types, and will have even smaller heads later in the season. **Violetto** is an elongated type that has a lovely purple color.

Arugula

This peppery, pungent green is not for everyone. Most people either love it or hate it. It is often included in mesclun greens mix, but can be used in many ways on its own.

GROWING Arugula is easily grown from seed and can be directly seeded into the garden bed or containers. The seeds may be broadcasted over the entire bed and thinned to the correct spacing, or planted in rows 12 inches apart, with plants spaced 8–12 inches apart. The seeds germinate and grow quickly. Sow every three to four weeks to have a crop all season long.

It grows in full sun, but will benefit from some afternoon shade in warmer climates (zones 7–10). The flavor gets stronger and the plants will bolt if they get too dry or are in too much sun. Use hoops and row cover to provide shade for milder arugula. It handles cold very well and light frosts will not harm it.

Flea beetles will leave tiny holes in the leaves. Cover plants with row cover to keep them protected. Seal the row cover tightly to keep these fast-moving insects at bay. Aphids are an occasional pest but are easy to wash off with a blast of water.

HARVESTING Within several weeks of planting, the arugula leaves can be trimmed with scissors and added to salads. Harvest them frequently to keep the flavor mild and delay blooming. The flavor gets very strong at bloom stage, but the white blooms are edible. Cut the flower stalks to the ground as soon as they appear to delay blooming. The leaves can be added to pesto, soups, omelets, and sandwiches. I love to use them to top a pizza fresh out of the oven.

VARIETIES **Astro** and **Apollo** are common cultivated varieties. **Sylvetta** is a wild perennial variety of arugula that has a stronger flavor and yellow flowers. It makes an attractive ground cover for part-shade gardens and self-sows readily.

Asian Greens

From sweet and crunchy Napa cabbage to the spicy tang of mizuna, Asian greens can play a starring role in salads, stir-fries, soups, and casseroles. They are more tolerant of warm spells during the cool season in the Southwest. There is a wide range of colors and sizes to choose from.

GROWING Seeds may be sown directly in the soil or planted as transplants in late summer or throughout the winter. Many of these greens will bolt or be prone to insects if temperatures are warm, so wait until temperatures are lower or shade new plantings to protect them.

Plant them in fertile soil in a sunny location. Be sure to thin as directed on the package. Mizuna and other Asian greens can be very large and should be thinned to 12–14 inches apart.

Asian greens may have problems with flea beetles, aphids, and worms. Use row covers to protect them as needed. Snails, slugs, and pillbugs can also be problems. Use beer traps or iron phosphate granules with Spinosad to control them.

HARVESTING Eat the thinnings as you trim them. Outer leaves of mizuna and Napa cabbage can be harvested and the plants will continue growing. Whole plants may be harvested as needed. Smaller leaves of mizuna add a spicy zest to salad mixes. Napa cabbage adds a nice crunch to salads also. Spicier tatsoi, mustard greens, and mibuna are best used lightly stir-fried, sautéed, or added to soups.

VARIETIES **Minuet Chinese Cabbage**, **Hon Tsai Tai**, **Komatsuna**, **Mibuna**, **Mizuna**, **Osaka Purple**, **Tatsoi**, **Shungiku Chysanthemum**, and **Vitamin Greens** are all excellent ways to diversify your winter greens selections.

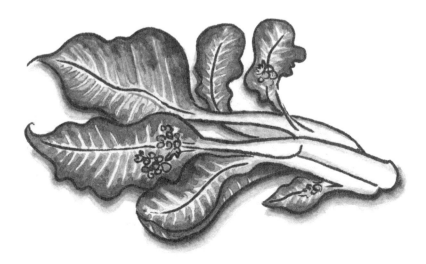

Asparagus

If your garden is large enough to allow a dedicated space for asparagus, there is no easier crop to grow and maintain, once established. The plants will produce delicious young shoots in spring, which are a good source of vitamins B and C, iron, and calcium. They are excellent cleansers for the urinary tract. The freshly harvested spears are so tender and delectable they are often consumed raw in my garden.

GROWING Select an out-of-the-way sunny spot for your asparagus bed as it will be unattractive and wild looking for many months of the year. Deep soil (18–24 inches) with lots of organic material will give it a good start. The bed should be at least 4 feet wide. Good drainage is essential or the asparagus crowns will rot.

One-year-old asparagus crowns may be purchased or ordered as bare root plants in late winter. Soak the crowns in compost tea or half-strength seaweed tea for 30 minutes before planting to plump up dry roots. Dig 12- to 15-inch-wide trenches, 6–10 inches deep (deeper for colder climates or sandy soils), in your prepared bed. Lay the crowns in the trenches, spreading out the roots, and cover them with a few inches of soil, watering gently to settle the soil. Allow 12–15 inches between each crown. Crowding them will reduce yields and produce spindly spears. Plant at least four or five plants for each person in your household.

Two weeks after planting, top the crowns with several inches of compost. Before temperatures get warm, make sure to top the entire bed with a generous layer of mulch, but avoid piling mulch directly over the crowns. Add additional compost and mulch throughout the growing season as needed and maintain even soil moisture. The sprouts that are not harvested become 4- to 6-foot-tall fern-like growths that remain green until the first hard freeze. I installed easily removed livestock panels around my asparagus bed to keep the fronds upright and out of the way. The panels can be removed for the harvest period. The leggy growths are feeding the roots to create the next harvest, so don't be tempted to prune them. The plants

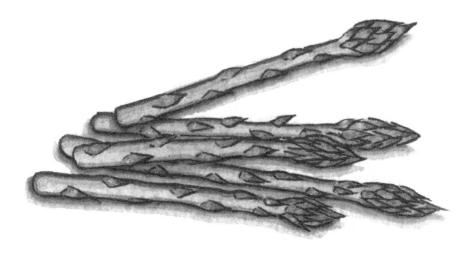

will benefit from foliar feeding of seaweed, fish emulsion, or compost tea.

Asparagus plants are either male or female. Male plants will produce more spears. Female plants produce seedpods that will turn from green to red. These seeds often germinate and can result in overcrowding. A thick layer of mulch can discourage that, but you may notice asparagus sprouting up in other parts of your garden. Some gardeners grow their asparagus from seed so that they can eliminate the female plants and have only the more productive male plants, but there is a much longer period before harvesting can begin when starting by seed.

Keep the dried brown foliage on the plants after it freezes. The dead foliage is not terribly attractive, but it protects the crowns. It should be cut back before new spears begin to sprout in spring.

A well-prepared and maintained bed of asparagus can produce for fifteen years or more, so it is worth the time to do it correctly. Keeping the bed mulched, weed free, and evenly watered will keep the plants in production for years.

Asparagus is recommended for zones 3–8. Warmer zones and wet areas will have trouble growing it. Pest problems are uncommon in asparagus beds. Asparagus beetles might appear but can be controlled with a soap spray.

HARVESTING It is difficult to watch those succulent spears coming up the first spring and not eat them, but it is best to let them grow to establish strong, healthy plants. You can begin harvesting in your second year. Cut the spears at or just below the soil level and continue harvesting until they begin to be smaller than a pencil. At that point you will want to leave the remaining spears to grow and feed the crowns. Apply an organic fertilizer around the crowns and mulch after harvest is over.

VARIETIES **Jersey Knight** or **Jersey Supreme** will have high higher percentages of male plants but may not produce well in warmer zones. **UC 152** and **Atlas** are recommended for warmer areas. **Mary** and **Martha Washington** are some of the older varieties available.

Beans

Beans are a valuable part of the southwestern garden and due to their high protein aid in soil building. Green beans are grown for their edible pods and shelling beans are grown for their mature seeds which are dried for long term storage. Shelling beans may also be eaten in their immature green stage.

Bush beans are self-supporting and produce more beans at one time, but will have a shorter duration of harvest than pole beans. Plant early rows of bush beans along the sides of beds with tomatoes or peppers; the beans will be finished when the other plants need more space and they will provide needed nitrogen. Bush beans are less tolerant of heat, so plant them as early as possible.

Half-runner or semi-pole beans will need a short fence or support for best yield and easier harvesting.

Pole beans need a structure of string, a fence, or a trellis to support them. Utilize the tall beans to provide needed shade for other vegetables. Pole beans will take a longer time to be ready for harvest but will produce a crop for a longer period. Most beans will continue to bloom when temperatures are above 95°F but will fail to make beans. The blooms give bees a reason to visit the garden and the plants will still be generating nitrogen, so leave them in the garden. Once temperatures cool down they will once again produce a crop.

GROWING Plant beans one to two weeks after the average last frost. Sow additional beans every two weeks for a continual harvest. Plant directly in the garden—transplanting is not recommended. Beans may be anywhere from 50 to 100 days to harvest. Pay attention to the number of days to harvest as you plant successive crops or you may have too many ready at one time.

Since beans produce most of their nitrogen, it is important to avoid adding too much nitrogen to the planting bed. Excess nitrogen will produce lush leaves and no blooms. Plant beans when soil is warm in spring. Plant the seeds $\frac{1}{2}$–1 inch deep and 2 inches apart. Depending on the variety, plants will need to be thinned to 3–8 inches apart once the plants are 3–4 inches high. Use a pair of scissors to cut the thinned plants at the soil line to avoid injury to the remaining plants. Plants will be stressed and more prone to disease and insects if they are not properly thinned. Birds, pillbugs, and cutworms will help themselves to the tender bean sprouts, so you need to plant extra seeds. Just be sure to eventually thin to the recommended spacing.

Dusting wet bean seeds before planting with the bacterial inoculant Rhizobium will boost nitrogen production. When beans are finished producing, cut plants at the soil line rather than pulling out the roots so that the nitrogen-rich roots will feed the next crop. If time permits, chop the aboveground portion of the bean plants and incorporate them into the garden bed. They will break down in a few weeks and add even more nitrogen to the soil.

HARVESTING Harvest the beans as the seeds start to swell and the pods are firm and crisp. Avoid handling or harvesting your bean plants when the foliage is wet to avoid the spread of disease. I always try to have some early green beans ready to cook with the new potatoes as they are being harvested—one of the great pleasures of spring!

VARIETIES Bush Beans: **Blue Lake**, **Contender**, **Dragon Tongue**, and **Romano**. Pole Beans: **Florida Speckled Butter Beans**, **Kentucky Wonder**, and **Rattlesnake** are standard heat-loving pole beans. **Fava Beans** or **Broad Beans** thrive in cool, damp weather. They are large bushes with attractive flowers and foliage. **Edamame** is another cool-season bean. **Calypso** and **Pinto** are great shelling beans, but I find Pintos delicious and productive as green beans as well.

Beets

Colorful, nutritious, and versatile, beets are easy to grow and provide a bonus harvest of vitamin-packed leaves. Garden-fresh beets have little in common with the ones that come in cans. They are an excellent source of iron—a cup of beet greens has as much iron as a hamburger!

GROWING Beets are planted by seed in soil amended with abundant organic material several weeks before the last frost in spring and when the worst of summer heat is over. The seeds come in bumpy seed capsules that may contain up to five seeds in each capsule. The seed coat is very hard and germination is improved by soaking the seeds in warm water several hours before planting. It is crucial to thin the beets to get uniform, well-shaped roots since they are already crowded in the seed capsule. Thin them to 3–4 inches apart when the leaves are several inches tall. Beets like rich, well-drained soil and sun, although they will tolerate more shade in warmer regions of the Southwest. They also thrive in containers. Make additional plantings every three to four weeks for regular harvests.

Leaf miners will occasionally infect leaves. Pull off affected leaves and discard in the trash. Wireworms can occasionally be a problem.

HARVESTING Harvest the greens while the leaves are young and tender for salads and juicing. Larger leaves can be sautéed and added to soups and stir-fries. The roots may be harvested when they have grown from 1 inch in diameter up to 3–4 inches. Remove the greens to prevent the roots from drying out in the refrigerator.

Young beets can be grated and added raw to salads. Roasting and grilling brings out the sweetness of beets. Beets are delicious when canned or pickled, and can be used to make borscht.

VARIETIES **Detroit Dark Red**, **Bull's Blood**, and **Red Ace** are deep red standard types. **Golden** are bright yellow with a mild, sweet flavor. **Chioggia** has alternating white and pink rings that give it the nickname "candy cane beet." **Cylindra** produces 6-inch-long and 2-inch-wide roots that chefs love for uniform slices, but it requires deeper, sandy soil for perfect form. **Early Wonder** has some of the tastiest beet greens and nice beet roots also.

Blackberries

This perennial plant requires some taming to keep it in check and to ensure good fruit production but the jewel-like juicy fruits are worth the effort. Zones 7–9 will have the most success with blackberries.

GROWING Plant rooted cuttings in late winter in well-prepared soil in a sunny location. Blackberries are often available throughout the spring and summer in 1-gallon containers. The plants can grow up to 5 feet tall and do best with some support. Prepare a bed next to a fence or provide a trellis to support the canes. Space them 2–3 feet apart in the prepared bed or plant several plants together in a hill. They are tolerant of a wide range of soil pH.

Prune out the two-year-old canes immediately after they have borne fruit to keep the plants in check. Prune suckers away from the base of plants also. Avoid pruning canes in winter or you will prune off the next season's fruit.

HARVESTING Collect berries as soon as they are fully colored and easily removed from the plants. The harvest will continue for several weeks. Cover the plants with netting to protect the juicy jewels from birds. Excess berries are easily frozen.

VARIETIES **Brazos**, **Choctaw**, **Womack**, and **Rosborough** are all good thorned varieties. Thornless types are generally not as productive but a new exceptionally vigorous one, **Natchez**, is an exception to that rule. Other thornless types are **Apache**, **Arapaho**, and **Navajo**.

Bok Choy

Asia's cabbage, there are many flavors, sizes, and colors of bok choy to choose from and they are more productive in warm climates than the typical cabbage types. And from salads to soups, bok choy is just as versatile.

GROWING Bok choy is easily grown from seed and may be direct seeded in the garden or planted as transplants. Some varieties are very large and need up to 12 inches of space. Baby bok choy can be spaced 4–6 inches apart.

Keep the plants mulched and well watered. Bok choy is fairly cold and heat tolerant. Protect the plants when temperature are below 25°F and provide shade when spring temperatures stress the plants. They have few insect issues but snails and slugs can be a problem. Use beer traps or iron phosphate granules for control.

HARVESTING Harvest just the outside leaves as often as needed or cut the entire plant. Bok choy grows much like celery. Unlike many other greens, the stems are actually the best part of the plant. Old or damaged leaves can be cut off and discarded.

Baby bok choy can be sliced in half and grilled or roasted. Larger bok choy stems have a delicious crunch and are used in salad, soups, and stir-fries.

VARIETIES **Mei Qing Choi**, **Joi Choi**, **Jade Pagoda**, and **Pak Choi** will give you a delicious mix of flavor and crunch all winter long.

Broccoli

A cool-season star in the garden, broccoli is easy to grow and more tolerant of temperature extremes than its relatives Brussels sprouts and cauliflower. A serving of broccoli can give you a whopping 303 percent of your daily need for vitamin C and is a good source of vitamin A, iron, calcium, and fiber.

GROWING Plant transplants in full sun in rich soil 15–18 inches apart. Put transplants a little deep in the soil, up to the first true set of leaves. Plant radish seeds, green onion sets, or lettuce seeds between the plants to be harvested out before the broccoli is ready. Broccoli can grow 2½–3 feet tall. Plant seeds directly in the ground several weeks before the last frost in spring and nine to twelve weeks before the first frost in fall. Shade the new seedlings to protect them from hot temperatures in late summer.

Cabbage worms are often a problem on broccoli plants. Check the undersides of leaves for worm eggs, pupae, and adults. These worms are active at night and in the early morning. Take a flashlight and a cup of soapy water to the garden to search and destroy the culprits. Aphids, slugs, pillbugs, flea beetles, cutworms, and cabbage root fly may also be problems for broccoli. Spring crops may have issues with grasshoppers, harlequin beetles, and other stink bugs if plants are stressed by warm temperatures.

Feed broccoli frequently with compost tea or seaweed to keep it healthy and minimize pest problems. Keep the soil moist and mulch the plants after the transplants have hardened off.

Showy broccoli plants can also be added to container gardens. Choose pots that are at least 15 inches in diameter and 12 inches deep.

Broccoli tolerates mild frosts and light freezes. Row cover can protect it from temperatures under 28°F. It will have a better flavor after experiencing some cold.

HARVESTING Broccoli crowns are flower buds. Cut stalks with a sharp knife at an angle when the crowns are still dark green and tight. If the crown starts to show yellow flowers, it is getting old. Harvest and use it quickly. Don't pull up the plant when the crown is harvested—it's not finished! Most broccoli plants will form smaller shoots after the main crown is harvested. You may harvest more, pound for pound, with the side-shoot harvest than with the initial crown.

Broccoli leaves are also delicious. Cut smaller leaves and steam, sauté, or add to soups.

When the side shoots become very small, I let them flower. Bees love the yellow blooms and it keeps them happy at a time when there are not many other things to feed them.

VARIETIES DiCicco, Packman, Waltham, Green Comet, Green Goliath, and heirloom-type Calabrese are all dependable dark green varieties that will produce plenty of side shoots. Romanesco is a lovely pyramid-shaped chartreuse form that looks and tastes like cauliflower. Purple Sprouting has a deep purple color that unfortunately turns green when cooked.

Broccoli Raab is a related plant that is also harvested in immature bud stage and has a stronger flavor than broccoli. It grows larger than broccoli, and is more productive and more tolerant of warm temperatures than broccoli. Harvest the shoots before the flowers open for use in salads, smoothies, casseroles, soups, or steaming. It is an heirloom plant also known as rapini, asparagus broccoli, and Italian broccoli. It is easy to start from seeds.

Brussels Sprouts

Mini cabbages with a robust flavor, Brussels sprouts can be tricky to grow in the warm Southwest. Recommended for zones 4–7, they will often not form sprouts in warm winters. Still, I love the flavor of homegrown sprouts, so I gamble on a few each year, but don't commit too much garden space to them.

GROWING These cool-season plants have a longer growing season than most vegetables—about three months from a transplant—so starting with transplants rather than direct seeding saves time. Plant the seeds for transplants eight to ten weeks before the first frost and keep the new plants shaded to keep them cooler. Protect the plants from freezes with row cover.

They need a well-prepared soil, high in organic matter. The plants can grow up to 3 feet tall so I use them at the back of a border planting or in the middle of garden beds. They need a lot of space—set them 15–18 inches apart and stake them if they start to flop. You can plant quickly maturing radishes or lettuce between the Brussels sprouts and harvest those before the sprouts are ready.

Trim away some of the lower leaves to allow the plant to concentrate production on the sprouts, but leave the upper leaves to feed and shade the sprouts. The trimmed leaves may prepared like other greens.

The same insects that attack all of the cabbage family, particularly aphids and cabbage worms, can be problems for Brussels sprouts.

HARVESTING The sprouts grow in the leaf axils and begin forming near the soil line. Harvest the sprouts when they are 1–1½ inches in diameter by gently breaking them from the stem. Sprouts will continue to fill out higher on the stem.

If they remain on the plant for too long or are exposed to excessive heat, the sprouts will split and be ruined for eating. The flavor of the sprouts will be sweeter when they have experienced some light frosts.

VARIETIES **Jade Cross** and **Franklin** are two varieties recommended for warmer areas.

Cabbage

European-type cabbage is inexpensive to buy and difficult to grow in the Southwest. It is a cool-season crop and it can struggle if our cool season isn't cool enough. I generally plant a few plants, but seldom have large heads of cabbage form. Even those softball-sized heads are worth savoring for their sweet and tender leaves. Savoy types have wrinkled leaves. Asian cabbage varieties like bok choy and napa can be more productive for us and they are very versatile in the kitchen.

GROWING Set out transplants several weeks before the last frost in spring or eight to ten weeks before the first freeze. Protect fall-planted transplants from excessive sun. Space transplants 12–15 inches apart in rich garden soil. Zones 8–10 will do best with fall planting only.

Insect damage can ruin cabbage heads at an early stage. Handpick caterpillars in early morning and evening or use row cover and spray or dust with *Bacillus thuringiensis* (Bti) or Spinosad spray to protect young plants. Snails and slugs can also leave large holes in leaves.

Keep transplants mulched and evenly watered. Cabbage tolerates light freezes and the flavor improves with cold.

HARVESTING Cut the heads away from the roots when they are well formed and firm. Cabbage stores well in a root cellar or in the refrigerator.

VARIETIES **Early Jersey Wakefield, Emerald Cross, Tenderheart**, and **Late Flat Dutch** are all green varieties. **Red Acre, Mammoth Red,** and **Ruby Ball** are deep red types.

Cantaloupe

These plants need a lot of space and the yields are not extremely high, but the flavor of a sweet, vine-ripened cantaloupe is the nectar of the gods.

GROWING Start seeds indoors several weeks before the last frost or plant seeds directly in mounds several feet apart. Plant four or five seeds per mound and thin to the strongest two plants. These plants will spread up to 10 feet in all directions but can be grown on a trellis to save space. I use pantyhose, fabric, or net bags from produce to make slings to support cantaloupes as they form on the trellis. Pillbugs, snails, and slugs can often damage fruit lying on the ground. Prop up the fruit with old compact discs or plastic lids to keep the fruit off the ground.

Reduce water to the plants several weeks before harvest to ensure that the melons are sweet. Adding mineral-rich fertilizers to the planting area will yield sweeter fruits also, especially if your soil is a bit alkaline.

Avoid wetting the foliage and blooms in the morning to ensure pollination of the flowers. (bees do not like soggy pollen). Plant herbs and flowers to attract bees near the melon patch to increase the pollination of the melons.

HARVESTING The fruits will separate easily from the vines when they are ripe. Handle them carefully to prevent bruising. Melons will store for about a week in the refrigerator, but that is seldom a problem for me. If you have more than you and your friends can consume, consider freezing melon chunks for future use.

VARIETIES **Ambrosia**, **Chantenais**, and **Hale's Best** are large, sweet, and delicious.

Carrots

. . . .

Carrots are finicky about soil. To get nice, long, sweet carrots you will need finely textured, perfectly drained soil that is fertile and free from rocks. If that doesn't sound like what you're working with, don't despair—there can still be carrots in your future.

GROWING Use a soil screen to clean sticks, rocks, and clods from the carrot planting area. Add plenty of compost to the planting area. If your soil is not ideal for carrots, grow them in a container with a loose, well-drained potting mix. Or choose one of the shorter-type varieties which grow well in heavier soil.

This cool-season crop is best direct seeded in the garden. I usually mix the seeds with radish seeds, which will germinate more quickly and give the carrots an assist with growing. Plant carrot seeds ¼ inch deep and ½ inch apart in rows, sow seeds on the edge of your garden beds or broadcast over a bed. Make additional plantings every three weeks for a continual harvest all season. Lightly mist the planting areas daily until seeds germinate. When seedlings are several inches tall, use scissors to thin the plants to 2 inches apart. Several weeks later, thin the carrots to 4 inches apart and eat the thinnings. Water the carrot bed with a fine-mist nozzle attachment to gently wet the soil and avoid compaction or crusting of the soil around the delicate roots. Pull soil up over the tops of carrots to keep them from turning green. Make additional plantings every two to three weeks for a continual harvest. Don't overfertilize carrots as it will produce lush top growth and stunted carrots.

HARVESTING Harvest carrots when they are large enough to eat. Roots will pull out more easily when the soil is damp. Cut the tops off before storing carrots as they will pull moisture from the carrots.

VARIETIES Small varieties include **Danvers Half Long**, **Little Finger**, **Parmex**, and **Oxheart**. **Danvers**, **Nantes**, **Imperator**, and **Red Cored Chantenay** are long types better suited for deeper soils.

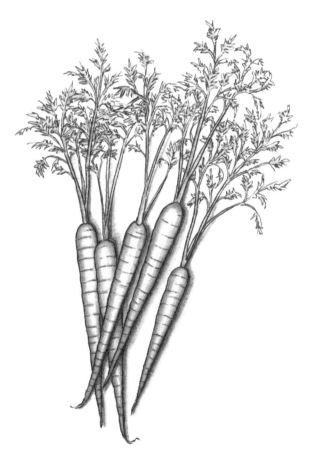

Cauliflower

This cool-season crop can be difficult to grow in zones 8–10, since it prefers to grow when temperatures are 65–70°F. Heads may fail to form or be small and grainy. Sweet, crunchy cauliflower is worth the gamble.

GROWING Plant transplants in well-prepared soil several weeks before the last freeze for spring or in fall. Keep the plants evenly moist throughout the growing period. Allowing cauliflower to go too dry will result in small heads that are uneven, bumpy, and unattractive. A thick layer of mulch will keep the plants moist.

Feed the transplants regularly; use seaweed, compost tea, or fish emulsion every two weeks.

Row covers can keep plants from being eaten by cabbage loopers or attacked by flea beetles and stink bugs.

HARVESTING Cut the heads when they are 6–8 inches across and the curds are still very tight.

VARIETIES New self-blanching cultivars have longer leaves that keep the cauliflower head shaded. Older varieties required tying leaves together over the crown to blanch or keep the heads white, creamy, and firm. White varieties include **Snow Crown** and **Snow King**. Orange **Cheddar** and purple **Graffiti** are beautiful and worth growing.

Citrus

Tropical citrus trees are sun and heat lovers—perfect for gardeners in the Southwest. There are many that grow well in containers and can be protected from extreme cold indoors or in a greenhouse. Those in zones 8–10 may plant some varieties outdoors as long as plans are in place for the occasional hard freeze. Most citrus will tolerate light freezes outside but protect them when temperatures are below 30°F.

GROWING Plant citrus trees outdoors in well-drained, nutrient-rich soil. The southern and eastern sides of your home will offer the most protection from the coldest winter winds. In containers, use a high-quality potting soil. Many citrus are grafted, so take care not to plant them so deeply that the graft is covered. If you notice new growth coming from the base that has trilobed leaves, cut them immediately. That is coming from the thorny Trifoliate Orange root stock below the graft.

Citrus trees are heavy feeders; fertilize them every other week when they are outdoors. I rotate special organic citrus food, coffee grounds, earthworm castings, seaweed, and fish emulsion to keep the foliage dark green. The trees will stay in constant bloom if they get enough to eat. Cut back the blooming branches and bring them indoors to enjoy the divine aroma. Trimming them keeps them compact and bushy.

Mulch the pots or planting beds with compost and wood-chips to keep the soil evenly moist and water them deeply.

HARVESTING The fruit will begin to ripen in late summer and fall. It can be harvested any time it has full color and it will store on the tree for a long time. Citrus can be refrigerated for several weeks or you may juice the fruit and freeze the juice.

VARIETIES **Improved Meyer Lemon** is one of the easiest to grow. It has delicious mild-tasting lemons. **Ponderosa** lemon has huge grapefruit sized bumpy fruits with pink flesh and a mild lemon flavor. One Ponderosa can make 2 quarts of lemonade. **Mexican Lime** and **Key Lime** produce many small limes of excellent quality. **Meiwa Kumquats** have a sweet rind and tart flesh and are excellent for eating fresh off the tree. **Calamondin Orange** grows well in containers or in the ground, and is very cold tolerant and extremely productive. The 1-inch oranges are quite sour, but can be used for marmalade when sweetened. The peels can be used to make a wonderful orange liqueur. They bloom prolifically and have fruit throughout the year, with the heaviest crop in fall. I would grow that one for the fragrance alone.

Collards

These vigorous greens are large, easy, and fast growing. Even though they match kale for nutrient density, they have not developed the superstar status of kale, despite centuries as a southern garden standard. Still, they deserve a spot in everyone's garden and kitchen. Black-eyed pea and collard green soup is a staple in my kitchen.

GROWING Plant collards in sun or partial shade in well-prepared garden soil. Since they grow so large and lush, they require a substantial diet. Sow the seeds ½ inch deep and 2–3 inches apart. Thin the seedlings to 15–18 inches apart—they get very large!

Caterpillars and aphids can sometimes be a problem but are easily controlled. Harlequin beetles, lygus bugs, and other stink bugs can damage the leaves and are usually more of a problem when the plants are stressed by warm temperatures in spring. That is my cue to pull them out and plant something else.

HARVESTING Harvest the large leaves by cutting them to the base of the plant. They will have a sweeter flavor after they have been exposed to a frost.

Collards are a popular food for New Year's Day; tradition says that a helping of collards ensures a prosperous new year.

VARIETIES **Morris Heading**, **Flash**, and **Georgia Southern** are common varieties. **Champion** hybrid has improved heat tolerance.

Corn

Corn is a vigorous warm-season crop that requires nutrient-rich soil, regular feeding and watering, and lots of space. Birds, worms, and raccoons may eat more of it than you do and you can expect two ears of corn per stalk at best. Despite all these issues, mouth-watering sweet corn fresh from the garden is worth the trials and tribulations—and unlike store-bought corn, you will know exactly what went into growing it.

GROWING Corn is wind-pollinated so it should be planted in clusters of four to six plants or in blocks of at least 4 feet wide so that the pollen from one plant can be transferred by wind to other plants. Avoid planting corn in single rows. Soil should be warm, at least 55–60°F. Plant organically grown seeds an inch deep and 4 inches apart. Thin to 8 inches after a few weeks. Cut plants with scissors rather than pulling to minimize root damage. Thin the corn to 12 inches apart for the final spacing.

Many gardeners like to get a jump-start on growth and avoid bird and insect damage by planting in containers and planting the corn seedlings when they are 4–6 inches tall.

Corn is a type of grass, so it requires regular nitrogen. Prep the soil with nitrogen-rich fertilizer or follow a planting of peas or a green manure. Plan to side-dress the plantings with compost and organic fertilizer or spray with fish emulsion when the plants are knee-high and again when the ears start forming. It has deep roots, so prepare the soil deeply and mulch to keep the plants moist. Kernels will fail to form if the corn is allowed to get too dry.

Stabilize the tall and top-heavy corn stalks with stakes and string wound around the outside of the cluster of plants. If high winds topple the plants, upright them and water well. They can recover quickly.

Cover plants early on with row cover or bird netting to keep birds from eating the young tender shoots of corn. Spray with hot pepper and garlic spray to deter raccoons, who seem to know just when the corn is ready and will raid your garden the night before you plan to harvest. Duct tape can come to the rescue, too. Some gardeners rely on taping the ears to the stalk just below the tip of the ear and an inch or so above the base of the ear just as the silks begin to turn brown. In my garden, my Rottweiler method of raccoon control has been very successful, too.

Corn earworms do most of their damage at the tip of the ear, where the eggs are laid by a light brown moth. Gardeners will treat the silks at the top of the corn ears with Bt (*Bacillus thuringiensis*) or mineral oil to kill the worms and deter the moths. You can also inspect the ears, remove and kill the worms, cut off the damaged tips, and enjoy the rest of the corn.

HARVESTING Check the ears after the tassels begin to turn brown. Once an ear feels plump, pull back the shuck and pierce a kernel with your fingernail. If the juice is milky, it is ready to harvest. Experienced corn growers will have the water boiling while the ears are being harvested because the sugars turn to starch quickly after corn is harvested. Refrigerate or freeze corn quickly after harvest if you are not eating it immediately.

VARIETIES **Ambrosia**, **Kandy Korn**, **Silver Queen**, **Early Sunglow**, and **Golden Bantam** are good sweet corn varieties.

Cucumbers

If I never eat another waxed, flavorless store-bought cucumber again, that will be just fine with me. Home-grown cucumbers are very productive, have more flavor and crunch, and come in a wide range of colors and shapes.

GROWING Plant cucumbers in pots three to four weeks before the last frost or direct seed outdoors after danger of frosts have ended. Plant seeds in mounds to improve drainage. Trellis plants to conserve space, allow pollinators better access to blooms, and make the cucumbers easier to harvest. Guide new vines onto the trellis to direct early growth. They will climb the supports by winding delicate tendrils as they grow.

Prepare the planting spot with lots of organic material and fertilize often throughout the growing season. Trim and remove any dead leaves or vines quickly to avoid spread of diseases. It is best to avoid watering the foliage of cucumbers to avoid powdery mildew. Drip irrigation is best. Watering the foliage in the morning will wet the pollen and interfere with the pollination work of bees. Plant basil and other flowering plants near your cucumbers to attract bees and ensure excellent pollination. Bitter tasting cucumbers are due to the cucumbers getting stressed from being too dry. Mulching will help to avoid stress.

Avoid touching the foliage or harvesting when the foliage is wet to avoid the spread of disease.

Cucumber beetles can spread bacterial diseases in the plants. Remove leaves that show trails of leaf miners and discard those in the trash. A regular fertilization program will keep the plants healthy and avoid most insect problems.

Cucumbers can also be grown in large containers. Add a trellis or stakes to train the vines up.

HARVESTING Cut ripe cucumbers from the vines with scissors or shears to avoid damaging the delicate vines. Watch the growth carefully—they can go from tiny to over-grown in a couple of days. Old cucumbers will have large, hard seeds, tough skins, and yellow color and should be composted or fed to the birds or chickens. Sometimes it is difficult to see them until they get quite large, so inspect the vines from several angles.

VARIETIES **Straight 8** and **Marketmore** are my most productive slicing types. **Green Fingers**, **Poinsett**, and **Sweet Slice** are also good. **Lemon** cucumbers are a round, pale yellow type that is quite productive. Unusual white varieties include **Blanche** and **White Wonder**. **Suyo Long** and **Armenian** produce very long cucumbers with small seeds that produce well in heat. **Mexican Sour Gherkin** is an unusual heirloom offered by Seed Savers Exchange. The vines are sturdy and vigorous and produced well in the hot-test and driest summer when everything else withered and died. The fruit are 1–2 inches long and look like tiny water-melons. They are crisp and a little sour, as though they have already been pickled.

Eggplant

Decorative as well as delicious, eggplant is easy to grow and extremely productive, even in the hottest days of summer. I often plant them with flowers in containers or even in ornamental beds. Their lavender flowers and brightly colored fruits will brighten any garden. They even thrive in shady locations. A bowl of brightly colored eggplant is a beautiful summer table decoration.

GROWING This warm-season plant can be a perennial in warmer zones. It likes a rich, well-drained soil and even soil moisture. Keep it mulched well to keep the blooms from falling off. Eggplant does not like cool temperatures, so don't plant it too early. I purchase 4-inch transplants and pot them up into 1-gallon pots and keep those in the greenhouse until night temperatures are above 45°F. Eggplants can grow into large plants and the heavy fruits can cause branches to droop. I use small tomato cages to support them.

Eggplants can be quite happy in containers of 5 gallons or larger. Use a well-drained, rich potting soil and add additional compost. Keep the pot mulched and move it to a location with afternoon shade when temperatures are over 95°F.

Eggplant is one of the few plants that deer don't seem to like in my garden.

HARVESTING Cut the fruits from the plants with scissors or shears to prevent damage to the plants. Harvest fruits when they are still shiny; dull eggplants are old and will be bitter. When temperatures are above 95°F, harvest the fruits when they are smaller. When temperatures cool down the fruits will be larger once again. Eggplant can be covered and protected from occasional frosts and be harvested until late in fall or winter.

Delicious grilled, roasted, or fried, and in soups, dips, and casseroles, eggplant can be prepared many ways.

VARIETIES The shiny neon magenta fruits of **Dancer** are my favorites. **Black Beauty** is the standard dark purple eggplant you will find in most markets. **Tycoon**, **Florida High Bush**, and **Dusky** are similar dark purple varieties. **Louisiana Long Green** and **Ravena** are light green and less likely to be bitter. **Thai Long** and **Ichiban** are long slender purple varieties that are easy to slice and grill or broil. **Casper** and **Ghost** are smaller and white-skinned and tend to have very mild flavor. **Listada de Gandia**, **Pinstripe**, and **Rosa Bianca** are lavender and white Italian types with very white mild flesh. **Fairy Tale** is a miniature eggplant with plentiful 3- to 4-inch purple and white fruits. It is ideal for smaller containers.

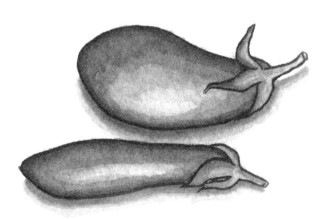

Fennel

I enjoy the mild licorice flavor of fennel fronds, and children love to chew the "licorice seeds," but the sweet, crunchy bulbs of the plant are the real star in the winter garden.

GROWING Plant seeds of bulbing fennel in late summer in rich garden soil. Fennel can grow in sun or partial shade. Transplants are usually available also.

The fronds of fennel provide an important larval food for swallowtail butterflies. Since the fennel is so large and prolific, I move the green-, yellow-, and black-striped caterpillars from the dill and parsley to the lush foliage of fennel.

The flowers will attract aphids to your garden, which in turn attract ladybugs and lacewings, so don't be in a rush to control the aphids.

HARVESTING Harvest the foliage any time. The seeds may be harvested when they are full and green or when they have dried and turned brown. The seeds can be chewed for indigestion and as a breath freshener in addition to cooking uses.

Cut the bulbs just under their rounded bases, leaving the roots in the ground. The plants will produce additional bulbs. Trim back the flower stalks to redirect the plant's energy into larger bulbs.

VARIETIES **Zeta Fino** and **Trieste** are Italian types with large bulbs. **Common** and **Bronze** are grown for their foliage and seeds and do not produce bulbs. They also are larval food for swallowtails.

Garlic

This pungent member of the onion family is used in every cuisine of the world and has amazing health benefits; it lowers cholesterol, reduces risk of cancer, and improves cardiovascular health in addition to providing delicious flavor in your cooking.

GROWING Plant organic or untreated seed garlic cloves in rich, loose garden soil in full sun. Garlic from grocery stores is usually treated to hinder sprouting. Separate the individual cloves and plant the largest ones with the pointed end up. In milder climates plant cloves 2–3 inches deep. Cold climates need to set the cloves 4–6 inches deep. Space them 5–6 inches apart and mulch well. Water the plants frequently as they begin to sprout and spray the foliage with seaweed and fish emulsion regularly to encourage growth.

Slow fertilizer and watering as the plants begin to form the bloom buds. Excess growth at this point can rot the bulbs. Cut off garlic bloom stalks as they begin to straighten up to get larger bulbs.

HARVESTING Green leaves of garlic can be cut and used in the kitchen, but leave most of them to feed the garlic cloves. Their flavor is milder than that of the cloves. Many gardeners love the flavor of "green garlic" and pull some of the stalks out to use like leeks.

When most of the leaves are turning yellow, the bulbs may be harvested. Gently ease them out with a garden fork rather than pulling the bulbs from the soil.

Dry the bulbs in a single layer in a well-ventilated, shaded location for several weeks. Once the outside layers are dry and papery the garlic can be braided and hung in mesh bags or pantyhose.

VARIETIES Softneck varieties rarely produce bloom stalks, are better suited to warmer climate zones, and store well for long periods. Most garlic sold in grocery stores is the softneck type. **Inchelium Red**, **California White**, and **Texas White** are softneck types. Hardneck types tend to have larger cloves and more varied flavors. They can be stored for longer periods. **Creole Red**, **Spanish Roja**, and **Persian Star** are hardneck types. **Elephant Garlic** produces large mild cloves but there are fewer cloves per bulb. It is actually a type of leek.

Kale

Kale has a well-deserved reputation for being the most nutritious vegetable available. It is a good source of vitamins A, C, and K, calcium, and iron and it is also rich in nutrients that fight cancer.

I plant kale in containers and in flower beds. Its tall, upright growth is the perfect backdrop for pansies, snapdragons, calendula, and other winter blooms and the leaves may be harvested continuously.

GROWING Kale grows easily from seed or may be grown as a transplant. Many varieties are available from garden centers as transplants. It needs fertile, finely textured soil, and appreciates regular feedings to keep up with the heavy harvesting it provides. Plant it in full sun. It is very cold tolerant and the flavor becomes sweeter with frosts. I cover it when temperatures below 25°F are expected.

Aphids are the biggest problem for kale. Blast them with a strong spray of water and step up the feeding schedule. Regular applications of seaweed will keep the plants insect free. Stink bugs may be a problem when temperatures climb and the plants become stressed by heat. Instead of spraying to control the bugs, I pull out the kale and plant something else.

HARVESTING Cut the outside leaves from the plants to keep harvesting the same plants all season long. The entire plant may be harvested as the season winds down.

VARIETIES **Nero di Toscana** is perhaps the most popular variety. If I only planted one type in my garden, this would be the one. It will often be 3 feet tall by the end of the season. It's nickname, "dinosaur kale," comes from the pebbly blue-green texture of the leaves, which might look like dinosaur skin. It is also known as Tuscan or lacinato kale. Curly kale varieties like **Redbor** and **Winterbor** have very frilly leaves. Make a colorful and nutritious Caesar salad with their young, tender leaves. **Red Russian** is often grown as an ornamental type. The red color will intensify with cold temperatures. Ornamental kale like **Nagoya** and **Peacock** are edible, just tough and not that tasty. They'll work okay as a garnish, but stick with the edible types for the best flavor and texture.

Kohlrabi

This unusual cool-season member of the cabbage family produces a round bulb above the ground. The bulb is crunchy, sweet, and mild and tastes like a mild turnip. It is delicious when peeled and thinly sliced and used for dips, chopped in salads, or added to stir-fries or baked.

GROWING Plant seeds directly in the garden or start indoors and transplant. Since the plants are only about 12 inches tall at mature height, they do well if planted along the edge of the garden bed. Kohlrabi needs fertile, well-drained soil and a layer of mulch. The plants are more heat and drought tolerant than many other cool-season greens. Kohlrabi can also tolerate some shade. Make several plantings in the cool season to ensure a continual harvest. Most types are ready to harvest in 50 to 60 days.

HARVESTING Harvest the bulb as soon as they are sufficiently large, about 2½–3 inches in diameter. Larger bulbs can be woody. Kohlrabi stores well in the refrigerator but remove the leaves before storing it.

The leaves of kohlrabi are also edible and you may pick a few leaves from each plant and use them in salads, or use larger leaves in stir-fries, steamed, or in soups.

VARIETIES **White Vienna** and **Grand Duke** are light green varieties. **Purple Danube** and **Kolibri** have a rich purple color. **Crispy Colors Duo** includes both colors in the packet.

Leeks

Leeks are so easy to grow that there is no reason to pay the high prices they command in grocery stores. They have many of the health benefits of garlic and onions, with a milder flavor.

GROWING You may find leeks sold in 4-inch pots or you can start seeds indoors and transplant to the garden when they are about ¼ inch in diameter. The seedlings are planted 4–6 inches deep and 6 inches apart. Pull the soil up around the leeks as they grow to increase the length of the delicious white part of the roots. Feed leeks with compost tea, seaweed, or fish emulsion and keep them evenly moist.

If leeks are left in the garden, they will form a cluster of small leeks. Dig up the clump, pull out the larger roots for kitchen use, and divide and plant the smaller leeks. Cut healthy roots with a couple of inches of white stems from purchased leeks and plant in your garden. Once they get going, you will never buy leeks from the store again.

Leeks have few issues with pests or diseases. They are an excellent companion plant for roses. When the leeks are dormant, the roses are lush and the roses go dormant when the leeks are actively growing. Many of the pests that bother roses are not fond of leeks.

HARVESTING Leeks may be used at any size. Discard most of the green leaves of leeks in favor of the tender white stem.

When leeks form a bloom spike they will be tough and stringy. Cut the blooms before the curled tips open and use in flower arrangements. When the round blooms are open, the garlicky smell is not welcome in most homes. Leeks will go dormant in late spring and disappear from sight. They will sprout again with cooler weather in fall.

VARIETIES **Tadorna**, **American Flag**, and **King Richard** are all easy-to-grow varieties.

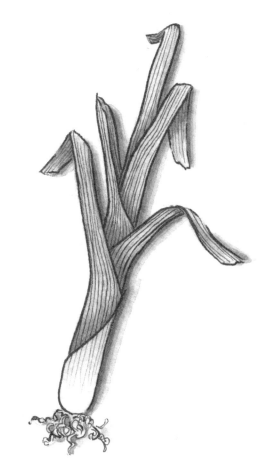

Lettuce and Salad Greens

Garden-fresh lettuce is strictly a cool-season pleasure and I look forward to the "salad days" of fall and winter.

GROWING Seeds may be planted in rows or broadcast on the surface of the soil. Make a raised lip around the edges of the broadcast lettuce bed so that seeds will not be washed off with watering and rain. Plant fast-growing lettuce seeds between slower crops like broccoli and cauliflower and harvest them as "living mulch" before the slower crops fill in and need the space. Plant the seeds with a very light covering of fine soil. Thin the seedlings to 2 inches apart and eat or transplant the thinnings to other spots. Final spacing for most lettuce should be 6–10 inches, depending on the variety. Lettuce may be started in pots and transplants are usually available for purchase.

Lettuce needs cool soil and cool temperatures. If temperatures are warmer than usual, shade the area where you want to plant lettuce for several weeks in advance to cool the soil. Water the planting area deeply before planting the seeds. Use lightweight row cover to keep the seed bed from drying out and crusting.

Prepare the soil with lots of compost and add minerals such as lava sand, greensand, and rock powders to improve the flavor of the lettuce. Feed lettuce regularly with seaweed or compost tea to keep it productive and healthy. The trace minerals in seaweed not only improve the flavor, they will help it withstand more cold temperatures.

Be prepared to cover lettuce when temperatures will be lower than 32°F. Shading lettuce will help it last a little longer in spring.

Colorful lettuce plants do well in container plantings and may be planted with winter annuals like nasturtiums, violas, and pansies.

Head-type lettuce requires cooler temperatures and does not perform well in warmer areas. Deep red lettuce and Romaine types will tend to bolt more easily with warm temperatures. Shade them or plant in the coolest part of the growing season.

HARVESTING Remove the outer leaves from young leaf lettuce plants. As the plants get larger, use scissors to cut the plant's center, leaving the outside leaves to feed the plant. The center will grow back again. Regular fertilizing will allow you to cut lettuce more frequently.

Use a salad spinner to remove excess water from the leaves after washing. Store the lettuce in the spinner basket with a small amount of water in the bottom of the bowl to increase humidity. Lettuce will stay fresh for up to two weeks in this manner.

VARIETIES **Buttercrunch** is a sweet dense butterhead lettuce. **Salad Bowl**, **Black Seeded Simpson**, **Red Sails**, **Lolla Rosa**, **Merlot**, **Oakleaf**, **Royal Oak**, and **Tango** are all excellent leaf-lettuce types. Romaine types include **Paris Island**, **Cos**, and **Valmaine**. **Mâche** or **Corn Salad** is a small, nutty-tasting salad green that is richly flavored and very cold tolerant. The seeds are very slow to germinate but worth the wait. The heads are about 4 inches across and high. Cut leaves or pull the entire head for salads.

Malabar Spinach

Not a true spinach plant, Malabar spinach is heat-loving, climbing plant from India that can make an attractive addition to the landscape. It seeds itself prolifically and will come back each year—abundantly—once established. The flavor is more intense than spinach and the leaves are thicker and more succulent. Like cool-weather spinach, Malabar is very nutritious; high in vitamins A and C, iron, calcium, and fiber. The leaves are popular in Asian and Indian cuisine.

GROWING Plant seeds or transplants 6 inches apart in spring when the soil is warm. It is not picky about soil and will grow in some shade but it does need a sturdy support. It will grow to about 4–5 feet tall. Pinch back the tips to encourage branching. Most families will not need more than two or three plants.

You won't need to help this plant much. In fact, I rip it out of the ground by the bucket-full. It makes a great addition to compost if you have more than you can eat and your chickens will also love the excess. I try to cut as many of the seeds off as I can in the fall to limit its growth, but I still always have too much of it. The juicy, purple seed capsules will stain your hands, so wear gloves. The plant will die back with the first freeze but reappear the following spring.

HARVESTING The young seedlings are tender and tasty and easy to pull up. Trim their roots and eat the leaves and tender stems raw or cooked like spinach. Trim the vine's tips or harvest individual leaves.

VARIETIES **Red Malabar** has deep red stems and green leaves. **New Zealand** spinach is similar, but has green leaves and stems. It likes warm soil and is more easily controlled than Malabar spinach.

Okra

This African native is quite at home in hot southwestern gardens. Tall, sturdy stalks are prolific producers from late spring until the first hard freeze. Its attractive yellow blooms and large leaves make it worthy of a spot in the flower garden.

GROWING Warm soil—at least 70°F—is a must for okra. Once my peas or potatoes have been harvested in late May, I have that spot for okra. If the seeds are planted in cool soil they will not germinate.

Soak the seeds several hours or overnight to speed germination. Plant them in full sun directly in the ground. Okra is a big plant—some types will grow over 10 feet tall—so it is a heavy feeder. Follow a nitrogen-rich bean or pea crop with okra and work lots of compost and organic fertilizer into the soil. One planting of okra will bear until frost. Give it at least a 3-foot-wide planting bed and plant the seeds an inch deep. Transplants of okra are available, but the roots get large so quickly that the transplants are often root bound and stressed before they get planted; I prefer to plant seed directly in the garden. Thin the seedlings until they are at least a foot apart. Once the plants are 10–12 inches tall, mulch them and water regularly. Okra does not like to be too wet.

Fire ants love okra, as do stink bugs. A funny insect called a leafhopper will play "hide and seek" with you in the garden. They suck the juices from the stems so they are not a good bug to have around, but okra is pretty tolerant of low levels of insect damage. Regular foliar feeding will allow you to grow successfully. Root-knot nematodes can make it almost impossible to grow okra, but applying Actinovate to the soil as directed can deal with the problem.

HARVESTING Plan to pick okra daily when harvesting begins. The pods can grow from usable to tough and woody overnight. Wear long sleeves to avoid the inevitable itching that comes from contact with the hairy leaves. Use scissors or garden shears to cut the pods from the plants. If the plants are getting too tall to harvest the tops easily, don't reach for the ladder; just cut a few feet off the top of the plants in late summer. That forces new growth in the lower parts of the plant and they will be bushy and easier to harvest.

Boiled and pickled okra tastes best with pods 2 to 3 inches long. Fried okra, stews, and gumbos can utilize the longer pods. It is important to keep the okra harvested. Like all annuals, once it produces mature seeds in the woody pods it will start to decline and picking it regularly will keep it in production much longer. Cut and compost any pods that are not easily cut with a knife. In late fall I like to leave some of the pods to dry on the plant and harvest them for use in fall arrangements.

Try eating young pods of okra raw. When no more than 3 inches long, the pods have a nice crunch and mild flavor. Use them with dips or just munch on them in the garden. Lightly brush okra with oil and put it on the grill or roast it in the oven until browned. It may also be sliced and frozen or even breaded and frozen for fried okra.

VARIETIES **Clemson Spineless**, **Emerald**, and **Louisiana Green Velvet** are some of the productive old varieties. **Burgundy**, **Cow Horn**, and **Red Velvet** are attractive and productive newer types. There are dwarf types like **Cajun Delight** and **Annie Oakley**, but I find they usually grow much taller than the package promises.

Onions

Sweet, flavorful onions are a kitchen essential. They contain sulfur compounds which fight cancer and heart disease and have antiviral and antifungal properties. If your garden space is limited, grow this useful crop in containers or tuck them between other garden plants. They don't take up much room and make excellent companion plants.

GROWING Onions may be planted from small bulbs called sets, pencil-thin seedlings, or from seed. Seeds may be started indoors in flats or started outdoors in warmer areas. Gently divide the seedlings while small and plant them in rich garden soil 4 inches deep and 2 inches apart. Later, thin the onions to 4 inches and eat the thinnings as green onions.

If you purchase bundles of onion seedlings, soak them for several hours in a dilute seaweed solution to rehydrate the roots and get them off to a faster start.

If your soil is less than ideal, feed onions regularly to create larger bulbs. Stop feeding them when the tops start to decline before harvest time.

HARVESTING Harvest as green onions any time they are large enough. Harvest bulbs when they are large and the tops have started to die back. Allow the onions to dry in a well-ventilated and shaded area for several weeks before storing in a cool, dry place.

VARIETIES Gardeners in warmer, southern areas will be more successful with short-day types of onions since we plant them in our cool season. Those include **White Grano**, **Texas Super Sweet**, **Yellow Granex**, **White Granex**, and **Bermuda**.

Gardeners in zones 4–6 can have success with long-day and intermediate-day onions. Intermediate-day onions include **Candy**, **Red Candy Apple**, and **Super Star**. Long-day types include Italian heirloom **Cippolini**, **Gladstone**, and **Southport**.

Multiplying or bunching onions do not make onion bulbs, but provide a constant supply of tender green onions in the cool season. They go dormant in hot weather but magically reappear with a heavy rain or cooler temperatures. **McCoy's** is a multiplying onion often sold in 4-inch pots in garden centers. Bunching onions come in white, red, and yellow types. To harvest, dig or pull up the clump, remove the larger onions for kitchen use, and replant the remaining smaller onions. Plant them in areas where they will not be disturbed by warm-season plantings. I have them located along the edge of a raised bed. You may need to find them online or in garden catalogs that specialize in onions, but they are worth the search if you like a constant supply of green onions without the tedium of planting tiny seedlings. Pull and dry the small bulbs in areas where the soil freezes.

Evergreen Long White Bunching is a bunching variety to plant from seed. It produces beautiful, straight, mild-tasting onions. I broadcast the seeds in fall and thin as they grow. One packet keeps me well supplied all winter.

Peas

∙∙

Peas can be a gamble for the southwestern gardeners. They don't want soil that is too hot or too wet or too dry or too cold—but gardening in the Southwest is usually extreme in one way or another. Sugar snap peas, snow peas, and green or English peas have similar growing requirements and can be extremely productive if you plant them at the right moment and the weather gods are smiling on you. If your timing is right and you get even a few delicious peas, you'll want to take your chances and make room for them in every winter garden.

GROWING There is generally a narrow window for planting peas in most zones, so don't delay. If you are having unseasonably warm temperatures around planting times for peas you can compensate by installing shade fabric or row cover over the planting area and irrigate the soil before planting to cool it. Continue to shade the bed after planting peas if the weather continues to be warm and sunny.

Direct seeding rather than transplanting is recommended for all peas. Soak the seeds in half-strength seaweed solution or compost tea to speed germination. Make sure the seeds do not dry out after planting. Give them a daily watering until they sprout. It is usually a good idea to make several plantings, beginning eight to ten weeks before your first freeze date.

Since peas are a legume they will not require much nitrogen, so use compost and a low-rate balanced organic fertilizer to prepare the soil. Too much nitrogen can lead to lush leaves and no bloom production. Inoculate the pea seeds after soaking them with Rhizobia bacteria to facilitate nitrogen production by the pea's root nodules. When the plants are no longer productive, cut the vines, add them to the compost pile, and leave the nitrogen-rich roots to feed your next crop.

Even though many seed packets will tell you that the plants do not require a trellis or stakes, I still prefer to use them. The vines grow straighter and the peas are easier to see and harvest. They are also less likely to have disease issues since air circulation is better. I use metal T-posts with sections of galvanized livestock panels 4 feet tall and

6 feet wide to support the peas. (These same panels are used for pole beans and cucumbers, but installed 6 feet tall and four feet wide.) Most winter peas will not grow taller than 5 feet. Utilize your tomato cages that have completed their work for the season for pea supports. I have used okra stalks for pea supports also.

Mulch the plants after they start to climb the supports and keep the soil moist. Remove any leaves infected by leaf miners and blast aphid attacks with water. Powdery mildew can be a problem in warm, wet winters.

HARVESTING Sugar snap peas have edible pods and can be eaten fresh from the vine. If any make it to the kitchen, they can be added to stir-fries and salads. Larger peas may require removal of strings on the sides of the pods. If the peas are allowed to fill out completely, the pods may be tough, but the peas can still be shelled out and eaten.

Shelling peas need to fill out completely on the vine, but harvest them before the pod starts to turn brown. The pods are not edible. Don't pull; trim the pods from the delicate vines with scissors.

Snow peas should be harvested while the pods are flat, before the peas start to swell inside the pod. They will be crisp and tender at that stage. The young tendrils or pea shoots of snow peas are also edible and are wonderful sautéed very lightly. Strings may require removal on larger pods.

The sugars in sugar snap peas will quickly convert to starch after being harvested, so pick them just before serving. Snow peas can be refrigerated for a few days or blanched and frozen.

VARIETIES Wando, **Sugar Spring**, **Sugar Ann**, **Sugar Baby**, and **Little Marvela** are great sugar snap varieties; **Dakota** and **Maestro** are great for shelling; and my favorite snow peas are **Mammoth Melting Sugar** and **Dwarf Grey Sugar**.

Peppers

Sweet and hot peppers come in an array of shapes, sizes, and colors. They love heat and are even tolerant of some shade. Both sweet and hot peppers will change from green to bright red, orange, yellow, and even purple when they are mature, but they can be eaten at any stage.

GROWING Peppers can put on a heavy load of fruit, causing branches to break and droop. I use small tomato cages to support them. Plant them in well-drained rich soil and keep them mulched and evenly moist. They appreciate a shade covering in the hottest part of summer, when temperatures go above 95°F, but will produce from spring until a hard freeze.

Peppers grow well in containers and will survive for years if they are protected. Since they are a tropical plant, bring them inside when temperatures go below 40°F. I kept a jalapeño in a pot for many years. The peppers would turn bright red in winter, so I decorated it and used it as a Christmas tree.

Feed peppers regularly. Give them a well-balanced fertilizer at planting time and side-dress the plants when they begin to bloom. Epsom salts used as a fertilizer drench—2 tablespoons per gallon of water—will push the plants into blooming stage.

HARVESTING Peppers may be harvested at any stage. Sweet peppers will have more vitamins and have a sweeter flavor when they have color. Don't pull the peppers from the stems. Use clippers and make a clean cut.

VARIETIES Among the sweet peppers, **Gypsy** produces small peppers but they turn color much more quickly than other types. They will often have several colors of peppers on the plant at one time. **Pimento** peppers are thick-walled, very crisp peppers that turn a rich red color. **Purple Beauty** turns a deep rich purple color when mature. **Chocolate Beauty** turns a deep rich brown. **Pinot Noir** is a brilliant magenta color when mature. **California Wonder**, **Keystone**, and **Jupiter** are also good sweet bell peppers. **Fooled You** jalapeño looks like a hot pepper and smells and tastes like a jalapeño, but has no heat.

For the hot peppers, **Chile Pequin** is a perennial pepper in zones 7–10. It freezes to the ground but comes back from the roots. Birds love the tiny red peppers also and spread the seeds. **Mucho Nacho** is a mild jalapeño that produces a large pepper. **Habañero**, **Serrano**, **Big Jim Green Chile**, **Cayenne**, **Hungarian Hot Wax**, **Tabasco**, and **Sweet Heat** are all excellent producers.

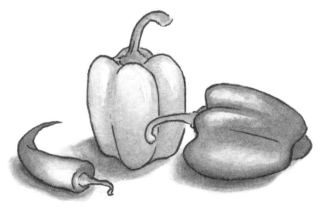

Potatoes

Potatoes are inexpensive to buy and take up valuable spring garden space, so why bother? Once you have sampled tender and tasty new potatoes from your garden, you'll never ask that question again. Plus there are many wonderful shapes, sizes, and a rainbow of colors of potatoes that are not generally available in your grocery store.

GROWING Purchase certified seed potatoes for planting. Potatoes from the grocery store have generally been treated to keep them from sprouting. The seed potatoes should be firm, with no mold or damaged spots, and with healthy buds. Golf ball–sized potatoes may be planted whole. Cut larger potatoes into pieces of golf ball or egg size with at least two or three eyes on each piece. Dust the cut pieces with sulfur powder to prevent fungal problems and place them in a single layer in a cool, dark place for several days. This will prevent the cut pieces from rotting in the planting bed.

Plant the potatoes in well-drained, rich garden soil in a trench 6–8 inches deep. Plant the potatoes 4–6 inches deep in heavy clay soil. Place a piece of potato every 12–14 inches. Crowding the plants will reduce the harvest. Press the potato into the soil with a healthy sprout facing up and cover with 4 inches of soil. Several weeks after planting, dark green sprouts will emerge from the planting trench. When the sprouts are 6–8 inches tall, pull the soil from the sides of the trench to cover the lower portion of the sprouts, leaving about 4 inches of greenery visible.

Potatoes grow from the stems of the tubers that were planted. The process of hilling up soil provides growing space for potatoes and protects the tubers from sunlight.

Exposure to sunlight creates a bitter green substance on the skin called solanine that can be highly toxic.

Once the potatoes have grown another 8 inches above the soil level, add a layer of mulch, partially finished compost, or grass clippings to mulch the bed. Side-dress the trench with coffee grounds if the foliage is not deep green and spray with compost tea, fish emulsion, or seaweed.

Protect the potato tops from freezes with row cover if necessary. Keep the bed consistently moist but not soggy. The tops may bloom. Once the tops turn yellow and begin to die, you can begin gently harvesting small new potatoes. Larger potatoes will be ready three to four months after planting depending on the type.

Potatoes can also be grown in large containers to save garden space

HARVESTING Cut the foliage back several days before harvesting and gently loosen the soil from the edges of the bed with a spading fork. Handle the potatoes carefully, gently removing excess soil, and spread them out in a single layer. Do not wash the potatoes. Let them cure in a dark, cool place with good air circulation for at least ten days.

VARIETIES **Red LaSoda**, **Pontiac**, and **Red Norland** are some of the most productive potatoes. **White Kennebec** is a reliable white potato. **Yukon Gold** is buttery yellow. **Purple Viking** and **All Blue** are blue varieties. **LaRatt**, **Austrian Crescent**, and **Yellow Finn** are smaller fingerling types. You should produce eight to ten pounds of potatoes for each pound of seed potatoes planted.

Purslane

Yes, that weed that you have trying to get rid of for years—I am telling you to plant it! It loves the heat and spreads easily but its shallow roots make it easy to get under control if it takes over. I harvest it so much it doesn't have a chance to get out of bounds. The succulent and crisp leaves are slightly sour and tasty in summer salads or added to eggs, stir-fries, soups, and smoothies. It is rich in vitamins A, C, and E, beta-carotene, and minerals, and is very high in omega-3 fatty acids.

GROWING Wait to plant seeds until soil is warm, at least 60°F. Water the seed bed and then press the seeds into the soil for good soil contact, but do not cover—they need sunlight to germinate. I broadcast the seeds and allow them to act as living mulch under peppers or eggplants. They come back each year once established and are easily transplanted to new locations. They will grow 12–15 inches tall.

Cut them back hard when they start to bloom to keep them in check. The tiny yellow flowers are not nearly as showy as those of hybrid purslane that we use as ornamental flowers. It is related to ornamental moss rose and portulaca.

They do well in containers with loose, very well-drained soil. They don't require a rich soil or much water but the leaves will be milder and more abundant with a little TLC.

Abundant volunteer purslane is an indication that your soil is healthy and well balanced.

HARVESTING Cut 3- to 4-inch-long pieces off of the plants. Rinse, drain, and wrap in a damp towel to keep it crisp. I prefer to harvest it just before use. It will turn to mush quickly in the refrigerator.

VARIETIES **Golden Purslane** grows taller than wild types for easier harvesting and has a milder flavor. It is a different species than the typical garden weed.

Radishes

Radishes are easy and fast growing. The seeds will sprout several days after planting and be ready to eat in a few weeks. They are often mixed with slower growers like carrots to help mark the planting site and assist delicate carrot seeds with breaking through the soil. Radishes can be planted between broccoli, cauliflower, and cabbage and will be harvested long before those crops crowd them out.

GROWING Loosen the soil and add lots of compost and a balanced organic fertilizer. Too much nitrogen will produce lush tops and spindly roots. Plant a few rows at a time, ½ inch deep and 1 inch apart. Space the rows at least 3–4 inches apart so that you can cultivate around them and pull soil up over the expanding roots. Tuck a few radish seeds into any bare spot in the garden. Plant additional rows every two weeks, making sure to label the rows and include the date they were planted.

Keep the soil evenly moist. Too much water will cause the radish roots to split and crack and too little will make them bolt and be too pungent to eat.

HARVESTING Once radishes have gotten to harvestable size they should be pulled out and eaten. Radishes that remain in the soil too long will be woody and hot. The leaves of radishes are also edible and they have a nice peppery flavor, similar to arugula. If some of your radishes happen to bloom, leave them in the garden. The tiny seedpods are crisp and delicious, with a peppery bite.

Cut the leaves off the radishes before storing them. The leaves will pull moisture from the roots and make them dry. Radishes will keep in the refrigerator for several weeks.

VARIETIES **Champion**, **Cherry Belle**, **Early Scarlet Globe**, and **Easter Egg** are colorful, round, fast-growing types. **Watermelon Radish** has a red center with a pale green skin. **French Breakfast**, **White Icicle**, and **Black Spanish** are longer radishes that prefer deep, sandy loam soils for a better shape. **Daikon** is a long white Asian variety that has a delicious mild flavor. It needs more space than other radishes. Thin to 6 inches between plants. Harvest the long roots with a trowel, rather than pulling them, to avoid breakage.

Southern Peas

These heat-loving peas include black-eyed peas, cream peas, crowder peas, and purple hulled peas. They are often referred to as cow peas and were grown as a livestock food crop and legume cover crop. They are high in fiber and full of protein and they leave the soil improved for the next crop. If you decide to give up the garden when summer temperatures make growing a challenge, plant a cover crop of southern peas. They will germinate even in the hottest soil.

GROWING Plant seeds directly in well-drained, sunny garden soil. Avoid adding excessive nitrogen to the soil and inoculate the seeds with Rhizobium bacteria to ensure abundant production of nitrogen by the roots. Some varieties will require some support or staking.

Chop the plants down and turn them into the soil to improve it before the next garden crop.

HARVESTING Pick the seedpods while still green and the seeds inside are plump. Immature green pods can also be gathered and included as snap beans in the bean pot. For dried peas, harvest the pods when they are brown and dry.

VARIETIES **Mississippi Silver** and **Brown Crowder** are popular large-seeded crowder-type peas. **White Acre** and **Lady** are light-colored, mild-flavored cream peas. **Big Red Ripper**, **Red Noodle**, **Texas Pink Eye**, and **Black Eye #5** are all good purple hull types. **Yard-Long Beans** are a prolific Asian variety that taste like black-eyed peas with pods that can be up to 2 feet long. They are vigorous climbers that require sturdy support. Like black-eyed peas, they produce two pods together at the terminal bud. They are usually chopped into pieces and added to stir-fries, roasted, or steamed.

Spinach

Popeye steered me wrong. That green stuff in a can led to years of avoiding spinach. Fortunately, succulent spinach from the garden bears no resemblance to the bitter, canned stuff. There are two main types: smooth leaved or savoyed, the type with bumpy leaves. Savoy types of spinach are better adapted and more flavorful in cold weather. Southwest gardeners may have better luck with the smooth types. The smooth leaves grow more upright so they are easier to harvest and they are much easier to wash. The savoy leaves must be washed carefully to avoid gritty spinach.

As Popeye knew, spinach has lots of vitamins A and C, calcium, and iron. It tolerates cold well and is a dependable crop all winter long.

GROWING Plant spinach seeds directly in the soil in fall and again in late winter for early spring harvest. It grows best in full sun and when temperatures are cool. Shade the seed bed to keep it cooler if necessary. Seeds will fail to germinate in warm soil. Broadcast the seeds over the bed or plant in rows. Spinach is generally available in transplants also.

Soak the seeds for several hours or overnight to speed germination.

Remove and discard leaves that show trails of leaf miners. Aphids may also attack spinach. Spray spinach with seaweed or compost tea every two weeks to keep it strong and healthy. Use row cover to protect it if temperature is below 25°F, but the flavor is sweeter after exposure to a little cold.

Mulch plants with compost to keep them growing well all winter.

Spinach is an attractive addition to containers. It has shallow roots so it will grow in a window box or shallow container. Mix it with pansies, violas, and nasturtiums for a useful and decorative winter display.

HARVESTING Cut the larger outside leaves of each plant. If you broadcast the seed in the planting bed, pull up entire plants and trim the roots until the plants are spaced 4–6 inches apart. Those tender thinnings are perfect for salads.

VARIETIES **Bloomsdale** and **Melody** are savoy types. **Monstreaux de Viroflay** and **Tyee** have large leaves and are very productive. **Renegade, Corvair**, and **Space** are smooth-leaf types.

Strawberries

....

Harvesting delicious red strawberries is a pleasure. Commercial strawberries are often picked before they are truly ripe so they have white, flavorless interiors. You will be able harvest your berries at the peak of perfection. You will be amazed at how good a strawberry can be!

GROWING Strawberries may be planted from container-grown 4-inch pots or as bare root plants in early spring. Choose a location with full sun and well-drained, fertile soil with an acidic or neutral pH. Make small hills and set the plants about 12–15 inches apart. The crown of the strawberry should be about halfway above the soil level to provide adequate drainage.

Coarse mulch like pine straw will prevent the plants from drying out and be less hospitable for snails, slugs, and pillbugs, which love the ripe berries also.

I prefer to grow the berries in containers where the fruit can spill over the sides. Insects and birds have a more difficult time getting to the hanging, ripe red jewels, though bird netting may be necessary to protect your crop. It is also easier to correct soil drainage and pH in a container planting.

Keep the soil evenly moist but not soggy, which can lead to disease issues.

HARVESTING Harvest as soon as the fruit is ripe and consume the berries quickly as they do not store well.

VARIETIES **Chandler**, **Sequoia**, and **Allstar** are some of the most reliable warm-climate berries.

Summer Squash

....

Summer squash is the thin-skinned type that does not store well. It is easy to grow, grows quickly, and can be quite prolific. There are many shapes, sizes, and colors to choose from. There are bush types and vining types that spread up to 12 feet wide. There is a squash for every garden.

GROWING Squash needs warm soil to grow well. Planting seeds directly in the soil is best, but you may start with transplants to save time. Plant in full sun in well-prepared, rich soil. Plant four or five seeds an inch deep in a raised mound for increased drainage. The raised soil will warm up faster also. Thin gradually until there are two strong plants left. Overcrowding will stress the plants and lower yields. Space the mounds 18–30 inches apart, depending on the variety.

Smaller bush-type squash may be planted in large containers of at least 7- to 10-gallon size. Use a well-drained potting soil and add additional compost to it.

Squash has a well-deserved reputation for having a number of pest issues. Cucumber beetles, squash bugs, and squash vine borers can wipe out your crop quickly. Avoid many pest issues by covering the newly planted squash immediately with lightweight row cover. Ensure that the cover is completely sealed so that the cucumber beetle or vine borer moth is not able to sneak in and attack.

The squash vine borer is the most serious pest for squash and can kill the plants before they ever bloom. Row cover prevents the vine borers from attacking the plants but will also keep pollinators from the blooms. I keep the row cover in place until the plants have both male and female flowers. The first squash blooms are all male blooms. The female bloom has a small fruit below the blossom. Some gardeners use the male flowers to pollinate the female blooms but I open the covers and let the bees do their work. The plants eventually succumb to vine borers but I get eight to ten weeks of harvest. I make another covered planting of squash to be ready to harvest when the vine borers start to do their damage in the first planting.

HARVESTING Squash flavor and quality is best when they are harvested small. Pick zucchini and yellow squash when they are 4–6 inches long and patty pan when it is 3–5 inches across. Larger fruits will stress the plants and lower yields. Baseball bat–sized zucchini is edible, but not the most flavorful. Use scissors or shears to cut squash from the stem and avoid damage to the plants.

Use the male flowers in salads, dips, or soups. They are often battered and fried. Chop them and add to cheese for quesadillas. Pick them just as they start to open.

VARIETIES **Yellow Crookneck** or **Straightneck** are reliable yellow squash. **Black Beauty** and **Dark Green** zucchini produce lots of richly colored squash. **Summer Scallop Trio** is a tricolor mix of yellow **Sunburst**, dark green **Starship**, and apple green **Peter Pan** squash. Harvest these when they are no more than 5 inches across. They are lovely stuffed and this color mix makes a lovely presentation. **Tatuma** or **Tatume** is a round green heirloom squash that may be used like zucchini and is more drought tolerant and resistant to squash vine borer than other types. Vines can grow to 12 feet. Pick the squash when it is around 3 inches wide. Larger squash will have a large seed cavity and hard seeds but can be hollowed out and stuffed. **Trombetta di Albenga** is an Italian heirloom that produces long (up to 2 feet!) curvy squash with firm flesh. This squash needs lots of room to roam. The vines can grow up to 25 feet long and will cover a fence, canopy, or trellis. I wind the vines around tomatoes and peppers for a lush, living mulch. The leaves are huge—over a foot wide. It gets vine borers but keeps on growing.

Sweet Potatoes

These plants grow rampantly and will not be possible for small-space gardens. Use them as a ground cover if you decide to take the summer off from your garden. The lush vines are attractive and with little effort you will harvest a bumper crop of sweet potatoes in fall.

GROWING Sweet potatoes need a long growing season (up to 115 days), lots of sun, and a neutral to slightly acidic, well-drained soil. Raised beds with sandy loam are ideal.

Sweet potatoes are grown from sprouts from the potato root called slips. Purchase certified disease-free slips online or from garden centers once soil is very warm. Plant slips 12 inches apart in wide beds that give the wide spreading vines plenty of room. Keep them watered regularly but avoid overwatering, especially near harvest time.

HARVESTING Let the sweet potato bed dry out two weeks before harvesting. Cut the vines back a few days before harvesting to help the potato skins to dry. Gently loosen the soil with a garden fork to expose the roots. Brush off dirt and place the sweet potatoes in a single layer in a well-ventilated and shady location to allow the skins to dry and cure for several weeks. Rough handling will bruise them and cause the potatoes to rot.

Check stored potatoes frequently for signs of damage. Well-cured sweet potatoes should store up to six months.

Mild-flavored sweet potato greens are also edible and can be cooked like spinach or Swiss chard or added to soups and egg dishes.

VARIETIES **Centennial** is a compact type with 90–100 days to harvest. It is a better choice for zones with shorter growing seasons. **Beauregard** and **Garnet** have deep orange flesh. **Jewel** has good nematode resistance. **Vardeman** and **Porto Rico** are compact varieties suitable for small gardens.

Swiss Chard

The brightly colored leaves of Swiss chard are as appropriate in a flower bed or container as in the vegetable garden. It has a wide range of heat and cold tolerance and withstands both wet and dry conditions.

GROWING Start from seeds or transplants and plant in full sun or partial shade in rich soil or in containers. Chard and beet seeds are similar; they are actually seed capsules with several seeds inside. It is important to give them adequate space and thin the plants. Fall-planted chard will often continue leaf production throughout the following spring and into summer, especially if given some afternoon shade.

HARVESTING Young chard greens can be used in salads and smoothies, while larger leaves are sautéed or added to soups, eggs, and casseroles. The plants can be continually harvested by removing the outer leaves. Cut or snap the leaves away from the base of the plant. When cooking with larger leaves, chop and sauté the stems for a few minutes, then add the chopped leaves.

VARIETIES **Bright Lights** has brightly colored stems of yellow, pink, red, and orange. If you wish to stick to a single color look for **Rhubarb Red**, **Golden Sunrise**, **Bright Yellow**, or **Magenta Sunset**. **Fordhook Giant** and **Lucullus** have deep green leaves with white stems, but why settle for plain vanilla when you can have the colors of the rainbow?

Tomatoes

Tomatoes are the most popular garden vegetable and for good reason. The rich, juicy, meaty flesh and incomparable flavor of a homegrown tomato has inspired poetry and songs. Store-bought tomatoes are grown more for their hardiness for shipping than for flavor. Timing is more important with tomatoes than most crops. Plant too early and they are damaged by cold, too late and they will not set fruit.

GROWING Start transplants indoors in a good-quality potting mix. Provide plenty of light to keep the plants from being stretched and spindly. A grow light that can be raised as the plants grow is ideal.

If purchasing tomato transplants, make sure they have been protected on cold nights. Early cold stress (below 45°F) may not kill the plants, but can damage them and make them more prone to disease. Avoid transplants that have purple veins and stems that indicate cold stress. Transplants in 4-inch pots that sport heavy blooms or fruit are probably root bound. It is better to buy a short, stocky plant than a tall, spindly one. Pot the 4-inch transplants into 1-gallon pots and keep them protected from cold. These larger plants will give you a head start when it is warm enough to plant them outdoors.

Wait until night time temperatures are above 45°F to set out transplants, or provide row cover or wrap tomato cages to protect the plants. When night temperatures reach about 75°F, tomatoes will stop setting blooms. That could be late April or mid-May in warmer zones. The fruit that is on the plant will continue to develop but the flowers will usually fall off after blooming. A cool rainy day or two could set additional fruit so don't give up on the plants.

Tomatoes are wind-pollinated and may not set fruit well if they are planted near a fence or building that blocks breezes. Give the cages a good shake in the morning to disperse the pollen.

Remove any lower leaves that touch the ground to reduce transmission of diseases from the soil. A layer of mulch will prevent disease spores from being splashed on the foliage. Uneven watering can lead to cracking, splitting, and blossom end rot. Water deeply and keep the plants well mulched to reduce water stress.

Don't be afraid to prune tomato plants. They are sturdy vines and are invigorated by pruning. Remove all damaged leaves, vines, and the stems where tomatoes were attached. Prune back the tops of tomato plants in summer to rejuvenate the plants. If the plants are healthy, take cuttings from the tops of the plants and root them in water to plant a fall crop.

Give healthy spring tomato plants a break from the hot summer sun with burlap, shade cloth, or row cover. A shade cover that blocks 25–30 percent of the sunlight will allow the plants a respite. When temperatures are cooler, remove the shade cloth and the tomatoes may set a bountiful new crop. I generally plant some fall tomatoes, but if the plants from spring still look fairly healthy I think it is worth a little pruning and shading to give them another chance to produce.

HARVESTING Cut tomatoes from the plant when they begin to show color. They will ripen indoors and be less likely to be damaged by insects and birds. Store tomatoes with the stem-side down for longer storage and never put them in the refrigerator unless they have been cut or cooked. Refrigeration destroys the delicate flavor compounds.

You can also cut green tomatoes and slice, batter, and fry them for delectable fried green tomatoes.

VARIETIES Grow the varieties recommended for your soil and climate. Warmer zones will have trouble growing the large beefsteak tomatoes. These are some of the best all-around types:

Celebrity has a lot of disease resistance built in and produces well. **Early Girl**, **Better Boy**, **Tycoon**, **Improved Porter**, and **Superfantastic** are all good slicing tomatoes. **La Roma**, **Viva Italia**, and **San Marzano** are Italian pear-shaped tomatoes that have a meatier texture and are excellent for drying, sauces, and soups. **Sun Gold**, **Large Red Cherry**, **Sweet 100**, **Sweet Million**, and **Juliet** are good cherry types. Cherry tomatoes will usually still continue setting fruit in hot weather. **Heat Wave** and **Heat Set** are supposed to continue to set fruit in warmer weather. I have not observed much of a difference.

Turnips

If you haven't tried turnips in a while, you should give them another chance. Newer varieties are milder tasting and the leaves have less of a bite.

GROWING Turnips need cool weather for optimum flavor. The roots will be tough and the leaves bitter in warm weather. Plant seeds in full sun in well-drained rich soil. Cover seeds with a quarter-inch of soil and thin seedlings to 4 inches apart. Eat the tender thinned plants in salads.

Keep soil evenly moist and mulch the plants with compost.

Flea beetles and caterpillars can damage the leaves. Use row cover or spray as needed to control damage.

HARVESTING Harvest the greens when they are 10–12 inches tall. Cut the outer leaves off of each plant. They cook down a lot, so harvest a good deal. The roots will have the best flavor when they are smaller than 3 inches in diameter. Turnips are wonderful sliced and eaten raw in salads or with dips. Roasting, steaming and mashing turnips are good ways to enjoy them. Cook the greens and add the diced roots to the pot.

VARIETIES **Purple Top**, **Royal Globe**, and **Shogoin** are good for turnips and leaves. **All Top** is grown just for the greens.

Watermelon

Summer isn't complete without a daily slice of watermelon to help you cool off after a stint in the garden. It has electrolytes to rehydrate you and is a good source of lycopene and vitamin A.

GROWING Most melons will require 70 to 100 days from planting to harvest. They need warm soil and plenty of sun. Plant four or five seeds in a mound and thin to the two strongest plants. Cut the plants at the soil line rather than pulling them out so that the roots of the remaining plants are not damaged.

Watermelon vines can spread up to 20 feet, so they are not advised for a small garden.

HARVESTING Watch for the stems connecting the melon to the vine to dry out and turn brown. The spot where the melon has been on the ground will turn from white to creamy yellow and the rind gets a dull finish.

Cut back on water several weeks before harvesting the melons to allow the sugars to intensify for a sweet fruit. Heavy rain or excessive watering may cause melons to split.

Freeze watermelon in cubes or small balls for refreshing drinks later on if you have more than you can manage fresh. Watermelon margaritas made with frozen melon are always a hit with my friends.

VARIETIES **Crimson Sweet**, **Sugar Baby**, and **Jubilee** all grow well. **Moon and Stars** is an heirloom type that has unusual moon and star markings on the outside.

Winter Squash and Pumpkins

Colorful, delicious, nutritious, and waiting for you for weeks or months until you have a need for them make these excellent crops to consider. Butternut, acorn, and other winter squash have lots of vitamins A and C, along with folate, fiber, calcium, and potassium, and are versatile and delicious.

The most important consideration in planting winter squash is the timing of the planting. Look at the days to harvest and then count the number of days until your first freeze. Hopefully there will be several weeks between those dates to pull in some squash for storage. For example, you're planting on 15 July and the variety needs 90 days until harvest. If your first freeze is expected on 1 October, you will not have enough time to get in a harvest. Count backward from your freeze date to determine the correct planting date. Most large pumpkins will need 90 to 120 days to reach maturity. They also need lots of room to spread. The vines will sometimes grow 20 feet long, so they are not a great choice for a small garden.

GROWING These are large, spreading plants, so prepare the soil well. Use lots of aged manure or compost and an organic fertilizer. Spraying with seaweed or compost tea is beneficial. Give the vines a thick layer of mulch once they are 8–10 inches tall and water deeply. Cover the plants with row cover to thwart squash bugs and squash vine borers until they require pollination.

Cover the plants with a frost blanket if an early cold snap threatens.

For a little fun in the pumpkin patch, while the skin of pumpkins and winter squash is still green, but starting to turn color, use a sharp nail, ice pick, or small knife to gently carve the skin. Try to cut only the skin. Carve a face, initials, or a message, and the cut areas will scab over and form a raised design. As the squash or pumpkin continues to grow, the lines often get twisted and distorted and a scary grin will get even weirder. When the squash is harvested it is already decorated for Halloween, and since it is uncut it will last much longer.

HARVESTING Depending on the variety you are growing, you will be looking for different cues to tell you the squash is ready to pick. Acorn develops an orange spot where it touches the ground. The stem for butternut and most pumpkins will turn brown and dry when it is time to be harvested. Store squash in a cool, dry place for a week to dry and harden the skins. Monitor the squash frequently during storage to check for moldy or soft spots. You can pick and use any of the squash immediately if the skin has not hardened sufficiently for storage.

VARIETIES **Ghost** is a round white pumpkin with a deep orange, flavorful interior. **Cinderella** makes a nice carving pumpkin and has richly colored and delicious flesh.

Butternut and **Acorn** squash are relatively fast-growing winter squash and store well.

Resources

A. M. Leonard, Inc.
www.amleo.com
Since 1885, the source for some of the best gardening tools on the market with reasonable prices and shipping rates.

Aggie Horticulture from Texas A & M University
http://aggie-horticulture.tamu.edu/
Fact sheets on insects, vegetables, fruit trees, herbs, and organic growing advice. Online courses are available. Great color photos to aid in insect identification.

Arbico Organics
www.arbico-organics.com
Source for comprehensive pest control solutions including beneficial nematodes, mosquito controls, and much more.

Central Texas Gardener
www.klru.org/ctg
Even if you don't live in Central Texas you will learn a lot from this show. Watch for my segment at the end of the program in Backyard Basics. Watch the program online, follow their blog, and look for my recipes and lots of good information on the website.

The Dirt Doctor
www.dirtdoctor.com
Howard Garrett's website is a rich source of organic information from where to buy organic products in your area to gardening guides, radio and television broadcasts, and a forum for gardening discussions.

Gardener's Supply Company
www.gardeners.com
Great source of organic products for gardeners who are unable to buy products locally. Easy-to-assemble raised-bed garden kits and planters for the would-be gardener without carpentry skills. The online garden planner and insect control information are very useful for new gardeners.

I Must Garden
www.imustgarden.com
A line of deer repellants, squirrel, rabbit, mosquito, and other critter repellents. Many of them actually have a pleasing scent and they work well.

Liquid Fence
www.liquidfence.com
They have deer, armadillo, mole and vole, and many other critter repellants available. They don't smell great, but they work.

Peaceful Valley Farm Supply
www.groworganic.com
Source for cover crops, vegetable seeds, and organic supplies

Texas Soil and Plant Lab
Edinburg, TX
www.texassoilandplantlab.com
Soil, compost, and plant tissue testing available. Helpful staff will help you understand how to manage your soil needs organically.

Texas Tomato Cage
877-983-4646
www.tomatocage.com
The last tomato cages you will ever buy! Sturdy, built to last and they fold flat for easy storage when not in use. Use their smaller cages for peppers and eggplants.

SEED AND PLANT SUPPLIERS

Baker Creek Heirloom Seeds
Mansfield, MO
www.rareseeds.com
Good source for rare and unusual plants and open-pollinated and non-GMO seeds. Seeds are untreated.

Seed and Plant Suppliers, continued

Botanical Interests
Broomfield, CO
www.botanicalinterests.com
Their seed packets are not only beautiful, they are filled with lots of growing information inside and out; a great resource for the beginner seed gardener. They sell seeds for flowers and herbs as well as vegetables.

Native Seeds
www.nativeseeds.org
A nonprofit organization dedicated to preserving the traditional agricultural heritage of the Southwest.

Plants of the Southwest
Santa Fe, NM and Albuquerque, NM
www.plantsofthesouthwest.com
Many varieties of drought tolerant vegetables, herbs, flowers, and landscape plants.

Renee's Seeds
Felton, CA
www.reneesgarden.com
Seeds are untreated and not genetically modified. Good selections of herbs, vegetables, and flowers.

Seeds of Change
Dominguez, CA
www.seedsofchange.com
One hundred percent organic seeds, including herbs, vegetables, and flowers.

Seed Savers Exchange
Decorah, IA
www.seedsavers.org
Old-fashioned and heirloom varieties ideal for gardeners who wish to save their seeds from year to year.

Territorial Seed Company
Cottage Grove, OR
www.territorialseeds.com
Source for organic, open-pollinated, and non-GMO seeds.

Further Reading

Adams, William D. 2011. *The Texas Tomato Lover's Handbook*. College Station, TX: Texas A&M University Press
   Not just for Texans, this the definitive guide to growing the country's most popular vegetable. (Since the state of Texas spans USDA climate zones 6–10, most books written for Texas are applicable to much of the Southwest.)

Bubel, Nancy. 1998. *The Seed-Starter's Handbook*. Emmaus, PA: Rodale Press
   A very complete guide to seed starting, from creating soil mixes and choosing containers to problem solving. It also includes seed-saving tips for specific vegetable crops.

Campbell, Stu. 1975. *Let It Rot: The Gardener's Guide to Composting*. North Adams, MA: Storey Publishing
   Everything you always wanted to know about building, tending, and using a compost pile.

Carr, Anna. 1985. *Good Neighbors: Companion Planting for Gardeners*. Emmaus, PA: Rodale Press
   This book helps you sort fact from fiction regarding the complex subject of choosing plant communities.

Clausen, Ruth Rogers. 2011. *50 Beautiful Deer-Resistant Plants: The Prettiest Annuals, Bulbs, and Shrubs that Deer Don't Eat*. Portland, OR: Timber Press
 A guide to understanding deer and their habits. Good lists of plants to avoid and ornamentals that can be successfully grown. Many control methods are discussed.

Garrett, Howard. 1995. *Texas Organic Gardening*. Dallas, TX: Taylor Trade Publishing
 Despite the title, the information on soil building, insect control, and planting techniques applies to all southwestern gardeners.

Garrett, Howard, and Malcolm Beck. 2005. *Texas Bug Book: The Good, The Bad & The Ugly*. Austin, TX: University of Texas Press
 Again, this book is relevant to the entire Southwest region. Good color photos of the various life stages of good and bad insects along with organic control information.

Garrett, Howard, and Malcolm Beck. 1999. *Texas Organic Vegetable Gardening*. Houston, TX: Gulf Coast Publishing
 A comprehensive guide to growing vegetables, herbs, and fruits in an easy-to-use format. Lots of color photos and good information on pests and diseases that might affect each crop.

Hart, Rhonda Massingham. 2005. *Deerproofing Your Yard & Garden*. North Adams, MA: Storey Publishing
 An excellent source for helping to deter deer in your landscape.

Hutson, Lucinda. 2010. *The Herb Garden Cookbook*. Austin, TX: University of Texas Press
 Both a growing guide geared toward the Southwest and a cookbook with beautiful photographs and mouthwatering recipes, this is an indispensable volume from a witty and wonderful garden writer.

Kourik, Robert. 2009. *Drip Irrigation for Every Landscape and All Climates*. Occidental, CA: Metamorphic Press
 From large to small drip systems, this guide can help you design and maintain water-saving drip systems. Good diagrams and information geared to beginners.

Lovejoy, Sharon. 2003. *Trowel and Error: Over 700 Shortcuts, Tips and Remedies for the Gardener*. New York, NY: Workman Publishing
 Entertaining and educational, filled with timesaving and problem-solving tricks that only a gardener with years of experience would know.

Nabhan, Gary Paul, 2013. *Growing Food in a Hotter, Drier Land: Lessons from a Desert Farmer on Adapting to Climate Uncertainty*. White River Junction, VT: Chelsea Green Publishing
 Age-old methods of farming that are more important than ever in our drought-stressed environment.

Ogden, Scott. 1992. *Gardening Success with Difficult Soils*. Dallas, TX: Taylor Trade Publishing Company
 Most of us are not blessed with cake-like sandy loam and this book will help you to cope with the challenges of clay, caliche, limestone, and more.

Organic Gardening. Emmaus, PA: Rodale Press, Inc.
 The oldest and still the best source of all things organic.

Stewart, Amy. 2005. *The Earth Moved: On the Remarkable Achievements of Earthworms*. Chapel Hill, NC: Algonquin Books of Chapel Hill
 Who knew reading about earthworms could be so interesting? All six of Amy's books merit a spot on your bookshelves. They are both educational and inspirational.

Index

Main entries for Edibles A to Z section appear in **bold type**.

leafhopper, 204
leaf miner, 183, 195, 207, 213
leeks, **201**
    as companion for roses, 149, 201
    harvesting times, 57, 65, 155
    hilling up, 154
    storage life of seeds, 68
    when to plant, 19, 57, 64, 65, 138, 146
leeks, recommended varieties
    American Flag, 201
    King Richard, 201
    Tadorna, 201
lemon grass, 114
lemon verbena, 114
lettuce, **202**
    cleaning and storing, 158–159
    companion planting with, 149
    in container gardens, 58, 145
    fall garden, 140
    frost and, 16
    harvesting times, 65, 84, 92, 100,
       129, 139, 146, 155
    red-leaf, 140
    soil depth for, 58
    storage life of seeds, 68
    succession planting, 44, 58
    sun and, 23
    temperature for seed germination,
      69
    thinning plants, 138, 145
    when to plant, 19, 20, 45, 57, 64, 65,
      74, 75, 84, 92, 100, 110, 120, 129,
      138, 145
    when to transplant, 92
    winter garden, 58
lettuce, recommended varieties
    Black Seeded Simpson, 202
    Buttercrunch, 140, 202
    Cos, 202
    Lolla Rosa, 202
    Merlot, 202
    Oakleaf, 202
    Paris Island, 202
    Red Sails, 202
    Romaine, 140

    Royal Oak, 202
    Salad Bowl, 140, 202
    Tango, 202
    Valmaine, 202
lima beans. *See* beans
lunar gardening, 20
lygus or leaf-footed bug, 176–177, 193

Malabar spinach, **203**
    harvesting times, 100, 120
    as heat-loving plant, 112
    when to plant, 84, 92, 100
Malabar spinach, recommended
    varieties
    New Zealand, 203
    Red Malabar, 203
March, 72–80
    fresh harvest, 75
    plan, prepare, and maintain tasks, 74
    sowing and planting, 74–75
    tomatoes, 73, 76–80
marigolds, 38, 149
May, 89–96
    fresh harvest, 92
    insect control, 93–94
    plan, prepare, and maintain tasks, 91
    poison ivy, 94–95
    sowing and planting, 91–92
    squash vine borers, 96
melons. *See also* cantaloupe;
    watermelon
    harvesting times, 120
    planting tip, 40
    seed saving, 122
    soil temperature and, 20
    stakes, trellising, or caging, 86
    storage life of seeds, 68
    when to plant, 57, 65, 75, 83, 84, 91,
      100
    when to transplant, 92
microclimates, 17, 19
microgreens, 57
mint, 115, 158
    Black Stem Peppermint, 115
    Chocolate Mint, 115

    Double Mint, 115
    Kentucky Colonel Spearmint, 115
    Wintergreen, 115
mosquitoes, 101, 111
mulches, 31
    for cold weather, 145
    for container plants, 148
    from cover crops, 148
    how to apply, 147
    newspaper as, 134
    for pathways, 39
    pine needles for, 148
    sheet composting as, 148
    texture of, 148
    for weed suppression, 67, 134, 138
    what to use, 147–148
    for winter weather, 147–148
mullein, 131
mustard and mustard greens, 38
    companion planting with, 149
    as cover crop, 160
    harvesting times, 57, 146
    storage life of seeds, 68
    when to plant, 138, 155
    when to transplant, 65

nasturtiums, 84, 124
nettles, 113
Nevada
    climate zones, 18
    frost dates, 14
New Mexico
    frost dates, 14
    wetter periods, 16
nightshade family, 45
November, 143–151
    companion planting, 148–149
    composting fresh leaves, 147
    fresh harvest, 144, 146
    herbs for winter, 150
    holiday herb bundles, 151
    mulching, 147–148
    overwintering plants, 147
    plan, prepare, and maintain tasks, 145
    watching for a freeze, 147

About the Author

TERRI OZYMY

Trisha Shirey is the director of flora and fauna at Lake Austin Spa Resort in Austin, Texas, and is the designer of their award-winning organic herb and vegetable gardens and organic orchard. She is also featured on the Central Texas Gardener program and an active speaker on organic gardening, native plants, wildflowers, xeriscaping, water gardens, and natural pest control.